Yinyang

The concept of yinyang lies at the heart of Chinese thought and culture. The relationship between these two opposing, yet mutually dependent, forces is symbolized in the familiar black and white symbol that has become an icon in popular culture across the world. The real significance of yinyang is, however, more complex and subtle. This brilliant and comprehensive analysis by one of the leading authorities in the field captures the richness and multiplicity of the meanings and applications of yinyang, including its visual presentations. Through a vast range of historical and textual sources, the book examines the scope and role of yinyang, the philosophical significance of its various layers of meanings, and its relation to numerous schools and traditions within Chinese (and Western) philosophy. By putting yinyang on a secure and clear philosophical footing, the book roots the concept in the original Chinese idiom, distancing it from Western assumptions, frameworks, and terms, yet also seeking to connect its analysis to shared cross-cultural philosophical concerns. In this way, the book not only illuminates a particular way of thinking, but also shows how yinyang thought has manifested itself concretely in a wide range of cultural practices, ranging from divination to medicine, and from the art of war to the art of sex.

Robin R. Wang is Daum Professor in the Bellarmine College of Liberal Arts, Professor of Philosophy, and Director of Asian Pacific Studies at Loyola Marymount University in Los Angeles. She is the editor of *Chinese Philosophy in an Era of Globalization* (2004) and *Images of Women in Chinese Thought and Culture: Writings from the Pre-Qin Period to the Song Dynasty* (2003).

This dynamic new series publishes books on the milestones in Asian history, those that have come to define particular periods or to mark turning points in the political, cultural, and social evolution of the region. The books in this series are intended as introductions for students to be used in the classroom. They are written by scholars whose credentials are well established in their particular fields and who have, in many cases, taught the subject across a number of years.

Books in the Series

Yinyang

The Way of Heaven and Earth in Chinese Thought and Culture

Robin R. Wang

Loyola Marymount University

CAMBRIDGE
UNIVERSITY PRESS

CAMBRIDGE
UNIVERSITY PRESS

32 Avenue of the Americas, New York NY 10013-2473, USA

Cambridge University Press is part of the University of Cambridge.

It furthers the University's mission by disseminating knowledge in the pursuit of
education, learning and research at the highest international levels of excellence.

www.cambridge.org
Information on this title: www.cambridge.org/9780521165136

First published 2012

A catalogue record for this publication is available from the British Library

Library of Congress Cataloguing in Publication data
Wang, Robin.
  Yinyang : the way of heaven and earth in Chinese thought and culture /
Robin R. Wang, Loyola Marymount University.
    pages cm. – (New approaches to Asian history ; 11)
  Includes bibliographical references and index.
  ISBN 978-1-107-00015-5 (hardback) – ISBN 978-0-521-16513-6 (paperback)
  1. Yin-yang. 2. Philosophy, Chinese. I. Title.
  B127.Y56W36 2012
  181′.11–dc23   2012012610

ISBN 978-1-107-00015-5 Hardback
ISBN 978-0-521-16513-6 Paperback

To Kelly & Mindy
A journey of a thousand miles starts with a single step.
千里之行, 始于足下.-----道德經

Contents

Figures

Acknowledgments

My research on the work of Dong Zhongshu (179–104 B.C.E.) in 2004 first awakened my interest in yinyang. I was investigating what appears to be a puzzling contradiction: on the one hand, yinyang seems to be an intriguing and valuable conceptual resource in ancient Chinese thought for a balanced account of gender equality; on the other hand, no one can deny the fact that the inhumane treatment of women throughout Chinese history has often been rationalized in the name of yinyang. These two conflicting observations are reflected in divisions within scholarly circles. Some scholars claim that the concept of yinyang can be a primary source for understanding Chinese gender identity and that it has much to offer to contemporary feminist thought. On the other hand, arguments have been given that the denigration and abuse of women in ancient China is a direct result of the idea of yinyang. This puzzle and the theoretical discussions around it led me to wonder what yinyang thought really meant in early Chinese texts, and why Chinese have for thousands of years continued to approach the world through the lens of yinyang. How can we understand the power of a way of thought that is both very simple and almost infinite in its applicability?

This project has been a transformative journey for me, and many minds, hearts, and hands have contributed to its development from those initial questions. I particularly wish to thank the following individuals for their intellectual insights and generosity in assisting me in this journey. At an early stage in its development I benefited much from discussions with Roger Ames, Philip J. Ivanhoe, Livia Kohn, Ronnie Littlejohn, Lisa Raphals, Weimin Sun, Bryan Van Norden, Zhihe Wang, Verner Worm, Wenyu Xie, Brook Ziporyn, and my dear colleagues in China: Su Yongli, Wu Genyou, Ding Weixiang, Zhang Xianglong, Gan Jianmin, Wan Junren, Zhang Zailin, Li Zhonggui, Lu Xichen, and Chen Xia. I owe a particular debt to Martin Schönfeld and Tao Jiang, who have always provided me with inspirational support. Li Ming has been a troubleshooter for me in resolving some obscure difficulties in my research. Special heartfelt thanks also to Hans-Georg Moeller for his constant encouragement and constructive suggestions throughout the process. I am also grateful to Kelly James Clark and Tom Plate for reading through the whole manuscript.

I have been able to test out much of this material with a variety of audiences. Nzazi Malonga (Master Zi) and Nisha Rodrigo gave me a platform to deliver a series of public lectures on yinyang at the InFocus Wellness Institute in Santa Monica. I also presented parts of this material to a group of physicians at Kaiser Permanente South Bay Medical Center and to a general audience at the Bower Museum. Finally, students in my upper division philosophy course on yinyang in Spring 2011 allowed me to test out draft versions of several chapters. The manuscript has benefited from feedback from these audiences, as well as presentations at academic conferences around the world.

I also want to thank Marigold Acland, my editor at Cambridge University Press, for her trust in me and her valuable guidance at each step of the way.

The research for this book was made possible by generous support from Loyola Marymount University, my intellectual home for many years. The Summer Research Grants, Rain Research Assistants, First Book Subvention Grant, and finally the Daum Professorship Award all supplied me with the time and resources to finish this project and lead a productive scholarly life.

This book would not have been brought into the world without the masterful editorial assistance of Franklin Perkins. Our years of collaboration are a perfect illustration of how a total interplay of yin and yang can generate human creativity, cognitive power, and a flourishing life. I will always be grateful for this *yuanfen*.

1 Introduction

The sage scrutinizes what is appropriate to the Yin and Yang and discriminates what is beneficial in the myriad things in order to enhance life.

Lüshi Chunqiu

Those charged with recording the Yin and Yang observe their interaction and can bring about order.

Xunzi

What is yinyang? This question is at once utterly simple and wildly complicated. Thorough scholarly attempts to answer this question are surprisingly few, given the prominence of this concept. This may be a result of that prominence itself. People generally think they know about yinyang, although they usually pronounce yang incorrectly (it should rhyme with the English words "tong" or "bong," not with "sang" or "hang"). Because yin and yang are the most commonly known concepts from Chinese philosophy, they have practically become English words themselves. This familiarity may suggest that their meanings are obvious or that the concepts contain little worthy of deep intellectual inquiry. This would be a serious mistake.

Chinese thinkers themselves have recognized the significance of yinyang in Chinese thought and culture since ancient times. In the *Yantie lun* 鹽鐵論 (*Discourse on Salt and Iron*, 81 B.C.E.), one of the most significant texts in early China, we read: "The middle kingdom (*zhongguo/* China) is in the middle (*zhong*) of heaven and earth and is at the border (*ji* 際) of yin and yang (中國, 天地之中, 陰陽之際也)."[1]

---

[1] K. Heng, 桓寬. *On Salt and Iron* 鹽鐵論, with commentary by Z. Li. 林振翰校釋 (Taipei: Commercial Press, 1934), p. 55.

1

China is framed here in two contexts: human beings live between heaven and earth and at the intersection of yin and yang. The word *ji* literally means the border or boundary of a land, but it applies just as well to interactions between things. This early text views Chinese culture within the borders of yin and yang. It is also possible to read this claim from the *Yantie Lun* slightly differently, as one contemporary Chinese scholar argues that "middle" and "border" should both be taken as verbs. According to this view, Chinese culture arises from the attempt to stay centered between heaven and earth and to maintain the appropriate relations between yin and yang.[2]

Another early view of the centrality of yinyang comes from a medical text unearthed at the Mawangdui Han tombs that was buried in 168 B.C.E. The "Ten Questions" (十問) begins with a dialogue between the legendary sage kings Yao and Shun:

> Yao asked Shun: "In Under-heaven, what is the most valuable?"
> Shun replied: "Life is most valuable."
> Yao said: "How can life be cultivated?"
> Shun said: "Investigate Yin and Yang."[3]

This statement identifies life itself as the most fundamental value for the myriad things, and the key to fostering life is yinyang. Yinyang is not only offered for matters of basic health but also for the highest levels of self-cultivation. Thus, the oldest extant Chinese medical treatise (written around 200 C.E.), the *Huangdi Neijing*,[4] (黃帝內經) known as *The Yellow Emperor's Inner Classic*, states that the "true person" (*zhenren* 真人) is one who can: "carry and support heaven and earth and grasp and master yinyang." (餘聞上古有真人者，提挈天地，把握陰陽).[5]

---

[2] Chen Yun takes this as the mission of Chinese culture: "Moreover, the 'middle' of the 'middle kingdom' functions as the middle between heaven and earth, and 'border' of yin and yang has a verbal sense, meaning that as a kind of civilization, China has the cultural mission of linking heaven and earth and connecting yin and yang." Chen Yun, "The Death of Hundun and the Deconstruction of the View of China-Centrism" 陳贇 "混沌之死"與中國中心主義天下觀之解構 in Discussion Forum for Chinese Thought, http://www.zhongguosixiang.com/thread-23589-1-1.html, October 7, 2010.

[3] D. J. Harper (trans.), "Ten Questions in Early Chinese Medical Literature," *The Mawangdui Medical Manuscripts* (London and New York: Kegan Paul International, 1998), p. 399.

[4] The date and author of this text are debatable. The text consists of two parts: the first is a series of questions and answers; the second section is known as the "Vital Axis," which deals with medical physiology, anatomy, and acupuncture. P. U. Unschuld, *Medicine in China, A History of Ideas*, 25th ed., (Berkeley: University of California Press, 2010), p. 108.

[5] Y. Zhang 張隱庵 (ed.), *Huangdi Neijing Commentaries* 黃帝內經素問集注 (Beijing: Xueyuan Press 學苑出版社, 2002), p. 7.

These passages, spanning four centuries, illustrate the importance attributed to yinyang at all levels, from governing the state to maintaining the health of the body. As Joseph Needham says, yinyang ideas "were the most ultimate principles of which the ancient Chinese could conceive."[6] The *Huainanzi* (淮南子), a synthetic work of the early Han Dynasty (200 B.C.E.) presents the human condition in a similar way: "Heaven as father, Earth as mother, yin and yang as warp, the four seasons as weft."[7] The metaphor suggests that without the binding thread of yinyang, the embroidery of human life would unravel.

Yinyang finds expression in numerous classical Chinese texts and commentaries, especially during the Han Dynasty (206 B.C.E.–220 C.E.), and it has retained its preeminence through thousand years of Chinese tradition, and even survived modernization. Popular discussions of yinyang now generally focus on three points. First, yinyang describes a condition in which there exist two opposite but related and interdependent ideas or objects. For example, one popular online dictionary defines yinyang as "Two complementary principles of Chinese philosophy: Yin is negative, dark, and feminine. Yang is positive, bright, and masculine. Their interaction is thought to maintain the harmony of the universe and to influence everything within it."[8] *Webster's Encyclopedia Unabridged Dictionary of English Language* in turn states: "Yin and Yang (in Chinese philosophy and religion): two principles, one negative, dark, and feminine (Yin), and one positive, bright, and masculine (Yang), whose interaction influences the destinies of creatures and things."[9] As we see in these dictionary entries, things like the earth, the moon, water, the night, the feminine, softness, passivity, and darkness all accord with yin, whereas heaven, the sun, fire, day, masculinity, hardness, activity, and brightness can all be attributed to yang. This division simultaneously emphasizes that these two elements are interrelated and interdependent.

Second, yinyang offers a normative model with balance, harmony, and sustainability as ideals. When one compares something to yin or yang,

[6] J. Needham, *Science and Civilization in China*, 7 vols. (Cambridge University Press, 1956), vol. II, p. 232.

[7] H. Roth (trans.), *The Huainanzi: A Guide to the Theory and Practice of Government in Early China* (New York: Columbia University Press, 2010), p. 241. *The Huainanzi* provides the most elaborate early philosophical account of the beginning of the universe. The picture of the universe is carefully drawn in a Daoist framework; however, it integrates many different schools. The text claims an important role in the Chinese intellectual tradition, having inspired approximately 200 commentaries over a span of 2,000 years.

[8] http://www.Dictionary.reference.com

[9] *Webster's Encyclopedia Unabridged Dictionary of English Language* (New York: Gramercy Publishing Company, 1994).

this usually suggests a way of dealing with things through the balance or harmony between two elements. Such advice is popularly applied to almost all fields of action: leadership, business, art, media, sports, and psychoanalysis. Consider a typical example, applying yinyang to parenting:

> In the context of parenting, it is typical of masculine energy to distance ourselves from our children, to push them away, while it is typical of feminine energy to draw them toward us, to open our arms and heart, and comfort them. Pushing away, at the right times, can be the perfect expression of love, because without it, our children will not learn to be independent. Children, therefore, provide women with opportunities to be yang as well as their general inclination to be yin.[10]

In science, there is a life cycle assessment and green chemistry in which one finds phrases like "the yin and yang of industrial ecology" or "the yin and yang of optimal functioning."[11]

Third, a more scholarly understanding involves conceptual construction, whereby yinyang is characterized as a "correlative" mode of thought or cosmology.[12] This "correlative cosmology" as a comprehensive system was formed between the third and the second centuries B.C.E. The focal point is "stimulus and response" (*ganying* 感應) among things and events. An event or action happening or performed in one domain affects corresponding factors in another domain. This cosmology is not based on linear causality between distinct entities, but rather on making a connection between entities and phenomena. In *Yinyang and the Nature of Correlative Thinking*, A. C. Graham explains Chinese cosmology in terms of correlative thinking.[13] Graham explicitly distinguishes this approach from that of the well-known French Sinologist Marcel Granet (1884–1940):

> In Granet's time, it was still natural to assume that in matters of fact as in geometry, demonstration can start from clearly defined terms independent of correlations, so that Yin-Yang thinking – not that he treats it

---

[10] http://www.modernphilosophy.com/philosophy/parenting.html

[11] E. Voit, *Design Principles and Operating Principles: The Yin and Yang of Optimal Functioning*. http://www.sciencedirect.com

[12] B. I. Schwartz, *The World of Thought in Ancient China* (Cambridge, MA: Harvard University Press, 1985), pp. 351–382. A. H. Black, "Gender and Cosmology in Chinese Correlative Thinking," in C. W. Bynum, S. Harrell, and P. Richman (eds.) *Gender and Religion: On the Complexity of Symbols* (Boston: Beacon Press, 1989); D. L. Hall and R. T. Ames, "Sexism, With Chinese Characteristics" in C. Li (ed.) *The Sage and the Second Sex* (Chicago: Open Court Publishing, 2001).

[13] A. C. Graham, *Yinyang and the Nature of Correlative Thinking* (Singapore: The Institute of East Asian Philosophies, 1986), p. 1.

unsympathetically – belongs to a stage which Greek logic put behind it once and for all. By now, however, it has come to seem that wherever you dig down towards the roots of analytic reason, you reach a stratum where thinking is correlative, so that it becomes necessary to look at Yin-Yang from another direction.[14]

Rather than taking it as a primitive form of thought, Graham takes correlative thinking as a fundamental element of all reasoning. In the Chinese context, this correlative thinking is yinyang thinking. For example, yinyang is not just an important tool for grasping the cosmic body, namely the universe; it is also applied to the micro body: "human flesh."[15] The human body bears the same rhythm and properties as the greater cosmic body. Yinyang presents a justification for this association and a conceptual tool for understanding it.

These common views show that yinyang places human flourishing within a rich and deep context involving the interrelatedness of the cosmos and human beings. These interpretations also demonstrate that these relationships and connections must be understood in terms of differentiation between related but distinct forces. This view of yinyang is frequently used to characterize the Chinese worldview as a whole, in a way that situates it in contrast to Western thought: the Chinese focuses on interconnection, immanence, and cyclical changes, whereas Western philosophers emphasize dualism, transcendence, and eternal principles.

Such generalizations are too broad, and they miss the complexity and diversity of both Chinese and Western philosophy. Nonetheless, yinyang can be thought of as a kind of a horizon for much of Chinese thought and culture. It serves as a horizon in the sense that although the terms are invoked in particular contexts for concrete purposes, they imply a deeper cultural background and a paradigm for thinking about change and effective action. Yinyang is a particular term, but it also represents an underlying structure in an enduring tradition. In this sense, we can consider yinyang as a thinking paradigm. Thomas Kuhn develops a concept of paradigm that signifies an exemplary model. He argues that paradigms precede and shape all the operations of rational thinking: methodology, theory building, the determination of facts, and perception. A paradigm is a conceptual configuration that is demonstrated and learned by example, providing a lens through which one can view the world.[16] Yinyang in

---

[14] Ibid., p. 3.
[15] Ibid., p. 28.
[16] T. Kuhn, *Structure of Scientific Revolution* (Chicago: University of Chicago Press, 1970).

Chinese culture fits this description. At the same time, yinyang can also be seen as a constellation of lay beliefs and practices, functioning explicitly and implicitly in activities ranging from philosophy to health care and from warfare to a way of life. To capture this broad structure, this book will use the term "yinyang," rather than "yin or yang," "yin-yang," or "yin and yang." This reflects the Chinese usage, in which the terms are directly set together and would not be linked by a conjunction.

Beyond Common Understandings of Yinyang

A careful study of early Chinese texts shows that common accounts of yinyang are far too simple. Yinyang embodies a wide range of linked meanings, many of which are in play simultaneously. The invocation of yinyang itself is always predicated on a particular situation, a unique moment in which we must engage in the world. As Granet points out, "Throughout the period from fifth to third century [B.C.E.], these terms of Yin and Yang are employed by theorists from very different orientations. This very wide usage of these two terms gives the impression that they signify notions inspired by a vast ensemble of techniques and doctrines."[17]

This book illustrates yinyang as a philosophical and cultural paradigm that has multiple dimensions that evolved over time, and lays out the ways in which yinyang works, examining some of the ways in which yinyang functioned as the warp and woof of Chinese thought and culture. The goal is to give a more nuanced, synchronic account of the roles of yinyang within various aspects of early Chinese thinking, while still bringing out common aspects of yinyang as a paradigm and strategy. We can take the metaphor of the tree in the *Huainanzi* to illustrate this. A tree has two basic parts, the roots (*ben* 本) and the branches and leaves (*mo* 末): "It is like the roots and branches of trees: none of thousands of limbs and tens of thousands of leaves does not derive from the roots."[18] Yinyang is like a root (*ben*) of the branches of Chinese thinking: "As soon as you stimulate the root, the hundred branches all respond; it is like the spring rains watering the myriad things."[19] A better understanding of yinyang thus helps to clarify many aspects of Chinese thought and culture.

---

[17] Marcel Granet, *La pensée chinoise* (*Chinese Thought*) (Paris: Editions Albin Michel, 1968), p. 73. Thanks to Sonya Ozbey who translated one chapter from French to English for this book.

[18] Roth, *The Huainanzi*, p. 241.

[19] Ibid., p. 796.

We can begin by considering three ways in which the common assumptions about yinyang are inadequate or misleading.

Lived Yinyang: A Multiplicity of Relations

The common understanding of yin and yang as related pairs often takes yin and yang as things or fixed qualities of things. In fact, yin and yang are not simply things, entities, or objects. They can be used to characterize structures in which things exist, but they can also be used to analyze the functions of a thing in any given condition. In Chinese terms, yinyang can be both *ti* 體 (structure) and *yong* 用 (function). In both cases, yinyang always applies in particular and relative contexts. As Alfred Forke puts it, "Ultimately, yin and yang do not mean anything in themselves at all, being only employed to express a relation; one notion is the opposite of the other, the one is positive, the other negative."[20] Even at its inception, yinyang was used to denote the function of the sun in the context of a hill, with yang referring to the sunny side and yin to the shady side. If yinyang is the result of the temporal interplay of the sun and the hill, then does yinyang exist in its own right if either the sun or the hill is absent?

Because of this dependence on context, a single thing can be yin in one way and yang in another. Again, Forke provides a nice illustration: "The left hand is Yang, the right hand is Yin, in this no change is possible, but raise both hands, then they are both Yang, and put them down, and they are both Yin, and no matter whether you raise them or put them down, when they are hot they are both Yang, and when they are cold they are both Yin."[21] These are not contradictory labels, and it would be absurd to argue whether the right hand is *really* yang or *really* yin. The qualities only make sense when one specifies a certain context. The fact that anything is simultaneously yin and yang mirrors the fact that things are always implicated in multiple relations at once. Moreover, which relation is in view depends on the particular purposes and priorities of the viewer.

Aside from the fact that yin and yang differentiate things only within particular relationships and contexts, the precise relationship between yin and yang could be characterized in different ways, many of which can be invoked simultaneously. It is important to point out that yinyang is neither dualistic in positing two absolutely independent entities, nor even simply dialectical in projecting one single pattern for change. Yin

---

[20] A. Forke, *The World-Conception of The Chinese: Their Astronomical, Cosmological and Physico-Philosophical Speculations* (London: Late Probsthain & Co., 1925), p. 214.

[21] Ibid., p. 215.

and yang contest each other in a temporal framework and in multiple ways. To better encapsulate the complexity and multiplicity of yinyang thought, we can generalize these different relationships into six forms.[22]

1) *Maodun* 矛盾: Contradiction and opposition. Although yinyang thought may prompt us to think of harmony, interconnection, and wholeness, the basis of any yinyang distinction is difference, opposition, and contradiction. Any two sides are connected and related, but they are also opposed in some way, like light and dark, male and female, forceful and yielding. It is the tension and difference between the two sides that allows for the dynamic energy that comes through their interactions. It is also this difference that enables yinyang as a strategy – to act successfully, we must sometimes be more yin and sometimes more yang, depending on the context.

This aspect of yinyang is often described in terms of *maodun* 矛盾, which literally means "shield-spear" and originates from a story in the *Hanfeizi* 韓非子 (280–233 B.C.E.). A person who sells shields and spears promotes his shields by saying they are so strong that nothing can penetrate them, whereas he promotes his spears by saying they are so sharp they can penetrate anything. Someone then asks him – what happens if one tries to use your spear to penetrate your shield?[23]

The *Hanfeizi* story raises opposites as logical contradictions. In this sense, something cannot be yang and yin (light and dark, masculine and feminine) in precisely the same way, at the same time, and in the same context. This approach to distinctions can be seen as the one of most fundamental in European philosophy. Such an approach, however, works only in the abstract. In reality, we not only find that opposites exist through interaction with and in dependence on each other, but also that the same thing can be considered to have opposite qualities depending on the context, as it is not a logical contradiction to say that one thing is small (in comparison to a mountain) but large (in comparison to an ant). In thinking about opposition and difference, Chinese thinkers concentrate much more on these latter aspects. The best-known modern example comes from Mao Zedong (1893–1976) who took *maodun* as the title of one of his essays, *On Contradiction* 矛盾論 (*Maodun Lun*), which highlights the unity of opposites as a force for class struggle and change.

---

[22] A further specification of the ways in which yin and yang can be related will be given in the discussion of the body in Chapter 5.

[23] Chen, Qiyou 陳奇猷. *New Annotation of Hanfeizi* 韓非子新校注 (Shanghai: Shanghai Guji Press 上海古籍出版社 New Commentary, 2000), p. 204.

2) *Xiangyi* 相依: Interdependence. One side of the opposition cannot exist without the other. This interdependence can be seen on several different levels. On one level, it points out the interdependence of opposites as relative concepts. In labeling something as "high," one must implicitly label something else as "low." One cannot have a concept of "good" without there existing a concept of "bad" (*Daodejing*, chapter 2). According to yinyang thinking, however, the interdependence of opposites does not simply refer to the relativity of our concepts, but also to how things themselves exist, grow, and function. One way that this interdependence appears most clearly is through the alternation of yin and yang. The sun is the best example of yang – bright, warming, stimulating growth, and giving a rhythm – but when the power of that yang is developed to the extreme, it is necessary for it to be anchored, regenerated, and sustained by the force of yin. The sun must set. Although yang is the obvious, it cannot thrive without attention to yin. This interdependence appears in traditional Chinese medical texts, where the surge of *yangqi* 陽氣 depends on the regeneration of the *yinqi* 陰氣 of the five internal organs. Without the *yinqi* of the organs, there will be no a surge of *yangqi* or its extension outward.

The *Gui Guzi* 鬼谷子 (*The Master of Spirit Valley*), a classic text of the school of *Zongheng* 縱橫 (School of Strategy) in the Warring States Period (451–221 B.C.E.), illustrates this interdependence, using an opening and closing door as a metaphor. To be a door, it must be able to open and close as two interrelated modes; otherwise, it will be simply a wall (that does not move) or an open space (that does not close). The *Gui Guzi* gives this a cosmic significance: "Opening and closing are the way of heaven and earth. Opening and closing change and move yinyang, just as the four seasons open and close to transform the myriad things."[24]

3) *Huhan* 互含: Mutual inclusion. Interdependence is linked closely to mutual inclusion. If yin depends on yang, then yang is always implicated in yin; in other words, yin cannot be adequately characterized without also taking account of yang. The same is true of yang – it necessarily involves yin. Regarding things themselves, even something that is strongly yang can be considered yin in some relations, as we have seen. The constant alternation between yin and yang also entails that yang always holds some yin and yin holds some yang. In the cycle of four seasons, summer is the most yang of the seasons, yet it contains a yin force, which will begin to emerge in the summer, extend through the fall, and reach its culmination

---

[24] F. Xu (ed.), 許富宏 *Gui Guzijishi*, 鬼谷子集釋, *Master of Spirit Valley* (Beijing: Chinese Press, 2008), p. 13.

in the winter. Winter is the highest stage of yin, yet it unfolds a yang force
that will attain its own full swing through spring to summer. This mutual
inclusion is best captured in the famous yinyang symbol that will be discussed in Chapter 6, which includes a small circle of yang within the fullest yin and a small circle of yin within the fullest yang.

Similarly, in the *Yijing* 易經 (*The Book of Changes*), all yin hexagrams
have a dominant yang line and all yang hexagrams have a dominant yin
line. This mutual inclusion has important consequences in terms of strategy because it indicates that, when one thing appears to you as present,
that thing also entails opposite forces that are hidden and in motion but
that have not yet appeared.

4) *Jiaogan* 交感: Interaction or resonance. Each element influences
and shapes the other. If yin and yang are interdependent and mutually
inclusive, then a change in one will necessarily produce a change in the
other. Thus, as yang ebbs in the autumn, yin strengthens, and as yin
declines in the spring, yang grows. For example, in Chinese traditional
medical diagnoses, too much yin in the body is a sickness of yang, and
too much yang in the body is a sickness of yin.[25] Changes in yin will affect
yang, and vice versa.

This mutual resonance is crucial to yinyang as a strategy because
it entails that one can influence any element by addressing its opposite, which in practice most often takes the form of responding to yang
through yin. The Eastern Han dynasty (25–220 C.E.) text, the *Taipingjing*
太平經 (*Classic of Great Peace* 31–7 B.C.E.), which is a valuable resource
for early Daoist beliefs and practices, applies this yinyang resonance to
oppose female infanticide, as we will see in Chapter 3.

In medical treatment, yin and yang should be fostered at the same
time. It is said, for example, that yin will not respond to the drug or acupuncture without a certain amount of yang. The *Lüshi Chunqiu* 呂氏春秋
(c. 240 B.C.E.)[26] takes this resonance as a general principle, approached
through the relationship between action and nonaction: "Not to venture
out is the means by which one does venture out; not to act is the means
by which one acts. This is called 'using the Yang to summon the Yin and
using the Yin to summon the Yang.'"[27]

---

[25] Zhang (ed.), *Huangdi Neijing Commentaries*, p. 46.

[26] The *Lüshi Chunqiu*, compiled around 240 B.C.E., is the one of the great monuments of
Chinese thinking. As Knoblock and Riegel put it, it is "a philosophical manual for the
universal rule of the coming dynasty.... It belongs in the first rank of classical Chinese
philosophy." J. Knoblock and J. Riegel, *The Annals of Lü Buwei: A Complete Translation
and Study* (Stanford: Stanford University Press, 2000), pp. vii–viii.

[27] Ibid., p. 410.

5) *Hubu* 互補: Complementarity or mutual support. Each side supplies what the other lacks. Given that yin and yang are different but interdependent, properly dealing with a situation often requires supplementing one with the other, which is a way of achieving the appropriate balance between the two. This relationship appears clearly in discussions of art and crafts. For example, the *Zhouli* 周禮 (*The Rites of Zhou*, 221 B.C.E.) describes the craft of making a wheel:

> The way of making the hub of wheel must be measured according to yin-yang. Yang is densely grained and thus is strong; yin is loosely grained and thus is soft. Therefore, one uses fire to nourish its yin, making it even with its yang. Thus, even if the wheel is worn, it will not lose its round form.[28]
>
> 凡斬轂之道，必矩其陰陽。陽也者，積理而堅；陰也者，疏理而柔。是故以火養其陰，而齊諸其陽，則轂雖敝不藃

This passage addresses the difficulty of creating a wheel that is firm but made of materials that are soft enough to bend into a circle. Here, softness and hardness complement and support each other. This complementarity is different from the submission of one to the other, because both sides stand on equal ground in performing different roles.

6) *Zhuanhua* 轉化: Change and transformation. One side becomes the other in an endless cycle. Yinyang thought is fundamentally dynamic and centers on change. In nature, there is decline, deficiency, decrease, and demise, as well as flourishing, surplus, increase, and reproduction. In the human world, life is filled with trouble, failure, exhaustion, and insufficiency, as well as fullness, fruition, mastery, and success. Considering these various states of being, one can derive that change is perpetual, never ending. Reversal (*fan* 反) is a constant theme in Chinese thought, especially in the *Daodejing*. It invokes the image of a circle, or more precisely, a spiral movement that forever continues in a ring formation. According to the *Daodejing*, reversal (*fan*) is the movement of *Dao* and the rhythm of life (Chapter 40).

The *He Guanzi*, 鶡冠子 (the *Pheasant Cape Master*), a text most likely from the Warring States Period (475–221 B.C.E.), gives an influential characterization of this movement: "Beautiful and ugly adorn each other: this is called returning to the full cycle. Things develop to their extremes and then reverse. This is called circular flowing. 美惡相飾，命曰復周，物極則反，命曰環流"[29] The character translated as flowing, *liu* 流, refers

---

[28] Y. Wang, 王雲五 (ed.), *Zhouli* 周禮今注今譯, *The Ritual of Zhou* (Taipei: Taiwan Commercial Press, 1972), p. 424.

[29] X. Wang, (ed.), 王心湛, *Collected Interpretations of He Guanzi*, 鶡冠子集解 (Shanghai: Guangyi Press, 1936) p. 9. The statement of *wuji zhefa* (物極則反), "a thing will reverse

most literally to the flowing of water, and the character itself contains the image of water on the left. The term for circular or ring is 環 *huan*. We might thus also translate the phrase as "flowing circulation."

The *Huangdi Neijing* often identifies yinyang interplay as a cycle (*huan*) without beginning or end: "Yinyang are mutually connected, like a cycle without beginning. Thus, one knows that attack and defense always follow each other. 陰陽相貫，如環之無端，故知榮衛相隨也." Another passage says: "Yinyang are interlocking like a cycle without limit, *yinyang* follow each other and internal and external interlock each other like a cycle without limit."[30]

We can see now the ambiguity and complexity in saying that two things "are like yin and yang." Everything is bound up in a plurality of relationships at the same time, related both to multiple things and to the same thing in multiple ways. These relations are not distinct but reflect the actual complexity of life and nature. Yinyang claims must be taken as a point of reference that is defined by location (*wei* 位) and time (*shi* 時). This study accentuates these complex, multidimensional frameworks to explore the wide array of practices that constitute yinyang understanding. The defense of this pluralistic picture of yinyang thought illuminates the diversity and variety within the paradigm itself, a diversity that has enabled yinyang to serve so many different functions throughout various aspects of Chinese culture.

Generation 生 *(Sheng) and Emergence*

The common understandings of yinyang, especially the emphasis on correlative thinking, have taken correspondence as their basis, recognizing the important role of yinyang in connecting heaven, earth, and the myriad things. These common views, however, often overlook one of the most important forms of change: *sheng* 生 (generation, growth, life).

The word *sheng* originally referred to a plant growing out of the soil. It can be a noun indicating life itself or a verb that conveys the generative

---

after developing to its extremes," has become a popular idiom in contemporary China. There is a term in contemporary Western science called "self-organized criticality," which refers to the tendency of large dissipative systems to drive themselves to a critical state, with a wide range of length and time scales. The idea provides a unifying concept for large-scale behavior in systems with many degrees of freedom. It has been looked for in such diverse areas as earthquake structure, economics, and biological evolution. It is also seen as "regression toward means."

[30] B. Niu 牛兵占 (ed.), *Huangdi Neijing*, 黃帝內經 (Shijiazhuang: Hebei Science and Technology Press 1993), p. 59.

living process. It is also the term for birth or giving birth. Even though cosmological correspondence is important to the use of yinyang as an explanatory tool, it is also necessary to consider the relationships between yinyang and the generativity that emerges from interaction. In fact, although we often think of yinyang as focusing on polarities, yinyang thought really is a type of triadic thinking centered on the thirdness that results from the interaction between yin and yang. The whole is made of the interactions between parts, not the individual parts, themselves.

Yinyang as a form of correlative thinking is evident in the thought of the Han Dynasty Confucian Dong Zhongshu 董仲舒 (179–104 B.C.E.),[31] however, it should be taken as only one of many possible ways that yinyang can explain changes. The contemporary Chinese scholar Pang Pu 龐樸 distinguishes between two types of generation: generation by transformation (*huasheng* 化生) and generation by reproduction (*paisheng* 派生). He describes *paisheng* as a chicken giving birth to an egg and *huasheng* as the egg hatching into a chicken. The products that stem from both of these kinds of generations bring out new phases of existence.[32] Yinyang plays a central role in such generative processes.

The *Huainanzi* explicitly links yinyang to generation and growth (*sheng*):

> Heaven, Earth and the four seasons do not [purposefully] generate (*sheng*) the ten thousand things. Spirit and illumination join, yin and yang harmonize and the myriad things are generated (*sheng*).[33] (天地四時，非生萬物也，神明接，陰陽和，而萬物生之).

A passage in the *Zhuangzi* 莊子 (third century B.C.E.) connects yinyang directly to life itself, referring to living things as "all the creatures taking shape between heaven and earth and receiving vital energy [*qi*] from the yin and yang."[34]

---

[31] Fung You-lan (1895–1990) claimed that the history of Chinese philosophy could be divided into two periods: the period before Dong Zhongshu ("the period of philosophers") and the period after Dong Zhongshu ("the period of Classical learning"). Dong Zhongshu was instrumental in making Confucianism the orthodoxy of the state at the expense of the other schools of thought and was prominent in the creation of the institutional basis for propagating this Confucian orthodoxy. For more discussion, see R. Wang, "Dong Zhongshu's Transformation of Yin/Yang Theory and Contesting of Gender Identity," *Philosophy East & West*, 55 (2005), 209–231.

[32] Pang Pu, 龐樸, *On Oneness Divided into Threeness* 淺說一分為三 (Beijing: Xinhua Press, 2004), p. 115.

[33] Roth, *The Huainanzi*, p. 803.

[34] B. Ziporyn (trans.), *Zhuangzi: The Essential Writings with Selections from Traditional Commentaries* (Indianapolis/Cambridge: Hackett Publishing Company Inc., 2009), p. 69.

It is the movement of yinyang *qi* that leads to the life or death of any living thing. Early Chinese texts tackled structural questions about the universe through yinyang as a way of highlighting the self-generative and self-organizing forces of complex phenomena. As Lauren Pfister contends, there is "an inherent necessity driving for transformation" in all aspects of reality, and "all transformation[s] are born within the hidden, invisible contexts."[35] Yinyang thought appeals to integrated processes rather than divided dualisms. It addresses what we could call a state of complexity, a term widely invoked in the field of contemporary science, particularly in relation to biological systems. The idea of complexity shows "the whole being formed of numerous parts in nonrandom organization."[36] In this sense, complexity is about seeing a thing in terms of its parts in connection with the whole. There is structure or order in the way in which the whole is composed of parts. The whole is greater than the sum of the parts.

Yinyang thought has been a kind of complexity thinking, in which the whole is perceived through multiple interactions. Any given existence is a complex system such that parts are arranged and their relations make its structure. Biological and organic processes, rather than the more abstract disciplines of physics or mathematics, were the favored conceptual sources for Chinese understanding of the world. This contrasts the analysis of the universe through geometrical logic and mathematical order more familiar in the West. This weight on biology prompted Zhang Xianglong 張祥龍, a contemporary Chinese scholar, to promote the idea that Chinese thinking at a fundamental level is gendered and that biological interaction between male and female is the ultimate model for Chinese philosophical speculation.[37]

One other aspect of the generative force of yinyang seen in many classical texts is an emphasis on probable reasoning with an open-end dimension. This again contrasts the common focus through most of the history of Western thought on certainty and universality, something that appears in Classical Greece, where geometry and reason were honed as tools for understanding natural phenomena.[38] This can be seen as reflecting a common human desire for stable and certain knowledge.

---

[35] L. Pfister, "Philosophical Explorations of the Transformative Dimension in Chinese Culture," *Journal of Chinese Philosophy*, 35:4 (2008), 663–682.

[36] S. D. Mitchell, *Biological Complexity and Integrative Pluralism* (New York: Cambridge University Press, 2003), p. 167.

[37] X. Zhang 張祥龍, "The Status and Consequences of 'Gender Difference' in Chinese and Western Philosophy" '性別'在中西哲學裡的地位及其思想後果, *Jiangsu Social Sciences*, 6 (2002), 1–9.

[38] L. M. Lederman and H. Christopher, *Symmetry and the Beautiful Universe* (New York: Prometheus Books, 2004), p. 121.

At the same time, however, human beings also have a need to develop the capacity for successful prediction to avoid danger. Such predictions are never certain and must go beyond abstract calculations. For the Chinese, the uncertainty involved in our ability to predict regularities was a practical matter of agriculture, not an abstract problem of philosophical skepticism. Facing an unpredictable world, we might lose confidence and feel as if there is no stability at all. Yinyang thinking emerged as a conceptual apparatus to ease the anxiety of lost control by creating ways of predicting and accepting the inevitability of change. At the same time, because there is no way one can exhaust the unknown, one must also have constant concern, *youhuan* 憂患, regarding the future. We will turn to this notion of anxious concern in Chapter 2.

Harmony and Strategic Efficacy

One of the most common ways to characterize yinyang has been through the idea of harmony (*he* 和). In fact, many interpretations of yinyang stop at this point, going no further than the idea of harmony or balance. However, what are the parameters for harmony? Can we give an unambiguous explanation of what constitutes a state of harmony? One might claim that an orderly society is a harmony of policy, institutions, and citizens; a healthy body is a harmony of different bodily functions; a delicious dish is a harmony of all its ingredients.

For example, the current Chinese government has been using "harmonious society" (*hexie shehui* 和諧社會) as a way to deal with the divergence between rich and poor brought out by economic development and to stabilize the Chinese society as a whole. As these examples suggest, "harmony" itself needs further definition and explanation. For example, Alan Chan formulates two models of harmony in ancient China: culinary harmony and musical harmony.[39] Musical harmony pays most attention to hierarchical relationships that require different elements or sounds working together in a coordinated way. In contrast, culinary harmony focuses on an integrated relationship that results from the interaction and blending of different elements. These two models have different practical implications, and both are present in the Chinese tradition.

In explaining yinyang and correlative thinking, A. C. Graham attempts to give a more specific formulation of harmony as it relates to yinyang. He

[39] A. K. L. Chan, "Harmony as a Contested Metaphor and Conceptions of Rightness (*Yi*) in Early Confucian Ethics," in R. A. H. King and D. Schilling (eds.) *How Should One Live? Comparing Ethics in Ancient China and Greco-Roman Antiquity* (Berlin: De Gruyter, 2011), pp. 37–62.

does this by articulating two different kinds of relationships: "paradigmatic relations" oriented around similarity and difference, and "syntagmatic" relations based on contiguity and remoteness, which he takes as also encompassing relations of part and whole.[40] Graham explains:

> The interaction of things are seen as either orderly or chaotic; they are orderly to the extent that in the symmetries of space and cycles of time the harmonious are together and the conflicting apart. To describe a phenomenon in its place and time within this order will be to select from conflicting (as paradigmatic A, B…) and to combine the harmonious (as syntagmatic 1, 2…).[41]

In other words, harmony and disorder are conceived through contiguity and distance, and finding harmony depends on combining contrasting elements into relations of contiguity. Harmony is ultimately a matter of integration, and this is the main function of yinyang thinking.

Although Graham insightfully brings out one important element of how yinyang thought relates to harmony, the function of yinyang cannot be limited to this goal. The most obvious inadequacy with a focus on harmony is that the focal point of yinyang as a strategy is not so much on achieving a static balance but rather on generation and transformation. This is the issue of emergence, which will be significant to this study, as it implies a thinking paradigm directed primarily toward self-organization and complexity.

A second key limit with an exclusive concern for harmony is that yinyang thinking, when considered as a strategy or guide, was used primarily to achieve concrete results, such as victory in battle, cultivating the body to attain longevity, and having constructive sexual intercourse. These goals are all relative to human purposes. The goal of yinyang thinking as a strategy is efficacy in general; harmony is frequently a means toward this goal as well as a manifestation of its success. Even so, from the perspective of nature itself, a long or short life, or the loss or victory in a particular battle, are probably all equally harmonious results.

However, the difference between them is crucial to the actors involved. Thus, an account of the aspirations behind the use of yinyang must go beyond harmony itself. This applies to how yinyang functions. In addition to using balance and harmony, yinyang as a strategy calls attention to and helps to organize the specific elements needed for efficacy, such

---

[40] Graham, *Yinyang*, p. 19.
[41] Ibid., p. 63.

as timing, situation, and background factors not immediately present. As we will see, presence (*you* 有) appears in a context of absence (*wu* 無). This attentiveness to the hidden background from which things originate and transform is an awareness of the yin side and is a common strategy of yinyang thought.

Methods and Structure of Chapters

This book employs three basic approaches for a comprehensive understanding of yinyang: the descriptive and historical, the paradigmatic and conceptual, and the pragmatic. The descriptive approach begins with the historical development of yinyang, attempting to establish the notion of "lived yinyang," that is, yinyang as a dynamic and changing system of thought and way of dealing with the world. This book traces the historical development and diversified manifestations of yinyang, drawing together the different uses and models of yinyang, starting from its origins in early classical texts. The focus is on works from the pre-Qin to Han periods, although later materials are sometimes used, as well. Although this historical aspect appears throughout the book, a historical overview of the development of yinyang thinking will be given in this chapter.

This book relies heavily on primary texts, with a careful interpretation of the claims and descriptions in each. Some of the texts, such as the *Daodejing* and the *Yijing*, are well known to Western readers, whereas others, such as the *Gui Guzi* (*Master of Spirit Valley*), *He Guanzi* (*Pheasant Cape Master*), *Wenzi* (*Master Wen*), or *Zhouyi Can Tong Qi* 周易參同契 (*The Three Ways Unified and Normalized of Zhouyi*), have attracted relatively little scholarly attention. One fundamental aspect of this book is letting the Chinese texts themselves disclose what yinyang is. I have tried not to impose an interpretation, especially those coming from Western terminologies, but rather let the texts themselves unfold the meanings of yinyang, frequently through quotations. This method supports the basic goal of giving greater specificity to conceptions of yinyang – we must recognize how different texts developed yinyang in specific ways and for different purposes.

This study brings together texts from different periods and contexts, which is the only possible way to reach the primary goal of this project: going beyond a simplistic explanation of yinyang to present a more complicated and diverse account. This approach, however, faces several challenges. First, as a study of yinyang, it must avoid becoming a simple survey of different viewpoints. Although grounded in a careful and thorough study of the sources and the development of ideas over time, it also needs some coherence. Second, given the centrality of yinyang in Chinese thought and culture, the amount of materials that could be included is nearly endless; of necessity, many interesting positions must be excluded. I have attempted to deal with both problems by selecting several exemplary positions in each chapter and focusing on specific texts expressing variations or developments of those positions. Thus, although each chapter is primarily organized thematically, these themes are linked to particular texts. At the same time, when illustrating a particular aspect of yinyang thinking, I have freely drawn in similar uses from other texts, even if they come from a different time or point of view. This balance between both the distinctiveness and continuity among various positions follows from the fact that even though each text takes up yinyang in its own way, yinyang provided a common vocabulary and framework, so that different positions still maintain some kind of "family resemblance."

Although emphasizing historical developments, the purpose of this work is not primarily historical. Instead, it is meant to articulate conceptual positions. This is the second main line of approach. In this sense, although grounded in Sinology, the book is intended to be philosophical. The study is not primarily intended to solve textual puzzles. For example, many texts used in this endeavor have disputed origins and dates. Was the "Neiye" chapter of the *Guanzi* written before or after the *Daodejing*? Did Dong Zhongshu actually write the *Chunqiu Fanlu*? These kinds of questions are beyond the scope of this book. The goal, instead, is to put many scattered, unexamined conceptual claims into a coherent whole – to build a yinyang-thought paradigm.

In putting yinyang on a secure and clear philosophical footing, this book strives both for internal coherence and faithfulness to the primary texts and traditions. It thus challenges us to remain rooted in the original Chinese philosophical vocabularies and issues, keeping away from Western philosophical assumptions, frameworks, and terms. That is, it intends to be philosophical, however, to develop these philosophical positions with Chinese terms and concepts. Because these positions developed in response to common aspects of human life, they frequently address shared cross-cultural philosophical concerns. Through such concerns, this book endeavors to open various routes by which contemporary Western readers can access and engage these early Chinese texts.

The paradigmatic approach centers on exemplars of yinyang usage, both in examining typical forms of yinyang reasoning and in showing how these are manifested in particular fields, such as cosmology, logic, social order, bodily cultivation, and visual presentation. Here, we will take a walk on a long path of Chinese texts. The flagstones on which we will tread are terms, each seemingly unique and strange. As we walk, however, we begin to notice that each term leads gently and logically to the other because of its link to yinyang. The *Dao* 道 (the way), *qi* 氣 (vital force or energy), *yi* 易 (changes), *taiji* 太極 (great ultimate), *lei* 類 (kinds), *shu* 術 (strategy), *xiushen* 修身 (body cultivation), and *xiangshu* 象數 (images and numbers) are interrelated on the basis of yinyang. These terms have many differences among texts and change over time, as there is not simply one unvarying yinyang position. At the same time, this book arranges these specific texts as paradigms to reveal resemblances that will illuminate consistent elements of yinyang thought and practice, even if these elements are not universal.

This emphasis on philosophy, however, should not obscure the fact that yinyang was not only a source of conceptualization but also a practical guide or strategy. Thus, the third way of approaching yinyang in this book is pragmatic, focusing on the role of yinyang in connection with specific practices, such as *fengshui*, city planning, military strategy, medicine, sexual practice, inner alchemy, and body transformation. This focus will not only specify the ways in which yinyang is applied as a theoretical structure but will also show how yinyang was used to guide actions in concrete contexts.

After the introduction in Chapter 1, the book is organized into five chapters, each centering on key concepts in Chinese philosophy. Chapter 2 highlights *xingershang* (形而上 above forms), a phrase with ancient roots but later used to translate the Western term "metaphysics." This chapter concentrates primarily on cosmology, showing how yinyang thought justifies and explicates a self-generating and self-transforming world. The chapter ponders the connections among four fundamental cosmological concepts: *Dao*, *qi*, *yi*, and *taiji*.

The concept of *Dao*, central to the *Daodejing*, illustrates many of the basic functions of yinyang thinking (although the *Daodejing* itself uses yin and yang only once). *Qi*, vital force or energy, is a key concept used for describing all kinds of natural processes. Yinyang has long been closely connected to the concept of *qi*, a link that goes back at least to the *Shangshu* 尚書 (*The Book of History*, 772–476 B.C.E.). In these cases, the *qi* of yinyang is the generative force underlying all existence and serves an indispensable role in making an ontological link between a unitary source and the diversity of the myriad things, *wanwu* 萬物 (literally, ten thousands of things). *Yi*, change, is in the title of the *Yijing* (*The Book of Changes*), which offers a rich resource for yinyang, both through the binary structure of the core text and the explicit discussions of yinyang in its various commentaries, particularly the "Xi Ci." These various cosmological views exemplify how the myriad things are tied into an interrelated net through yinyang, which explicates the general rules and the myriad small details.

Chapter 3 examines the world of *xingerxia* 形而下, what is "below forms." Yinyang is an underlying rhythm animating all existence or all things "under heaven," *tianxia* 天下. One of the basic functions of yinyang is as a system for classifying and relating things and events in both the human and natural world. This is based on the concept of *lei* 類, kinds or categories. Everything and every event can be seen either as yin or as yang, and then related with other things on this basis. If the legacy of Greek logic is the Aristotelian deductive pattern of reasoning and the Euclidean vision of geometry, then the legacy of Chinese thought is this kind of yinyang *lei* thinking. It functions by linking phenomena across various levels and forms. This kind of categorizing through yinyang forms a deep-seated way of thinking that is found in political systems, ethical orientations, art, and city planning. Yinyang, thus, supplies a rational and coherent basis for social structures and human behaviors.

The social function of yinyang categorization will be discussed along several lines. The yin and yang distinction is an obvious way to account for the differentiation between women and men, articulated most fully in the work of the influential Han Confucian Dong Zhongshu. Even so, several issues need to be clarified. If yin (woman/femininity) and yang (man/masculinity) are both necessary for any healthy human being, then the devaluation of yin (the feminine) will lead to a weakening of other indispensable parts, that is, the yang (the masculine). This point contrasts the prominence Dong Zhongshu himself gives to hierarchy.

Another question to be considered is the role of yinyang in the field of ethics. In particular, how does yinyang bring together the two sides of proper action, appearing in the two main contemporary Chinese terms for morality or ethics, *daode* 道德 (the way and its power) and *lunli* 論理 (patterned human relations)? On the one hand, yinyang furnished a sense of human connection to broader processes of the universe, which is highlighted in the term *daode*; on the other hand, it structures human obligations through particular human relationships and hierarchies, which is emphasized in the term *lunli*. This leads to an important question: how does yinyang present the integration of human actions with the patterns of the cosmos and the rules of social order?

Yinyang is a way that interweaves being, thinking, and doing. Chapter 4 turns our attention to *shu* 術 (strategy or method). The notion of *shu*, a strategy or technique, enables one to function effectively in any given circumstance. The development of strategies for functioning effectively in the world is one of the most fundamental aspects of the yinyang paradigm, and this integration of knowledge and action might be the main strength of yinyang thought.[42] As a strategy, yinyang is applied to everything from thriving in different natural environments to succeeding in battles to having skillful sexual encounters. This chapter will articulate several broad kinds of methods or *shu*: *daoshu* 道術 (the method of the *Dao*) and *xinshu* 心術 (the method of the heart/mind). All of these forms of *shu* address living skillfully and efficaciously. While yinyang strategy involves many elements, there are two orientations that are most critical. The first is the skillful use of existing resources, conceptualized as the timing of heaven and the benefits of earthly terrain. The second is a focus on the importance of yin as background and what is non-present or unseen.

Chapter 5 underscores the significance of yinyang in relation to *xiushen* 修身 (the cultivation of body). The term here for the body, *shen* 身, is also the ancient Chinese word for the self, indicating the fundamental importance of the body in Chinese thought. Many classical texts assert that the order of the world lies in sages governing their own bodies well, thus relating the body to the state, family, and self. Yinyang is the hub for understanding what the body is, how it functions, and how it can be strengthened and cultivated. It was a common belief in early China that the human body is a yinyang body, particularly in medical texts and practices. All internal bodily functions are the work of yinyang, according to at least three variables: (1) the rhythm of yinyang (*jiezou* 節奏): either yang or yin is too fast or too slow; (2) the balance of yinyang (*pingheng* 平衡): too much or too little yang or yin; and (3) the transformation of yinyang (*bianhua* 變化): yang or yin changing too much or too little.

Health involves all three factors, establishing proper rhythm, balance, and change. Disease comes when any of these three is disrupted. Given the connection between the body and the self, the importance of body cultivation naturally leads to spiritual transformation. The human body is taken as a gateway for going beyond current physical, mental, and social conditions. This journey is not simply becoming attuned to the hidden cycles of nature, but is also a kind of spiritual conversion.

---

[42] Paul U. Unschuld comments, "The yin-yang and Five Agents doctrines are relational science. They may be well suited to explain some relationships and their effects in society and in humankind's natural environment. They may even explain a Chinese superiority in social, economic and military strategies over the west." Unschuld, *Medicine in China*, p. xxix.

Chapter 6 moves into the field of visual presentations, something called *xiang* 象 or "image" thinking, an approach that has been dominant in the interpretation of the *Yijing*. *Xiang* thinking is basically a kind of analogical reasoning in which one image schema is used to conceptualize another domain and, thus, derives implications from it. This chapter will map out the image-making tradition of *xiangshu* (images and numbers), which has often been neglected in Western academic work because of its complexity and peculiarity. The aspiration will be to recognize how yinyang was represented and what these representations reveal. This will guide us in determining how to "read" the famous yinyang symbol. Beyond indicating various characteristics of yinyang, there is a thinking model presupposed in this symbol, suggesting a type of visual thinking. The yinyang symbol is a graphic representation of an image schema, the circle with the growing colors visually depicts the dynamic forces involved, and the seeds of the opposite color symbolize the shift from one to the other that occurs when one reaches its largest point, leading to a circulation without end. The yinyang interaction itself goes beyond yinyang as merely reciprocal, complementary, and interdependent. The symbol itself depicts the emergence of thirdness as the result of this interplay. This discussion of yinyang as shown in the yinyang symbol will serve as a conclusion of the book.

The Origins of Yinyang in Relation to the Sun

There are three main written sources for learning about early Chinese culture. One are the oracle bones, primarily from the Shang (Yin) Dynasty (seventeenth–twelfth century B.C.E.). The second are the bronze inscriptions from the Western Zhou Dynasty (twelfth century–770 B.C.E.), and the Spring and Autumn Period (770–221 B.C.E). The third are transmitted written texts, primarily the *Shangshu* 尚書 (*The Book of History*) and the *Shijing* 詩經 (*The Book of Odes*), parts of which go back to the Western Zhou and continue through the Spring and Autumn Period.

The terms *yin* or *yang* do not appear in early oracle bones or the bronze inscriptions, however, there are a few words that might be related to the creation of the characters for yin and yang, particularly the character for yang, given its close connection to the sun.[43] Three of the earliest six Chinese characters that have been found in Dawenkou culture 大汶口文化

---

[43] H. Xiao 蕭漢明, *Yinyang: Great Transformation and Human Life* 陰陽大化與人生, (Guangdong People's Press, 1998), p. 15.

1.1. The earliest six Chinese characters found in Shangdong Dawenkou culture.

(4300–2500 B.C.E.) are related to the sun[44] (Figure 1.1: 1, 2, 6). Given the fundamental importance of the sun and its connection to yang, the

[44] Da Wenkou culture is based around Shangdong. The six characters were found on pottery. For more discussion see, ibid., p. 14.

character for yang might have appeared earlier than did the character for yin (Figure 1.1).

In the *Shangshu* (*The Book of History*), the term yang appears six times in the "Yugong" chapter. Five out of the six characters refer to mountains or the south side of a mountain. The term yin appears three times in this book, referring to the north side of a mountain. From this, we can see that in the *Shangshu*, the terms yang and yin are geographical terms used for specifying a location.

In the *Shijing* (*The Book of Odes*), the term *yang* appears sixteen times, and yin appears ten times. The first written record of using the two characters together is found in the *Shijing*: "Viewing the scenery at hill, looking for yinyang (既景迺岡, 相其陰陽)."[45] This line indicates that yin and yang in their earliest usage were separate terms that were connected to label the result of the sun reflecting on the hill. The sunny side of the hill is yang, and the shady side is yin. This original usage already displays primary aspects of yinyang thinking, suggesting the intersection of one thing (the sun) with a complex context, so that yinyang depicts the interplay between the sun, a hill, and the light. This usage implies a concrete reference and an observable fact. At the same time, yinyang is not a particular object but rather a phenomenon: the features of the sun as they relate to other things. In this sense, yang is quite different from the sun itself, *ri* 日. The sun is an entity, a being, a particular object, however, yang is the effect of this entity and not the entity itself. In their earliest uses, yin and yang are not substances but functions of something, and they are inevitably attached to relationships or contexts. Any fixed definitions of yinyang will, thus, lead to a problematic understanding of the terms.

As we can already see, yinyang thought was inspired by human experience of the sun. This original association of yang (and yin) with the effects of the sun has consequences for how the terms function in later Chinese thought. We can reflect on some of these implications here. The sun plays at least three important roles in early Chinese life. First, it provides a clock for daily routines. Farmers depend on it for light, which in turn dictates the daily rhythm of human life. As the *Shijing* says, "When the sun is coming out, one goes to the fields, and when sun is going down, one goes to rest."[46] (日出而作，日落而息) The steady rhythmic alternation of yin and yang can be seen as expanding from this basic

---

[45] Z. Zhou 周振甫, *Commentary on Shijing* 詩經 (*The Book of Odes*) (Beijing: Chinese Press, 2002), p. 437. James Legge translated the word *yinyang* as "the light and the shade." See J. Legge, *The Chinese Classics*, 5 vols. (Taipei: SMC Publishing Inc., 1994), vol. IV, p. 488.

[46] Z. Zhou, *Commentary on Shijing* (*The Book of Odes*) p.232.

human experience. Thus, Granet takes the fundamental dimension of yinyang thinking as being "the idea of rhythm."[47]

In keeping with the effects of the alternation of day and night on human beings, yang is associated with movement and action, whereas yin is associated with rest and stillness. The *Zhuangzi* in "The Way of Heaven" states: "Those who know the joys of Heaven, during their life act like Heaven, and at death transform with things. In their stillness they possess the same virtue [*de*] as yin, and in their movement they flow the same as yang."[48]

Second, the effects of the sun offer parameters that designate appropriate living conditions, as well as burial sites for the dead. The two terms convey geographical location and direction in relationship to the sun – sunlight and its absence; coldness and warmth. The sun passes over the myriad things equally, however, the space one occupies on earth varies the quality and effects of the sunlight. The sun makes certain spaces brighter or warmer, and plants on the south side of a mountain will grow better. Therefore, humans have to figure out how yinyang is distributed, which is known as yinyang *fenbu* 陰陽分布. It is beneficial to choose a location that faces the sun/yang because it imparts the most light and receives the most warmth, another functional aspect of yang. We see the legacy of this orientation toward yinyang in names used to refer to geographical locations.

Many place names in China today originate from yinyang's connection with the directions. The south and east side of mountains are yang. The north and west of mountains are yin. Thus, the city of Huayin 華陰 in Shanxi is located on the northern side of Hua Mountain. When the relationships to rivers, lakes, or other bodies of water are relevant to a location, the west side and north side will be yang. The city of Luoyang 洛陽 is north of the Luo River, and the city Huaiyin 淮陰 is on the east side of the Huai River. Rivers and mountains both act as focal points, however, opposing directions are named yang, because they relate differently to the sun.

Third, as with many other primitive cultures, reverence toward the sun was an important part of human culture in early China, and the sun remained significant to Chinese religion. In the Zhou Dynasty, the highest divine force was *tian* 天, conventionally translated as "heaven," however, a term which could also mean the sky. The *Zuozhuan* 左傳 (*Chronicle of Zuo* or *Commentaries of Zuo*), an early history text covering the period from

---

[47] Sonya Ozbey translation of Marcel Granet, (*Chinese Thought*) p. 75.
[48] G. Chen 陳鼓應, *Commentaries on Zhuangzi* (Beijing: Chinese Press, 1983), p. 341.

722–468 B.C.E., and one of the most important sources for understanding the history of the Spring and Autumn Period, claims that "from the sun one will know there is the way of heaven" (是以日知其有天道也).[49] In early times, the commands or mandate of heaven (*tianming* 天命), were revealed in the movements of the constellations.[50] The movement of the sun, moon, and stars were all expressions of heavenly will. Because the will of heaven is apparent through events in the sky, one can look to the sky to know the will of heaven. The *Guoyu* 國語 (*Discourses of the States*), a supposed record of various states from the Western Zhou to 453 B.C.E., asserts confidently that heavenly affairs must be expressed through heavenly images (天事必象).[51] Heaven also expresses its will through the different seasons, which are produced by the sun.

In particular seasons, heaven manifests specific commands. Human action must be synchronized with the movement of the sun. In fact, the word for seasons, *shi* 時, is also the word for acting in a timely way. The character itself contains an image of the sun: 日. The use of the movement of the sun to structure time and place comes together with reverence for the sun most clearly in the fields of astrology and calendrics.

The development of yinyang thought was largely concomitant with the theorization of Chinese astrology. The sky concerns both the calendar and the seasons as they relate to farming and ritual. It has a central place in people's lives. In China, sun worship was closely associated with the making of the calendar, which was one of the most important duties for any ruler. How does one choose the proper date for various important tasks, ranging from rituals to farming? On which day should one perform what kinds of sacrifice? What time during the day should one carry out a particular ritual? Successfully choosing these dates was thought to secure a desirable outcome. Here we see the interconnection of different levels of phenomena, something typical of yinyang thought.

The *He Guanzi* tells the way in which seasons are determined, based on the position of the Seven Dippers:

> If it points east, in the world it will be spring; if it points north, in the world it will be summer; if it points to west, in the world it will be fall; if it points to north, in the world it will be winter. (*huanliu* chapter)[52]

[49] M. Li, (ed.), *Zuozhuan Yizhu* 左傳譯注, (Shanghai: Shanghai Guji Press, 1998), p. 673.
[50] See more discussions in D. Pankenier, "The Cosmo-Political Background of Heaven's Mandate," *Early China*, 20 (1995), 121–176.
[51] Wu Guoyi 鄔國義, (ed.) *Guoyu* 國論譯注 (Shanghai: Shanghai Guji Press,1994), p. 289.
[52] Wang, (ed.), *Collected Interpretations of He Guanzi*, p. 11.

The term translated here as "world" is literally what is "under heaven" (*tianxia* 天下). Thus, heaven/sky and the earth that is under or below heaven are viewed through a lens of relatedness. They are not separate or isolated entities. Similarly, human events depend on these relationships – in spring we plant, and in the fall we harvest. In the *Hanshu* (*The Book of Han*), a classical history text finished in 111 c.e. and covering the history from 206 b.c.e. to 25 c.e., four related elements are distinguished but connected together to form a whole: heavenly images (*tianxiang* 天象), weather and climate (*qihou* 氣候), the developing stages of things (*wuhou* 物候), and human affairs (*renshi* 人事). The images of heaven (*tianxiang*) provide the timing for all kinds of actions, including the ruler's policies for scheduling punishments and rewards. The condition of the weather (*qihou*) guides farmers to plant or harvest. The stage of things (*wuhou*) indicates the proper timing for ordinary people. All of these factors are integral parts of human affairs (*renshi*).[53]

This whole structure of time was conceived through the flowing of yinyang, thus making yinyang the basis for human activities. The chapter called "Four Seasons" in the *Baihutong* 白虎通 (*Comprehensive Discussions in the White Tiger Hall*), the official transcript of an imperial conference on the Confucian classics convened in 79 c.e, makes this point explicitly: "Seasons [timing] are periods of time, the periods of the waxing and waning of yinyang."[54] 時者, 期也, 陰陽消息之期也.

Thus, the passage concludes that one needs to follow the decline and growth of yinyang (陰陽消長). The early Chinese calendar is called the "joined yinyang calendar," *yinyang heli* 陰陽合歷, because it was based on the movement of both the sun and the moon. The moon's cyclical movement from full to crescent is called the yin calendar; the movement of the sun, which sets days and seasonal changes, is called the yang calendar. The sun and moon, joined together, provide a guide for farming. The classical Chinese "day" (*ri* 日) is the same word as "sun," just as "month" (*yue* 月) is the same word as "moon." The moon has an indispensable role to play, because individual days (*ri*, representing the sun) are situated within months (*yue*, representing the moon). When you decide what you want to do this particular day, you must also consult with the moon, the background, or the context. This understanding is what allows one to act effectively. The month that a day falls within is much more important in the traditional calendar than is the year. The sun and moon are

[53] Ban Gu, *Hanshu* 漢書 (*The Book of Han*), (Beijing: Chinese Press), p. 1079.
[54] L. Chen, (ed.), *Baihutong* 白虎通, *Comprehensive Discussions in the White Tiger Hall*, (Beijing: Chinese Press), p. 2376.

the most vital information for farmers; however, they cannot be viewed as isolated bubbles of elements, but rather related to each other to set the particular context for any decision. Situating oneself in any configuration of forces requires attention to both yin and yang, although the yin commonly is the context and background outside of one's main focus. It is worth noting here that the moon also signifies water, the yin. Water bears live-giving power. Several myths describe women who become pregnant by touching water.[55]

We can see from these examples that yinyang is an early attempt to reconcile human life with the sun. The traditional characters for yin and yang are rooted in this affiliation. The character yin 陰 shows a mound on the left side, with a cloud on the bottom left, below the symbol for "today." The traditional character for yang 陽 shows a mound on the left side, with a sun on the top right. Part of yang in Chinese is ri 日, sun. The right side of the yang character can further be grouped as dan 旦 (daybreak; i.e., the sun coming over the horizon) and yang 昜 (bright; i.e., light streaming off the sun), which both directly relate to the interpretation of yang as "sunny." The simplified forms of the characters now used in China show this connection even more explicitly – yang is a mound next to the sun 阳, and yin is a mound next to the moon 阴. Similarly, the word for sun even in contemporary Chinese today is taiyang 太阳, the absolute or greatest yang.

From the Terms Yin and Yang to Yinyang Thinking as a Paradigm

The terms yin and yang gradually developed from ways of naming relationships with the sun into a complex way of thinking, which we can call "yinyang thinking." Many building blocks contributed to the formation of this thinking pattern. Historically, although the term yinyang was not a dominant concept before the Han Dynasty, proto-yinyang thought already existed and had given rise to a particular thinking model. We can distinguish three main constituents that contributed to this formation of yinyang thought.

The first source is practices of divination. In the Shijing, sun and moon divination is used to predict good or ill fortune: "The sun and moon announce ill fortune, not keeping to their proper paths."[56] As we

---

[55] E. T. C. Werner, Myths & Legend of China (New York: George G. Harrap & Co. Ltd., 1922).

[56] Zhou, Shijing, p. 300.

know from oracle bones, in the Shang Dynasty, divination was consulted widely for a broad range of activities. Is it a good day for going hunting, getting married, or going to war? All of these questions were divided into "yes" or "no" – two aspects.

This kind of binary structure appears most clearly in the *Yijing* (*The Book of Changes*). The *Yijing* makes known two kinds of divination. One is *pu*, which uses the tortoise shell. The diviner would make marks on the tortoise shell, then burn it and read the cracks. Another method is *wu*, which uses stalks or other sticks that are divided and shuffled according to a certain procedure. The cracked lines or the arrangement of the sticks all point toward one of two possible results: well-fortuned or ill-fortuned, yes or no, going or stopping, failure or success, gaining or losing. The binary structure of these divination methods reveals a value and belief system that became deeply integrated with yinyang thinking. Edmund Ryden asserts, "Binary terminology is a feature of much early Chinese philosophy. Indeed it is perhaps also a feature of the Chinese language."[57] Such a binary system underlies the structure of the *Yijing*; this system was explicitly connected to yinyang through the *Yizhuan*易傳, (*Yi Commentaries*), which were probably written in the late Warring States Period. For example, the "Shuo Gua" ("Explanation of Hexagrams") declares, "The way of establishing heaven is yin and yang; the way of establishing earth is softness and hardness; the way of establishing human being is benevolence and righteousness."[58]

Although associated with divination, yinyang also signified a rationalizing tendency in relation to natural processes. According the contemporary Chinese scholar Chen Lai 陳來, in the Spring and Autumn Period, there was a growing tension between worldly political and moral consciousness and the tradition of spirit worship.[59] The tension concerned whether divination (*wu*) or virtue (*de*) should come first. One key distinction involved in this tension was the separation between yinyang and *jixiong*吉凶 (well-fortuned or ill-fortuned). Here, yinyang stands for human intellectual power to explicate natural events, in which case, human knowledge does not depend on divination or spirits. Natural phenomena result from yinyang movement as opposed to anything mysterious or dependent on the divine.

[57] E. Ryden, *The Yellow Emperor's Four Canons, A Literary Study and Edition of the Text from Mawangdui* (Taipei: Guangqi Press, 1997), p. 11.

[58] H. Gao 高亨, *Commentary on Zhouyi* 周易大傳今注 (Jinan: Qilu Press, 1998), p. 455.

[59] Chen Lai, *The World of Ancient Thought and Culture: Religions, Ethics and Social Thought in the Spring and Autumn Period* (Beijing: SDX Joint Publishing Company, 2009), p. 16.

We can consider an example from the *Zuozhuan*. In the Spring and Autumn Period, the officer in charge of astrology used yin and yang to explain the condition of weather and changes of season. The *Zuozhuan* records two exceptional events in 644 B.C.E. that supposedly happened in the state of Song. One was a shooting star, and the other was six birds flying backwards. The king of Song asked Shi Shuxing whether these were signs of being well- or ill-fortuned. Shi Shuxing responded that these are "the events of yinyang, not issues of being well or ill fortuned."[60] This is a bold claim, because it marks a transitional time when yinyang was used as a conceptual tool to clarify natural phenomena and when it provided a break from treating those events as auspicious signs determining human events. The *Xunzi* 荀子 (298–238 B.C.E.) later presents a more explicit and systematic account in the chapter, "Discourse on Heaven":

> When stars fall or trees groan, the whole state is terrified. They ask what caused this to happen. I reply that there was no specific reason. When there is a modification of the relation of Heaven and Earth or a transmutation of the Yin and Yang, such unusual events occur. We may marvel at them, but we should not fear them.[61]

The second aspect of proto-yinyang thought relates to the paradoxical interdependence of opposites. The earliest detailed view of this way of thinking appears in the *Daodejing*, a text expressing thought that probably developed in the fifth century B.C.E. According to Liang Qichao 梁啓超 (1873–1929), the terms yin and yang in the Shang and early Zhou were primarily descriptions of natural phenomena and did not yet form a philosophical system. He argues that the significant change in the meaning of yinyang began with the *Daodejing*.[62] Although there is only one use of the term yinyang in the *Daodejing*, the text has a persistent orientation toward the paradoxical interdependence of opposites in the world. In chapter two, there are six situations that consist of distinct but interrelated and interacting forces:

> Everybody in the world knows the beautiful as beautiful. Thus, there is already ugliness. Everybody knows what is good. Thus, there is that which is not good. That presence and non-presence generate each other, difficult and easy complement each other, long and short give each other shape,

---

[60] Li Mengsheng (ed.), *Zuozhuan Yizhu* (Shanghai: Shanghai Guji Press, 1998), p. 247.

[61] J. Knoblock (trans.), *Xunzi: A Translation and Study of the Complete Works*, 3 vols. (Stanford: Stanford University Press, 1988–1994), p. 543.

[62] Liang Qichao 梁啓超. 陰陽五行說之來歷, "The Origin of Yinyang and Wuxing" in Gu Jiegang, (ed.) 古史辨 *The Debate on Ancient History* (Shanghai: Shanghai Guji Press, 1982), vol. V, p. 347.

above and below fill each other, tones and voices harmonize with each other, before and after follow each other is permanent.[63]

Overall, the *Daodejing* presents at least thirty-five such pairs of opposites, and they exhibit many of the same characteristics later taken up by yin-yang theory. For example, these forces engage in constant transformation and generation. More specifically, the intertwined pair of fullness (*shi* 實 or *ying* 盈) and emptiness (*xu* 虛 or *kong* 空) is discussed in chapters 9, 11, 15, and 32, as exhibited in a river, a wheel, and a house. According to the *Daodejing*, emptiness is a necessary part of fullness. That corresponds to the later relationships between yin and yang. We will turn to this point in the discussion of Chinese painting in Chapter 4.

The third aspect of proto-yinyang thought is the link between *qi* and yinyang, a point already noted earlier. *Qi* became one of the most basic concepts for explaining change in the natural world. As Sandor P. Szabo explains: "Numerous thinkers believed that there is a material substance, a 'basic stuff' in the universe, the primary material of universe...the coming into being of all the existing things is the result of the concentration of *qi* and their decay is the result of the dispersal of *qi*."[64]

We can again take the *Zuozhuan* as an example. The *Zuozhuan* lists yin and yang as two of six heavenly *qi*:

There are six heavenly *qi* which descend and produce the five tastes, go forth in the five colors, and are verified in the five notes; but when they are in excess, they produce the six diseases. Those six *qi* are denominated the yin, the yang, wind, rain, obscurity, and brightness. In their separation, they form the four seasons; in their order, they form the five (elementary) terms. When any of them is in excess, there ensure calamity. An excess of the yin leads to diseases of cold; of the yang, to diseases of heat.[65]

Yin and yang denote the generative forces of the universe, however, at this point they are two of six kinds of *qi*. The development of *qi* theory elevated the role of yinyang as the dominant modes of *qi*, thus as explaining all kinds of natural phenomena.

Building on these proto-yinyang sources, an explicit yinyang thought paradigm emerged throughout many texts in the late Warring States

---

[63] Hans-Georg Moeller, (trans.). *Daodejing: A Complete Translation and Commentary*, (Chicago and La Salle: Open Court, 2007), p. 7.

[64] S. P. Szabo, "The Term Shenming – Its Meaning in the Ancient Chinese Thought and in a Recently Discovered Manuscript," *Acta Orientalia Academiae Scientiarum Hungaricae*, 56 (2003), 261.

[65] Translation slightly modified from James Legge, *The Chinese Classics, The Ch'un Ts'ew, with Tso Chuen, The Chinese Classics*, V, The She King, p. 580.

Period and early Han Dynasty. In the first stage, yinyang was taken up as part of a variety of specific techniques or skills, gaining popular acceptance as a way of thinking and doing. An important transition seems to have occurred during the time the Jixia Academy (稷下學院) was founded around 318 B.C.E., which was a gathering point for scholars and practitioners in Linzi, the capital of the state of Qi.

Several important texts associated with this academy make significant contributions to yinyang thought. The *Guanzi* 管子 (the *Master Guan*), an encyclopedic compilation of philosophical materials named after Prime Minster Guan Zhong in the seventh century B.C.E., is particularly significant in giving a detailed account how yinyang and *wuxing* 五行 (five elements, phases, processes) were linked together.[66]

At this stage, yinyang theory was applied to many more fields, such as health and body cultivation. This development was connected to Zou Yan 鄒衍 (305–240 B.C.E.) and what came to be called the Yinyang School (*yinyangjia* 陰陽家). The full expression of yinyang thought then appears in a group of late Warring States or early Han texts, such as the *Yueling* 月令 chapter in the *Liji* 禮記 (*Record of Rituals*), the twelve annals (*ji* 紀) of the *Lüshi Chunqiu* (*The Annals of Lu Buwei*), the *Huainanzi*, the *Taiping Jing*, and the *Huangdi Neijing*. Although many of these have disputed dates and genealogies, the usage of yinyang in these texts was prevalent and conveyed some shared features that lead to the formation of a unique yinyang paradigm. In these texts, we begin to see the central aspects of yinyang thought described: the complex relationship between opposite forces, the emphasis on generation and growth, and the use of yinyang as a strategy for living well. All of these texts will be encountered in the following chapters.

The Yinyang School

Although the concept of yinyang extended across all schools of thought from the early Han Dynasty on (202 B.C.E.–220 C.E.), the concepts of yin and yang were not found in early Confucian texts such as the *Analects*, *Mengzi*, *The Great Learning*, or *Zhongyong*, and there is only one mention in the *Daodejing* (chapter 42). The schools we have come to call Confucianism and Daoism, however, were only a small part of the wide range of positions and views in what later became known as the period

---

[66] The Han Dynasty scholar Liu Xiang edited the received *Guanzi* text circa 26 B.C.E., largely from sources associated with the fourth century B.C.E.

of "a hundred schools." Among these was an influential group that came to be called the Yinyang School (*yinyangjia* 陰陽家). Unfortunately, its works have been largely lost, and its thought and practices have been ignored in academic studies as a result of the limited sources and its difficulty and obscurity.

In his essay *Lun liujia yaozhi* 論六家要旨 contained in the *Shiji* 史記, (*Records of the Historians*), Sima Tan 司馬談, the early Han period 前漢 (206 B.C.E–8 C.E), historiographer, listed the Yinyang School as the first of six Chinese intellectual schools.[67]

He describes Yinyang school:

> The secret observations of the method [*shu*] of yinyang greatly emphasizes good fortune [*xiang* 祥] and has a multitude of prohibitions and taboos, it restrains people and multiplies what they fear. So regarding the order of the four seasons, it is greatly following along that cannot be lost.[68] (嘗竊 觀陰陽之術，大祥而眾忌諱，使人拘而多所畏；然其序四時之大順，不可 失也).

He then provides this more specific explanation:

> Yinyang, the four seasons, the eight positions, the twelve measures and the twenty-four restrictions all have their own teachings and commands. One who follows them will flourish, and one who goes against them, if they do not die, will decline. But it is not necessarily like this, and thus I say "it restrains people and multiplies what they fear." In the spring, things are born, in the summer they grow, in the fall they are gathered, and in the winter they are stored. This is the great order of the way of heaven. If it is not followed then one lacks the warp and woof of the world. Thus I say, "regarding the order of the four seasons, it is greatly following along that cannot be lost."[69]

We can see in these descriptions that yinyang was caught up in various particular practices and that Sima Tan himself is skeptical of at least some of these.

The "Yiwenzhi" chapter of the *Hanshu* supplies further details about the Yinyang School. The *Hanshu* traces the origins of each of the early schools of Chinese thought to different kinds of *shi* 士, the class of intellectuals and specialists who were government officials and advisors. For example, the school of the Confucians (*Rujia*) came from *shi* who

---

[67] The other five are Confucians, Mohists, Legalists, Logicians, and Daoists.

[68] Sima Qian, 司馬遷, *Shiji* 史記 (*Records of the Historians*) (Beijing: Chinese Press, 2003), chapter 130, p. 3289.

[69] Ibid., chapter 130, p. 3290.

practiced rituals and music. The Yinyang School also came from these specialists (*shi*), however, they were *fangshi* 方士 (specialists in techniques) who engaged in a wide array of practical skills, from reading the oracle bones and observing seasonal transformations, to analyzing political events and cycles of histories, to devising military strategies. Graham calls these *fangshi* "men of secret arts."[70]

More specifically, the *Hanshu* describes the Yinyang School as arising in the following way:

> The course of the Yinyang School probably came from officials for astrology, reverently following great heaven, the calendar, moon, sun, and stars. They reverently gave out the proper timing [*shi*, seasons] for the people, and this is what they were strong in. When it comes to enacting restraints, then they were bound by prohibitions and taboos and sunken in minor numerology, abandoning human affairs to rely on ghosts and spirits.[71] (陰 陽家者流，蓋出於羲和之官，敬順昊天，歷象日月星辰，敬授民時，此其 所長也。及拘者為之，則牽於禁忌，泥於小數，舍人事而任鬼神).

The same chapter explains further the basis of these practices:

> Yinyang is following the time to issue out; going forward by *xingde*, in accordance with the stars [*douji*] and five elements, relying on the five conquering and using the assistance of the ghosts and spirits.[72]

This passage raises three technical terms associated with particular methods, or *shu*, involved with astrology and numerology. The first is *xingde* 刑德, which is a method associated with the five elements: water, wood, metal, earth, and fire. *Xingde* was closely connected to yinyang, such that the *Records of the Historian* says, "In order to clarify yinyang, one needs to examine *xingde*" (明於陰陽, 審於刑德).[73] *Xing* refers to yin-conquering (*yinke* 陰克), and *de* refers to yang-generating (*yangsheng* 陽生). The second technical term is *wusheng* (五勝), "five conquering," which also concerns the mutual relationships among the five elements. Water will conquer fire, fire conquers metal, metal conquers wood, wood conquers earth, and earth conquers water. The third specific technique mentioned is *douji* (鬥擊), which was a form of divination based on the position of the Big Dipper, which could be used to predict the outcome of battles, depending on which direction it pointed.

---

[70] Graham, *Yinyang*, p. 13.
[71] Ban Gu, *Hanshu* 漢書, p. 1734.
[72] Ibid., p.1760.
[73] *Shiji* 史記 (*Records of the Historians*), chapter 128, p. 3231.

The use of yinyang in these *fangshi* practices continues and develops positions we have already seen, particularly in the link between yinyang, the sun, and divination. One of the main functions of the *fangshi* was in astrology and in making the calendar.[74] In fact, the *fangshi* were involved in all kinds of divinatory practices, including reading cracks in tortoise shells and reading people's facial appearances, a method known as *xiangfa*. These *fangshi* also interpreted the cycles of history.[75] Another central area of concern was in relation to health and the pursuit of immortality, and the *fangshi* included practices of medicine, herbal regiments, and sexual gymnastics.

The Yinyang School also dealt with mathematical figures and numbers, and yinyang was often connected with numerology. For example, the *Guanzi* says, "Fu Xi invented the hexagrams in order to calculate the fluctuations of yinyang. He also invented the nine-nine numbers in order to harmonize with the way of Heaven, and all things under heaven were transformed by it."[76] The *Houhanshu* 後漢書 (*The Book of Later Han*) connects geometrical shapes to the form of the natural world itself. Heaven is a circle, and earth is a square: "Yang takes the circle as its form and its nature is movement. Yin takes the square as its structure and its nature is stillness. The number of movement is three and the number of stillness is two. In using yang to generate yin, one doubles it. In using yin to generate yang, one quadruples it."[77]

As these descriptions illustrate, the *fangshi* did not form a coherent group or school but rather included many different practices and methods. These groups were linked by a common use of yinyang, leading to their later designation as the Yinyang School. Many of these practices relied on divination, divine forces, and occult practices, much of which we might now label as "superstition." We have seen that Sima Tan's description itself had a critical element. In the early twentieth century, the prominent intellectual and reformer Liang Qichao took this view

---

[74] For a discussion of these aspects of Chinese astrology, see C. Lai, *The World of Ancient Thought and Culture*, p. 76.

[75] According to *Yiwen Zhi*, 七略, Fangshi had six teachings: (1) astrology (*tianwen*); (2) calendrics (*lipu*); (3) five phases (*wuxing*) for analyzing the alternation of dynasties; (4) tortoise shell divination (*zhuguai*); (5) fortune telling based on dreams and visions (*zazan*); and (6) face reading (*xiangfa*).

[76] Modified translation from W. A. Rickett (trans.), *Guanzi, Political, Economic, and Philosophical Essays from Early China* (New Jersey: Princeton University Press, 1998), p. 499.

[77] H. Fan, (ed.), *Houhanshu* 後漢書, *The Book of Later Han* (Beijing: Chinese Press, 1965) p. 3055.

of yinyang: "The theory of Yinyang and Five Phases has been the root of superstitions for two thousands years. It has an influential power in society even up to today."[78] Even though Liang Qichao made this comment in 1930s, the notion of yinyang remains a central apparatus for all kinds of popular folk practices in contemporary China. At the same time, we have seen that yinyang thinking also could signify a turn away from superstitions and toward more naturalistic accounts, and the Yinyang School is closely connected to the development of science and technology in China. For example, one contemporary Chinese scholar, Li Ling 李零, states that the Yinyang School had the most advanced technology in ancient times.[79]

Some members of this group constructed philosophical interpretations of these particular practices and developed broader theories and positions. The main person was Zou Yan, who was from the state of Qi and was a participant at the Jixia Academy. He was supposed to have studied Confucianism during the earlier period of his life, and his biography in the *Shiji* (*Records of Historians*) is included in the "Confucius and Mengzi" chapter. In China in the 1930s, there was a lively debate about whether Zou Yan was a Confucian or Daoist.[80] In fact, he seems to have had a position different from both, and he is commonly considered as the founder of the Yinyang School. Donald Harper argues that Zou Yan "spawned a new kind of practitioner in natural philosophy and occult knowledge."[81] Liang Qichao takes Zou Yan as the first of three people who was responsible for the spread of Yinyang and *Wuxing* theory in early Chinese history, the other two being Dong Zhongshu and Liu Xiang.[82]

According to the *Hanshu*, Zou Yan established a theory based on the transformation of yinyang. He had a profound knowledge of yinyang theory, on which he had written around 100,000 words. He seems to have been quite prominent in his time. Yinyang thinkers were much more popular than those now well-known thinkers like Confucius and Mengzi. Confucius was hungry when he traveled through different states and was seen as a "dog who had lost his home." Mengzi also was driven from state to state, trying to find a ruler who would listen to him. In contrast, when

---

[78] Liang Qichao, "The Origin of Yinyang and Wuxing" in Gu Jiegang (ed.), in *The Debate on Ancient History* 古史辯, (Shanghai: Shanghai Guji Press, 1982), vol. V, p. 343.

[79] Lin Ling, 李零, *The Only Regulation: Sunzi's Philosophy of Conflicts* 唯一的規則:孫子的鬥爭哲學 (Beijing: San Lian Press, 2010).

[80] Gu (ed.), *The Debate on Ancient History*, vol. V, pp. 738–745.

[81] Harper (trans.), *The Mawangdui Medical Manuscripts*, p. 50.

[82] Liang, in Gu (ed.), *The Debate on Ancient History*, vol. V, p. 353.

Zou Yan traveled around the states of Wei, Zhao, and Yan, kings came to the city gate to welcome him as an honored guest.[83] Harper explains, "Perhaps in the context of third century B.C.E. natural philosophy and occult thought, Zou Yan stood as the master of the ultimate secrets of the cosmos."[84] Unfortunately, none of Zou Yan's works have survived, although we can rely on references in other texts to grasp some of his views.[85]

The most significant contribution Zou Yan made to the yinyang theory is his integration of yinyang with the five phases (*wuxing*) theory.[86] Before the Han Dynasty, the terms yinyang and *wuxing* were separate and developed out of different contexts. Yinyang originally focused more on the rhythm of time, whereas the *wuxing* was more attuned to the position and direction of terrain. Zou Yan may have been the first person to link them. He took resonance as an operative principle between yinyang and *wuxing* and, thus, integrated the yinyang theory into a broader conceptual ground. Yinyang is the nature or potency (*xing* 性) of the five phases, and the five phases are the properties (*zhi* 質) of yinyang. This marriage of yinyang and *wuxing* enriched and complicated the yinyang theory.

Given this connection, we can briefly explain the doctrine of five phases (*wuxing*). There are two hypotheses about the origins of *wuxing* theory. One holds that the concept of *wuxing* resulted from the idea of the five directions: east, west, south, north, and center. Others contend that the five phases arise from accounting for seasonal changes.[87] The term *wuxing* (five phases) first appeared in the *Hong fan* 洪範 ("Great Plan") chapter of the *Book of History (Shangshu)*. It refers to five material things with certain functional attributes: "Water is said to soak and descend; the fire is said to blaze and ascend; wood is said to curve or be straight; metal is said to obey and change; earth is said to take seeds and give crops."[88] These five phenomena are not static entities, but rather five phases that move according to their own internal natures. Although *wuxing* has sometimes been translated as "five elements," they are not fixed kinds of stuff but rather different functions and moments of change. As

[83] *Shiji*, 史記, chapter 74, p. 2345.

[84] Harper (trans.), *The Mawangdui Medical Manuscripts*, p. 50.

[85] Ma Guohan 馬國翰 (1644–1911) has collected all surviving fragments of Zou Yan's work in the collectaneum *Yuhanshanfang jiyi shu* 玉函山房輯佚書.

[86] For a detailed discussion, see Y. Liu, *On The Cultural Connotation of Yin and Yang and Their English Translation* (Changsha: Hunan University Press, 2010), pp. 114–117.

[87] For a more detailed discussion see Lang, "The Origin of Yinyang and Wuxing" in *The Debate on Ancient History*, Gu (ed.), vol. V, pp. 343–353.

[88] Wang Shishun (ed.), *Shangshu Yizhu* 尚書譯注, (Sichuan: Sichuan People Press, 1986), p. 119.

Joseph Needham states, the five phases are "five forces in ever-flowing cyclical motion, and not passive motionless fundamental substances."[89]

The importance of *wuxing* lies not in the five forces themselves, but rather in how they relate. In the book *Great Meaning of Wuxing* (*Wuxing Dayi* 五行大義), Xiao Ji 蕭吉, a scholar from the Sui Dynasty (581–618), clearly formulates the two interlocking sequences or cycles by which the phases alternate: *xiangsheng* 相生 (mutually generating) and *xiangke* 相克 (mutually conquering). The generating sequence is: water generates wood; wood generates fire; fire generates earth; earth generates metal; and metal generates water. The conquering sequence is: water conquers fire; fire conquers metal; metal conquers wood; wood conquers earth; and earth conquers water. These are two standard functions of the five phases.[90]

Another critical dimension of *wuxing* thought goes beyond mutual generation (*xiangsheng*) and mutual overcoming (*xiangke*), generating patterns of mutual controlling (*xiangzhi*) and mutual transforming (*xianghua*). Mutual controlling refers to a complex pattern in which one phase generates a second phase that controls a third phase that itself controls the first phase. An example will clarify this: metal can conquer wood, however, wood can generate fire, which controls metal. From one perspective, wood is conquered by metal, however, wood can fight back by producing fire to control metal, using its generating function against the controller. The pattern of mutual transforming relies on the use of generation to resolve tensions. For example, metal can conquer wood, however, metal can also generate water, which then generates wood. Water conquers fire, however, water also generates wood, which itself generates fire. These are indirect effects reflecting a concern with complexity and interrelatedness rather than a linear way of thinking.

We can consider an example of how *wuxing* is used to deal with complex relationships. In Chinese medicine, *wuxing* is used to adjust a wide range of human emotions. Anger belongs to wood, happiness belongs to fire, worry belongs to earth, sadness belongs to metal, and fear belongs to water. These set up certain relationships between the emotions. One can use sadness (metal) to conquer anger (wood), use anger (wood) to conquer worry (earth), use worry (earth) to conquer fear (water), use anxiety (water) to conquer happiness (fire), and use happiness (fire) to conquer sadness (metal). At the same time, these emotions are connected to the

---

[89] Needham, *Science and Civilisation in China*, vol. II, p. 244.

[90] G. Liu, *Research on the Great Meanings of Wuxing* (Shenyang: Liangning Education Press, 1999).

five organs: anger affects the liver, happiness affects the heart, worry affects the spleen, sadness affects the lungs, and anxiety affects the kidneys. With these connections, one attempts to alleviate health problems by transforming emotions. Worrying (earth) can generate fear (water), and the only way to control worrying is through anger (wood). Although we might now be skeptical of the basic set of categories, their application leads to complex and often effective accounts of the emotions and their relationship to physical health. Derk Bodde observes that "these attempts to fit the universe into numerical categories, though absurd to us today, represented in their time a very real effort toward the use of a scientific method."[91]

We can consider one other important application of the five phases, which has been attributed to Zou Yan himself. Zou Yan draws the five phases theory from descriptions of natural phenomena, however, he applies it to the human world and to Confucian moral codes to explicate the change of dynasties. This is known as "Theory of the Beginning and Ending of Five Forces" (*Wude Zhongshi Shuo*五德終始說). The theory holds that the historical changes in dynasties were the result of the generating and controlling functions of five phases, thus making a wide connection between the movement of natural forces and human events. Each dynasty was identified with one natural force: Xia Dynasty 夏 (seventeenth to fifteenth century B.C.E.) with wood, Shang Dynasty 商 (seventeenth to eleventh century B.C.E.) with metal, Zhou Dynasty 周 (eleventh century–221 B.C.E.) with fire, and Qin Dynasty 秦 (221–206 B.C.E.) with water. Just as fire will naturally melt metal, the Zhou Dynasty, thus, had a natural and inevitable propensity to replace the Shang (Yin) Dynasty. However, it would itself be conquered by water, in just the way that fire will naturally melt metal but will itself be extinguished by water.[92] This theory led Qin Shihuang (259–210 B.C.E.), the first emperor of a unified China, to define the Qin Dynasty as water so that it would necessarily take over Zhou, based on fire. It also led to important debates in the Han Dynasty about whether it should be water (thus excluding the Qin as a legitimate dynasty) or should be earth (thus naturally overcoming the Qin).

The main point is that because each dynasty has its own natural propensity to conquer or replace the other dynasty or phase, these dynasties

---

[91] D. Bodde, "Types of Chinese Categorical Thinking" in C. Le Blanc & D. Bore (ed. and introd.), *Essays on Chinese Civilization* (Princeton University Press, 1981), p. 143.

[92] Y. Kuan 楊寬, *History of the Warring States* 戰國史 (Shanghai: Shanghai People's Press, 1955), p. 390.

alternate in a natural process, just as metal triumphs over wood, fire overcomes metal, and water puts out fire. This gives a naturalistic justification for dynastic change, as opposed to more traditional models that explained the change of dynasties through the mandate or command of heaven based on the virtue of rulers.

2 Yinyang Cosmology: *Dao*, *Qi*, *Yi*, and *Taiji*

The "what" is in constant flux, the "why" has a thousand variations.

Marcus Aurelius, *Meditations*

All civilizations seek to understand what awesome forces, rules, or laws drove the sequence of events from which the physical world materialized. By whom or by what canon is an entire universe created? In what language must the story be told? Can all of the questions ever be answered?

Leon M. Lederman, Nobel Laureate, *Symmetry and the Beautiful Universe*

All of the key concepts we will look at this chapter – *Dao*, *qi*, and *Taiji*, as well as the system of the *Yi* – remained at the core of Chinese metaphysics. They were used in a variety of ways to construct metaphysical systems of varying complexity, particularly through and in response to encounters with Buddhist philosophy.

The Huangdi Neijing (*The Yellow Emperor's Inner Classic*) offers the most comprehensive definition of yinyang:

> The Yellow Emperor claims that yinyang is the *Dao* of heaven and earth, the net (*gangji* 綱紀) of the ten thousand things, the parent (*fumu* 父母) of transformations, the origin (*benshi* 本始) of life and death, and the residence (*fu* 府) of spirit and insight. To heal illness one must seek in this root.[1]

In this passage, yinyang is taken as a pattern embedded in the nature of all beings, thus providing the foundation for a coherent view of the

---

[1] Y. Zhang 張隱庵 (ed.), *Huangdi Neijing Commentaries* 黃帝內經素問集注 (Beijing: Xueyuan Press 學苑出版社, 2002), p. 41.

41

world. This worldview weaves together human beings, heaven, and the
Dao 道 (the way) in a way that creates a reality of dynamic wholeness
pervaded by and mediated through the interaction of yin and yang. That
is why yinyang is called the "net" (*gangji*) of the ten thousand things.
The term *gangji* comes from the image of silk fabric. *Gang* 綱 is the main
strand to which all other threads are attached, whereas *ji* 紀 represents
the mesh of the other threads. Together, they show that the ten thousand
things are tied to an interrelated net or web through yinyang. This chapter will explore this *gangji* through four of the most significant concepts
in Chinese cosmology: *Dao* (the way), *qi* 氣 (vital energy), *yi* 易 (change/
ease/constancy), and *taiji* 太極 (great ultimate). Even though these concepts have developed over centuries and take many diverse forms, we
will concentrate on yinyang and the emergence of the world from *Dao*
in the *Daodejing* (道德經), yinyang and the transformations of *qi*, yinyang
and configurations of change in the *Yijing* (易經) (*Book of Changes*), and
yinyang and the great ultimate in the metaphysics of Zhou Dunyi (周敦
頤1017–1073) and Zhang Zai (張載 1020–1077).

Let us begin with a popular Chinese myth about the origins of the
universe – known as *Pangu Kaitian* 盤古開天 (*the hero Pangu opens up
the sky/heaven*) – which will give us a glimpse of early Chinese views
of the cosmos. Although there are different versions of the myth, the
core narrative is shared by all early texts. The earliest recorded version
is in Xu Zheng's (徐整) book *Sanwu Liji* (三五曆紀) (*Three and Five
Calendars*), written during the time of the Three Kingdoms (220~280
C.E.).[2] According to the myth, in the beginning, the universe was like
an egg in a condition of chaos and indistinctness, called *hundun* 渾沌
(chaos); this cosmic egg did not take any shape or form. The hero Pangu
was born and slept in its middle where, after 800,000 years, he woke up
and faced utter darkness. He decided to open up this *hundun* to let in
light, so he made a break across the *hundun*. When Pangu grew one *zhang*
丈 (around ten feet), heaven also expanded one *zhang* higher, and the
earth descended one *zhang* lower, a process that continued for another
800,000 years. Eventually, Pangu could grow no more and died, however, by then heaven had reached its highest stage, and earth had attained
its deepest level. Pangu's body then transformed into the myriad things:
his breath became wind and clouds, his voice became thunder, his left
eye was the sun, and right eye was the moon. His four limbs and five
body parts became the four directions and five mountains. His blood

[2] The date has been questioned. Some suggest that it was composed in 184, 190, or 208
C.E. The tale itself has been repeated in many classical texts.

became rivers and oceans, his nerves the earthly lines, his muscles the soil, his hair the stars, his skin the grass and plants, his teeth and bones the stones, and his sweat the rain.

We are not sure when this myth arose, however, it reflects a general explanatory pattern for the universe, a pattern that appears in a wide range of early texts. We can note three implicit cosmological assumptions. First, the most primordial state of the universe is described as *hundun*. In this original state, there was no heaven and earth, no light and no forms, only undifferentiated oneness. The wholeness of the universe is rooted in its emergence out of such oneness.

In the *Huainanzi*, this *hundun* is depicted as a chaotic beginning: "Cavernous and undifferentiated Heaven and Earth, chaotic and inchoate [*hundun*] Uncarved Block, not yet created and fashioned into things: this we call the 'Grand One.' Together emerging from this unity, so that each acquired its distinctive qualities, there were birds, there were fish, there were animals: this we call the 'differentiation of things.'"[3]

The unitary origin, *hundun*, is not an external independent entity beyond or outside the myriad things but is always an integral part of the world. This original state of undifferentiated chaos has a complex two-fold relationship to the myriad things that compose the concrete world. On the one hand, *hundun* comes first and is in some sense distinct from what arises after it. On the other hand, *hundun* continues as the basis of the myriad things. That is, it is not just that the myriad things come from one source, but that they remain with that source.

The second implicit assumption visible in the myth is that the diversification of the universe happens through the interaction of two forces, called variously the light and heavy, clear and turbid, or in more general and abstract terms, yang and yin. When Pangu opened *hundun*, one part became heaven, and the other part became earth, bringing with them light and dark as well as the distinction between the shaped/formed and the shapeless/formless. Yinyang as light is the first sign of this opening of the universe. One difficult question is contained within this narrative: do heaven and earth generate yin and yang, or do yin and yang generate heaven and earth? Clear and bright forces become heaven, whereas turbid or muddy forces become earth: in this sense, yin and yang generate heaven and earth. However, in so far as yin and yang are also cold and warm, winter and summer, dark and light, they are generated by heaven

---

[3] Harold Roth (trans.), *The Huainanzi: A Guide to the Theory and Practice of Government in Early China* (New York: Columbia University Press, 2010), p. 536.

and earth.[4] We have already seen that labels of yin and yang depend on context, and thus, they can be applied on multiple levels.

The third aspect of the myth is that the entire universe is considered as analogous to the human body. In the myth, all natural forces or phenomena, such as wind, clouds, thunder, sun, moon, mountains, and oceans, form from the body of Pangu. This analogy between the parts of nature and the parts of the human body suggests that the world is conceived as a living organic whole on the model of a human body. On a fundamental level, the driving forces of the universe are generation and growth, which become the basic structure of the world. In the same way that the nature of motion became a focus for Aristotle and Newton, the way things are generated and transformed from one unitary source captured the attention of early Chinese thinkers. It is not a story of creation *ex nihilo* but a vision of spontaneous growth and transformation.

Yinyang in/with *Dao* and Myriad Things

The term *Dao* (*Tao*) has become one of the most widely known Chinese concepts, and it was central to most Chinese accounts of cosmology. In its original usage, *Dao* had two basic meanings. First, it is the road or path upon which one walks. The first usage of the word *Dao* appears in an imaginative character form found in bronze inscriptions, which shows one's head hidden in cloth or one's head covered by cloth while still walking. With one's eyes covered, one will be slow and probing in walking.

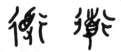

Another form shows one's head walking on a windy, snakelike road.

---

[4] For more discussion on this issue, see Q. Wang 王巧慧, *The Naturalistic Philosophy of Huainanzi*, 淮南子的自然哲學思想 (Beijing: Science Press 科學出版社, 2009) p. 132.

This image again suggests a path that must be traversed with caution. In the recently excavated texts at Guodian, buried around 300 B.C.E., the character is written with an image of a person between two sides of a path. Thus, the initial meaning of *Dao* is road or path or way. From this, it extends to a way of acting, a way of living, or even a way of functioning, so that the way of heaven is called *tiandao* (天道).

Second, *Dao* means guidance. To follow a path is, of course, different from being lost, wandering aimlessly, or going nowhere. Furthermore, the character implies that one does not simply walk on the road mindlessly and aimlessly but with a direction and with mindfulness. As a guide, *Dao* is a map for the journey through life, or, as G. E. R. Lloyd puts it, "an internalized mode of being and doing."[5]

Gradually, *Dao* developed into a complicated and multilayered term. In the Spring and Autumn Period, there are two traditions around the notion of *Dao*, which we might designate as the "way of human beings" (*rendao* 人道) and the "way of heaven" (*tiandao* 天道). The first is explicitly differentiated from "the way of heaven" in the *Ru* 儒 (Confucian) tradition. As the early Confucian *Xunzi* 荀子 says, "The way is not the way of Heaven and is not the way of Earth but is the way of human beings and the way followed by gentlemen."[6] The Confucian *Dao* refers primarily to a human way of life centering on ethics, politics, and culture.[7] For example, we read from *Analects*, chapter 29, "The Master said, human beings can broaden *Dao;* it is not the *Dao* that broadens human beings."[8] In this passage, the *Dao* is a part of human action and human life, not an independent cosmic guide. For the *Ru*, the way is the way by which human beings live, and it is the traditional way that developed over centuries.

The other tradition draws on an astrological account in which the *Dao* is the regular movement of the sun and other celestial bodies. The *Dao* reveals an infinite cyclical movement, the "way of heaven" or "heavenly Dao" (*tiandao* 天道). The *Dao* of heaven simply means the movement of sky, such as the sun's daily rising and setting and the moon's monthly cycle.[9] The heavenly *Dao* points to the movements and changes of

---

[5] G. E. R. Lloyd, *Adversaries and Authorities: Investigations into Greek and Chinese Science* (New York: Cambridge University Press, 1996), p. 8.

[6] Modified translation from Knoblock (trans.), *Xunzi*, p. 168. Perhaps the earliest explicit distinction of *rendao* is in the excavated Ru text, the "Xing Zi Ming Chu," strips 41–42.

[7] L. Chen 陳來, *The World of Ancient Thought and Culture: Religions, Ethics and Social Thought in the Spring and Autumn Period* (Beijing: SDX Joint Publishing Company, 2009), p. 78.

[8] B. Liu 劉寶楠 (Qing Dynasty), *Analects* 論語正義 (Beijing: Chinese Press, 1990), p. 636.

[9] Chen, *The World of Ancient Thought and Culture*, p. 80.

constellations and galaxies, linked closely with ancient astrology. Heaven has its own route and path, its own regularity and patterns. This heavenly *Dao* is different from the other humanistic account of *Dao* because it is a construction based on empirical evidence, resulting from the observation of the five planets and twenty-eight constellations. In addition, this heavenly *Dao* was also used to track the changes of the seasons and, thus, to determine the agricultural and political calendar.

The *Daodejing* is a milestone for the richness of the concept of the *Dao*, a term which appears seventy-three times in the text. It is the earliest text to elevate the *Dao* to its apotheosis by forging a metaphysical connection between *rendao* and *tiandao* – the human way and the heavenly way. The *Daodejing* exclaims explicitly that not only human beings but also heaven itself emerges from the *Dao*. Thus, the *Dao* is the unitary source of heaven, earth, and human beings, and it is the model or pattern they all follow (*Daodejing* 25). *Dao* becomes the source of all existence such that there is nothing beyond the *Dao*. Although there are many different interpretations of the meaning of *Dao* in the *Daodejing*, *Dao* is generally taken as the ultimate origin, source, and principle of the universe and the myriad things. Perhaps the most important point is that *Dao* provides a unitary source, analogous in function to *hundun* in the myth with which we began.

We have already discussed the *Daodejing* as a fundamental source for proto-yinyang thought. Although the terms *yin* and *yang* appear only once in the *Daodejing* (chapter 42), many of the basic structures of yinyang underlie the text. At the same time, yinyang thought developed through many concepts that first appear in the *Daodejing*. For both reasons, we can begin with an account of *Dao* and yinyang, focusing on the *Daodejing*.

In chapter 42, the *Daodejing* gives a specific account of *Dao* and the origination of the world: "Dao generates oneness, oneness generates twoness, twoness generates threeness, and threeness generates the ten thousand things. The ten thousand things carry yin, embrace yang, and blend *qi* to create harmony."[10]

This origin story has some analogies with the myth of Pangu. The concrete world originates from a unitary but indistinct source, a source that even precedes what could be labeled as "one." That source is the *Dao*. The movement from that source toward the tangible world is again a process of specification and differentiation, from one to two to three

---

[10] Hans-Georg Moeller, (trans.), *Daodejing: A Complete Translation and Commentary*, (Chicago and La Salle: Open Court, 2007) p. 103.

and to the myriad things, literally the "ten thousand things" (*wanwu* 萬物). In the *Daodejing*, yinyang is woven into the condition of the myriad things, which are said to "carry yin and embrace yang." (負陰抱陽) This intrinsic link between yinyang and the myriad things became a common view. For example, the *Liji* (*Record of Rituals*), one of the Five Classics of the Confucian canon edited and reworked by various scholars during the Han Dynasty (202 B.C.E.–220 C.E.), says, "When yinyang harmonize, the myriad things come into being."[11]

The preceding passage describes *Dao* as the origin and source of the myriad things, which entails that it in some sense exists before those things. This leads into the same question we raised about the relationships between *hundun* and the concrete world – how does *Dao*, as the source of all the myriad things, connect with the myriad things? Is the source of the world the same as the fabric of the world? This ambiguity is built into the concept of *Dao*, which is not just the origin but the structure (*ti*) and the functioning (*yong*) of the world, as well as a guide through it. The question pertains directly to the status of yinyang, which on the one hand is produced by the *Dao* but on the other hand is its function and serves as a guide.

The *Guanzi* 管子 (26 B.C.E.), for example, says, "Accordingly, the Yin and Yang are the primary organizational principle of Heaven and Earth, and the four seasons are the primary pattern of the Yin and Yang"[12] (是故陰陽者, 天地之大理也, 四時者, 陰陽之大經也). The yinyang is patterned after the *Dao*, whereas the *Dao* is in essence the interaction between yin and yang.

From these texts, we can see that yinyang plays a substantial role on two levels: first the *Dao* in/with yinyang; second the myriad things in/with yinyang. We can formulate three specific ways to explicate the *Dao* by showing the primary role of yinyang: *Dao* is oneness; *Dao* is spontaneity (*ziran* 自然); *Dao* is the female body.

The Oneness of Dao

The term *yi* 一 (oneness) is at the core of *Dao* in the *Daodejing*. *Yi* refers both to one and unity or, as a verb, to make one or to unify. When the ultimate *Dao* is identified with the one, this oneness is not simply the

---

[11] Wang, Mengou, 王夢鷗 (ed.) *Liji*, 禮記今註今譯 (*Record of Rituals*), (Taipei: Taiwan Commercial Press, 1981), p.416.

[12] W. A. Rickett (trans.), *Guanzi, Political, Economic, and Philosophical Essays from Early China* (New Jersey: Princeton University Press, 1998), p. 111.

first in a numerical sequence, but a unity and wholeness permeating all existence. In the *Daodejing* 22, "the sage holds on to oneness to be the shepherd of the world"[13] (是以聖人抱一為天下式). *Dao* ties together heaven, earth, and human beings, all of which are generated from the *Dao* and model its spontaneous and generative capabilities. *Dao* animates the whole world and leaves nothing out, giving this world unity and coherence. The world is not constructed from individual pieces, but rather is an indivisible whole taking patterns and processes of interrelatedness as its fundamental structure.

In speaking of the mother or origin of things, the *Daodejing* calls it *Dao* or "great," but in a similar passage, the *Lüshi Chunqiu* calls it the "great one":

> It is the nature of *Dao* that when we look for it, it is invisible; and when we listen for it, it is inaudible, for it cannot be given material form....The *Dao* is the supreme instance of the seminal essence, for it cannot be given shape or name. Forced to give it a name, I would call it "Great One" (*Taiyi* 太一).[14]

The text known as the *Taiyi Shengshui* 太一生水 (*Great Oneness Generating Water*) was found with the Guodian *Daodejing* and also names the origins of the world as the great one, with the beginning of the universe coming when "the great one gives birth to water."[15]

Dao permeates space and time, without being identical with any particular place or moment. Thus, the *Huainanzi* states: "The passing of the past and coming of the present is called time [*yu* 宇]; the four directions and up and down are called space [*zhou* 宙]. Dao is located between them, and none can know its location."[16] The "Original Dao" chapter works out this relation to space and time specifically in terms of unity and oneness:

> Oneness is the unity of up and down, independently going up to the nine skies and go down to the nine lands....Looking one cannot see its form; listening one cannot hear its sound; hiding one cannot get its body. The shapeless generates the shaped. Therefore, having comes from lacking and fullness comes from emptiness....Dao establishes the oneness and then the myriad things are generated."[17] (道者, 一立而萬物生矣).

---

[13] Moeller, *Daodejing*, p. 55.

[14] Knoblock and Riegel, (trans.) *The Annals of LüBuwei: A Complete Translation and Study* (Stanford: Stanford University Press,), p. 138.

[15] Liu Zhao 劉釗 (ed.), *Taiyi Shengshui*（太一生水）, strip 1 in *Guodian Chujian Jiaoyi* 郭店楚簡校釋 (Fuzhou: Fujian People's Press, 2003), p. 42.

[16] Modified translation from Roth, *The Huainanzi*, p. 415.

[17] Modified translation from ibid., p. 65.

This oneness or unity is built on the oppositional forces of reality. There would be no point in emphasizing the one if differentiation were not already assumed, and there would be no way for the *Dao* to explain the movement and patterns of singular things. At the same time, the distinction of opposition like yin and yang is not a matter of seeing reality through a dualistic or atomistic lens. Newton's world, in which all physical phenomena can be reduced to the mechanics of their elementary units, long dominated the modern world of philosophy. This deterministic and mechanistic framework goes hand in hand with dualism. In contrast to this conception, the early Chinese view approaches the whole as greater than the sum of its parts, as a result of the multileveled interaction within yinyang.

The Western Han scholar Yang Xiong 楊雄 (53–18 B.C.E.) characterizes yinyang as a threeness (*Yinyang Bisan* 陰陽比叁).[18] According to him, there is yin, there is yang, then there is the combination of yinyang, which is *taixuan* 太玄 (a great profoundness). It is the smallest unit that generates all things under heaven.[19]

Commitment to oneness leads to a search for the link between ultimate oneness and the ten thousand things. The vision of *Dao* as generation includes an association between the oneness of the source and the multiplicity of the myriad things. However, if *Dao* is eternal, ultimate, and the mother of the myriad things, then how does *Dao* connect to the myriad things themselves? To comprehend how *Dao* and yinyang can unify diverse phenomena, we should be more precise with our understanding of the Chinese term translated as "things" in the phrase "the ten thousand things" (*wanwu* 萬物). *Wu* (物, *things*), in Chinese, does not mean "entities in isolation" (what in European philosophy would be "substances") but rather phenomena, events, and even histories. It is said that heaven (*tian* 天, the sky) has its seasons; earth (*di* 地, territory) has its advantages; and *wu* (things/events) have their stages (*hou* 候). To attain success, one needs to be attuned to the stage of things. For example, crops need sunlight and rain, however, they also must grow according to their own phases or stages. The timing of things is rooted in how things come into being and transform, as well as how they emerge in a broader context. *Wu* are always becoming. This indicates that position and change are paired. If you are imprecise measuring change, you will be imprecise measuring position and vice versa.

---

[18] Sima Guang 司馬光, *Collected Commentaries of Tai Xuan* 太玄集注 (Beijing: Chinese Press, 2003), p. 10.
[19] Ibid.

More specifically, the difficulty of linking the oneness of *Dao* to the multiplicity of the myriad things is addressed through yin and yang inter-action. Yinyang is the cause of things as becoming and is also embedded in all things as their structure. The *Huangdi Neijing* claims, "From ancient times, the communication with heaven, the root (*ben* 本) of life, has been rooted in yinyang."[20] (夫自古通天者生之本, 本於陰陽天地之間). The more the unity of *Dao* is developed, the more the need for the notion of yinyang is increased. Yinyang is the mechanism for this vast network, which is why it is called the net or warp-and-woof (*gangji*) of things. The organism is a constitutive totality of interdependent compo-nents rather than a sum of simple parts. Yinyang clarifies these dynamic connections.

Existing as one in many, *Dao* can explain identity in difference and unity in plurality. It entails a sense or vision of *Dao* as the single unifying force within phenomenal reality, while seeing this reality in all its com-plexity. In particular, along with constant change there is an underlying stability both in things and their patterns. Yinyang relations elucidate this invariance, which applies to phenomena of organized complexity. One passage from a chapter of the *Lüshi Chunqiu* directly on upholding one-ness states:

> Heaven and earth, yin and yang, do not alter yet they complete the myriad things in their differences. Eyes do not lose the clarity of sight yet they can perceive the black and white; the ear does not lose its keenness of hearing yet it can make distinctions between treble and bass sounds. The true king holds oneness so that the myriad things are correct. One is the order, two is chaos.[21]

Unity is the basis from which to address complexity and plurality, just as the singular function of eyes to see is nevertheless able to perceive multi-plicity. Another passage from the *Lüshi Chunqiu* says: "A man capable of employing the One to govern the world, keeping cold and heat balanced, wind and rain seasonal, then becomes a sage. Thus, he who understands the One is enlightened, but he who glorifies the dual is demented."[22] This illuminates why maintaining unity or oneness becomes so central throughout the Chinese tradition, particularly in later Daoist practice.

Returning to the *Daodejing*, chapter 10 asks, "When you nourish the soul and embrace oneness, can you stay undivided?"[23] It also assigns

---

[20] Zhang (ed.), *Huangdi Neijing*, p. 17.
[21] Knoblock and Riegel, *The Annals of Lü Buwei*, p. 434.
[22] Ibid., p. 139.
[23] Moeller, *Daodejing*, p. 25.

different ways to describe oneness, such as "holding fast to the one" (*zhiyi* 致一) or "maintaining/guarding the one" (*shouyi* 守一). The vision and method called *shouyi* is described: "If one knows guarding the one, then the myriad things will be complete."[24] The *Taipingjing* 太平經 (31–7 B.C.E.) illuminates, "Oneness refers to the heart/mind (*xin* 心), intention (*yi* 意) and will (*zhi* 志). It is the spirit (*shen* 神) of one's body."[25] As this passage suggests, oneness has great significance for governing and cultivating the body. This will be discussed later in the Yinyang body chapter.

Transformation, Spontaneity, and Order

We have discussed the important processes of becoming and transformation. The fundamental connection between *Dao* and generation appears already in the claim that the *Dao* generates the one, which generates the two, then three, leading to the myriad things. This yinyang progression depends on motion or activation. Without this movement, being itself could not come about. We have also seen the centrality of growth in the myth of Pangu. *Dao* is a dynamic process, and its dynamism depends both on multiplicity and unity. The unity is what allows things to function well. Chapter 39 of the *Daodejing* says: "Heaven received oneness – to be clear; earth received oneness – to be at rest; spirit received oneness – to be animated; valley received oneness to be full; lords and kings received oneness – to set the world straight."[26]

At the same time, oneness itself cannot generate anything. The *Huainanzi* makes this point explicitly: "*Dao* begins in oneness, yet one cannot generate, so it divides into yin and yang. The harmony (*he* 合) of yin and yang generates the myriad things."[27] *Dao* divides into yin and yang; then yin and yang interact and harmonize to generate the diversity of our lived world.

The tension and relation between the distinct forces generalized as yin and yang naturally and intrinsically lead to changes and transformations. This view of unceasing change is articulated in the *Yijing* as *sheng* 生 (creating and generating). These processes of change can be divided into two types. One kind of change or transformation is growth, which is

---

[24] Ibid., p. 95.
[25] Yang Jilin 杨寄林 (ed.). *Taipingjing* 太平經 *Classic of Great Peace*, (Shijiazhuang: Hebei People's Press, 2002), p. 861.
[26] Moeller, *Daodejing*, p. 95.
[27] Modified translation from Roth, *The Huainanzi*, p.133.

a movement toward increasing complexity. Things grow up from seeds, and sexual intercourse generates offspring who grow into adults. The *Dao* is thus closely connected with life itself. As the *Zhuangzi* says, "if something receives or possesses *Dao*, it will be alive; but without it, that thing will die."[28]

The other kind of change is a cyclical alternation. Summer follows spring, and fall follows from summer in an endless cycle. These two kinds of change are closely related – the progression of the seasons is a pattern of growth (and death) for living things, and the reproduction of things creates recurring cycles that form generations. In the *Taiyi Shengshui*, we find a new dimension to this connection, showing explicitly that creation is not just a single direct line, but is a circle of cooperation in which one element is contained in the next. It tells that the Great One (*Taiyi*) generates water, which then turns back and assists (*fanfu* 反輔) the Great One in generating heaven, which then turns back to assist in creating earth. The end of this process is the sustainable cycle of the seasons, rooted in the alternation of yinyang.[29]

Dao is most associated with these perpetual cycles. The *Lüshi Chunqiu* devotes a special chapter to discussing the circularity of the *Dao*. First, it explains why the *Dao* of heaven is circular and the *Dao* of earth is square: "The vital essence and *qi* alternately rise and fall, revolving in a complete cycle that is never interrupted or impeded....Though the myriad things are distinct in categories and forms, each has its own place and function, and these cannot be interchanged."[30]

This cyclical movement derives from immediate observation of nature: the alternation of sun and moon, day and night, cold and hot, life and death. This concentration on cyclical movement and change contrasts conceptions of motion in early modern European physics, as in the Newtonian mechanical laws of nature, in which motion fundamentally existed as a straight line. We might connect this conception to an underlying view of the universe itself as linear, starting from its creation by God and moving toward a certain endpoint. However, the Chinese conception of motion – and of history – was focused on circular movement, perhaps expressing the agrarian roots of Chinese society. This difference has enormous consequences. If motion is constant in a circular fashion, there is no need for external forces to move the heavenly bodies

---

[28] Chen Guying, 陳鼓應, 莊子今注今譯, *Commentaries on Zhuangzi*, (Beijing: Chinese Press, 1983), p. 279.

[29] Liu Zhao (ed.), *Taiyi Shengshui*, strip 1, p. 42.

[30] Knoblock and Riegel, *The Annals of Lübuwei*, p. 110.

because there is no need for a starting point. One need not to seek out a first cause or an unmoved mover. The only necessary explanation is an account of what happens inside that circle and what sustains that movement. This is what the *Zhuangzi* called the axis of the *Dao* (*daoshu* 道枢) in all motions.[31]

The explanation for this eternal generation is the fact that the *Dao* itself contains yin and yang. Yin and yang are internal and inherent elements, not external forces added by grace or will. As the *Lüshi Chunqiu* describes:

> The Great One [*Taiyi* 太一] brought forth the dyadic couple; the dyadic couple brought forth yin and yang. Yin and yang metamorphose and transform, the one rising, the other falling, joined together in a perfect pattern, spinning and pulsing.... The myriad things that emerged are created by the Great One and transformed by Yin and Yang.[32]

The assumption that order and generation are implicit in the fabric of being is most apparent within the concept of *ziran* (自然), which most literally means self (*zi*) so (*ran*). *Ziran* can be translated to "spontaneity" or "naturalness." It refers to what is so of itself, without any external force or coercion. There are many interpretations of this term and its connection with *Dao*, and many scholars take it as the most central concept of the *Daodejing*.[33] Here, the focus will be on the relation between *ziran* and yinyang. Yinyang is the source and manifestation of *ziran*. The *Daodejing*, in chapter 25, lays out a sequence culminating in the claim that the *Dao* itself is modeled on *ziran*:

> There is a form that becomes in indifferentiation, coming alive before heaven and earth.
>
> Soundless, shapeless, standing alone but unaltered, it can be considered the mother of heaven and earth.
>
> Its name is unknown, but it is styled "*Dao*"; if I am forced, I name it "great."
>
> Great says passing away, passing away says distant, distant says return.
>
> Heaven is great, earth is great, *Dao* is great, the king is great. In the state there are four greats, the king is one.

---

[31] B. Ziporyn (trans.), *Zhuangzi: The Essential Writings with Selections from Traditional Commentaries* (Indianapolis/Cambridge: Hackett Publishing Company Inc., 2009), p. 12.

[32] Knoblock and Riegel, *The Annals of Lü Buwei*, pp. 136–137.

[33] Liu Xiaogan 刘笑敢, *Laozi Gujin* 老子古今 (*Laozi, Past and Present*) (Beijing: Chinese Academy of Social Sciences Press, 2006).

People model earth, earth models heaven, heaven models the way, the way models self-so-ing *ziran*.[34]

This passage addresses the problem of infinite regress – human beings model the earth, but what does the earth follow? It follows heaven, however, what does heaven follow? It follows the *Dao*, however, what does the *Dao* follows? The *Dao* follows *ziran*, however, *ziran* is not a model. It is simply spontaneity. Ultimately, the *Dao* is so of itself. The regress ends with spontaneity.

Ziran is not only an element of the world but also the most potent mode of action for human beings. Chapter 17 of the *Daodejing* says that when work is completed, people declare that it happens "self-so" by *ziran*. This is the highest stage of human action, where there are no external forces or power compelling things to happen. However, one must ask: why rely on spontaneity? How does *ziran* differ from randomness? Confidence in *ziran* is grounded in confidence in yinyang. *Dao* itself is a self-generating force (as yin and yang), so one should rely on this internal force and allow it to operate as it is. *Ziran* lets things be, in their own natural or raw state, just as heaven and earth have their own state (that is, *ziran*).

To fully grasp this reliance on *ziran* and yinyang, we must consider the place and origins of order. This order is harmony (*he* 和), the configuration and sequence of different elements in space and time. Although yinyang does not work from a rational or intentional plan, it is harmonious, with the endless variety of the world finely organized into a systematic and coordinated complexity. As with transformation, this order is emergent and implicit in the continuity of things rather than an independent principle. *Dao* combines in itself continuity, novelty, and indeterminateness.[35]

---

[34] Modified translation from Moeller, *Daodejing*, p. 63.

[35] R. Ames, (trans.), *Yuan Dao, Tracing Dao to Its Source* (New York: Bellantine Books, 1998), p. 38. This view of order as emerging spontaneously rather than being externally imposed (by a creator or designer) is commonly discussed in a contemporary context by evolutionary biologists. They see the spontaneous emergence of order and the occurrence of self-organization as an answer to the question: "What are the sources of the overwhelming and beautiful order which graces the living world?" S. A. Kauffman, *The Origins of Order: Self-Organization and Selection in Evolution* (New York: Oxford University Press, 1993), p. xiii. Biology, mathematics, chemistry, and physics all reveal the power of self-organization and spontaneous order in complex systems. There are self-ordering properties in complex living systems. As Kauffman says, "The unexpected spontaneous order is this: Vast interlinked networks of elements behave in three broad regimes: ordered, chaotic, and a complex regime on the frontier between order and chaos." Ibid., p. xvi.

The claim that *Dao* is *ziran* encompasses a view of uncertainty and novelty, that is, a "mysterious efficacy" (*xuande* 玄德).[36] We cannot definitively know whether or not it will be sunny tomorrow, however, we are able to prepare what we will do if the sun comes out (go to the beach) or not (stay at the library). Nature is not working from a rational plan that we can discern and use as a cookbook, so there is only a general rhythm for human beings to follow and with which to align themselves. The importance of yinyang lies in this sense of working with uncertainty. Uncertainty as a worldview calls for a mechanism or system to negotiate it, and yinyang fills this conceptual role. Finally, this element of uncertainty and indeterminacy shows that order – or at least an order good for human beings – is not simply taken for granted. Yinyang imparts a strategy for maintaining order, as we will see in later chapters.

Dao as Female Body

The spontaneous potency of the *Dao* is associated with the female body, which is a common metaphor for *Dao* in the *Daodejing*. It reveals not just the importance of yin and its generative force, but also designates a yin origin that is hidden, implicit, or empty. In the *Daodejing*, there are two sets of terms in relation to femininity: *pin* 牝 appearing three times and *ci* 雌 appearing twice. Both sets have been translated as female, whereas in fact *pin* refers to female animals in general. *Ci* refers to hen, as opposed to *xiong*, which refers to rooster.[37] In later texts, such as the *Guanzi*, *Huainanzi*, and *Shuoyuan*, *pin* and *ci* are explicitly defined as yin.[38]

Pin and *ci* are ways to demonstrate two noteworthy aspects of yinyang. One is the importance of yin and its generative force. The terms used in classical Chinese texts for the origin of the myriad things incorporate a sense of "life" and "birth," both of which are encompassed in the Chinese term *sheng* 生 (generation). For example, the origin is called the ancestor (*zong* 宗), mother (*mu* 母), the gate of the mysterious female (*xuanpin zhimen* 玄牝之門), the female (*ci* 雌), the root of the heaven and earth (*tiandi gen* 天地根), or the beginning (*shi* 始).[39]

We read from the *Daodejing* 6, "The spirit of the valley does not die – This is called mysterious femininity [*pin*]. The gate of mysterious femininity [*pin*] is the root of heaven and earth."[40] Here the *pin* is mysterious,

---

[36] Moeller, *Daodejing*, p. 121.
[37] For more discussion on these two pairs, see Ryden, *The Yellow Emperor*, pp. 29–36.
[38] Ibid., pp. 34–5.
[39] See discussion in Ames, *Yuan Dao*, p. 14.
[40] Modified translation from Moeller, *Daodejing*, p. 17.

the root of heaven and earth, an unlimited resource. This link between generation and the feminine naturally leads to the priority of yin forces.

The second aspect emphasizes the greater power of the feminine, as in chapter 61: "A large state is lowly waters, the female [*pin*] of the world, the connection of the world. The female [*pin*] overcomes the male by constant stillness. Because she is still, she is therefore fittingly underneath."[41]

Insofar as the feminine is associated with generation (and, thus, with the *Dao* itself), one can notice the yinyang distinction going in two directions. On one hand, there is what we might call the horizontal level in which yin and yang are counterparts embedded in the myriad things. On the other hand, there is a vertical level in which yang refers to the things before us, while yin refers to the origin that is hidden, implicit, or empty. The *Daodejing* 10 asks: "When heaven's gate open and close, can you be female [*ci*]?"[42] Chapter 18 suggests: "Knowing *xiong* (male) and guarding *ci* (female), it is valley or mountain stream."[43]

In this context, we must also consider the pairing of *you* 有 and *wu* 無. *You* literally means "to have," whereas *wu* means "to lack." To say that something exists in classical Chinese is literally to say that it "is had," whereas to say it does not exist is to say it is not had or possessed. By extension, these terms come to denote something like "being" and "nonbeing" or "presence and absence." *You* coordinates with yang, and *wu* with yin.

The texts under consideration attribute an unseen force to all existence. This non-presence is always a part of yinyang presence. We have already seen that the *Dao* cannot be perceived or singled out in experience. This characteristic of non-presence or emptiness is what permits the efficacy of the *Dao*. The ultimate *Dao* is the source of everything, however, it is also empty or void. *Wu*, non-presence or nothingness, is the beginning of all existence.

The *Daodejing* uses the word *wu* (lack/nothingness/absence) 101 times. In the oracle bones, *wu* is the symbol for dancing. In fact, there are three closely related characters with the same pronunciation: *wu* 無 meaning nothingness, *wu* 舞 meaning to dance, and *wu* 巫 meaning a female shaman. The earliest comprehensive dictionary of Chinese characters, the *Shuowen Jiezi* (說文解字) by the Han scholar Xu Shen 許慎 (58–147 C.E.), explicates the link: *wu* 巫 (shamans) are women who can perform

---

[41] Ibid., p. 141.
[42] Ibid., p. 25.
[43] Ibid., p. 71.

service to *wu* 無 (the shapeless) and make the spirits come down by *wu* 舞 (dancing). Dancing was the way to communicate with and worship *shen* 神 (spirits).[44] However, these spirits are unseen and formless; only through dancing activities can one communicate with *shen*. *Wu*'s dancing is something present, yet they are working (*shi* 事) with *wu* (nonpresence).

In its origin, *wu* (nothing) is not emptiness, loss, or absence but rather the unseen, hidden, and invisible. It is not a mere nothing but is the undifferentiated source of potency and growth that lets things function, much as the empty spaces between joints and muscles are what allows Cook Ding to cut with such ease in the famous story from the *Zhuangzi*. The aspects of yang might represent the explicated order, whereas the aspects of yin relate to the enfolded hidden implicated order. This aspect will be further discussed in the chapter on yinyang strategy.

Yin and yang are inseparable as *you* and *wu*, or foreground and background. This mutual implication is already suggested in the unity of full potency with emptiness or void (*xu* 虛). An interesting symbolic illustration is ancient Chinese coins or "square-hole currency." The outside edge of the coin is circular, however, there is a square hole in the center. The circle represents heaven, and the square represents the earth.

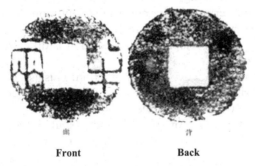

Front   **Back**

Standard ancient Chinese currency

What is most interesting is that the formless heaven is expressed with a solid metal circle with the concrete earth expressed by the square void. This symbolically shows the inherent connections between having (*you*)/lacking (*wu*) or fullness (*shi*)/void (*xu*). Excavated versions of the

[44] Shen Xu, 許慎, *Shouwen Jiezi* 說文解字 (ed.), Duan Yucai, 段玉裁 (Shanghai: Shanghai Guji Press, 1981), p. 201.

Daodejing support this unity. In the received version, chapter 40 says that the myriad things come from being (*you*) and being comes from nonbeing (*wu*). The Guodian version of the text, however, reads slightly different, saying, "the myriad things come from being, come from nonbeing."[45] In other words, the myriad things form simultaneously from *you* and *wu*, the foreground and background, yin and yang. The contemporary Chinese scholar Liu Xuyi (刘绪义) explains the importance of this version of the *Daodejing* chapter 40:

> The myriad things are generated in *you* (having or to have) and *wu* (nothing). Here *you* (having) and *wu* (nothing) are not connected in a sequence, one leading to other but rather they are parallel, *Dao* generates *you* and also generates *wu*. *You* and *wu* exist at the same time. *You* refers to a general existence that has a form in formlessness. Yet *wu* is formless, independent and unchanging. *Wu* is a part of *you*.[46]

Liu illustrates this with the example of a young girl and a mother. A young girl has not given birth, so she is *wu*, however, she still has the potential to exercise her reproductive ability to become *you*, or a mother.[47] So this description of *Dao* follows the biological ability and development of female body. However, how does one seize the *Dao*'s unity of *you* and *wu*? A young girl becoming a mother is the way of the *Dao*; Laozi's *Dao* is the mother of all myriad things. Another important point is that, as the soil to a seed, the mother provides a nourishing condition that allows things to grow and flourish, just as the female body supplies all nutrients for a fetus to survive and develop. This appreciation is different than simply one event of creation.

Dao has a strong tendency for reproduction. This association between metaphysical origins and biological reproduction, of course, appears in other cultures, as well. For example, Diotima, in Plato's *Symposium*, says, "All of us are pregnant...both in body and in soul."[48] One of her definitions of love is the desire to give birth in beauty. The *Dao* as the source of generation and reproduction in the world is based on such biological models, with concrete things being born through the interplay of *you* and *wu*, yin and yang.

---

[45] X. Liu, *Laozi, Past and Present*.

[46] X. Liu 刘绪义, *The World of Heaven and Human Being: A Study of the Origin of Pre-qin Schools* (Beijing: Beijing People's Press, 2009), p. 75.

[47] Ibid., p. 287.

[48] Plato, *The Symposium*, R. E. Allen. (trans.) (New Haven: Yale University Press, 1993), p. xix.

The relationship between *you* and *wu* also implies interplay between background and foreground that is crucial to how yinyang theory functions as a way of skillfully operating in the world. We will turn to this in the strategy chapter.

Qi and Yinyang

Qi 氣 is among the most important, cherished, and widely applied concepts in Chinese intellectual history. As a shared notion underlying all schools, *qi* is believed to be a dynamic all-present, all-penetrating, and all-transforming force animating every existence in the universe. Although *qi* is an abstract idea, it also is a common and integral part of one's perception and experience. It is woven into language: the air one breathes, the force that drives the fusion of blood, the food one eats, the strength of one's mind, the flow of one's thoughts, the deepest urges of one's heart. Tang Junyi 唐君毅 (1909–1978) captures some of this diversity in saying that, in Chinese philosophy, *qi* could mean "either something spiritual, as in ambition (*qizhi* 氣質) or something vital, as animation (*shenqi* 神氣), or something material, as geogaseity."[49]

The character for *qi* 氣 can be traced back to Shang Dynasty oracle bones, however, in its earliest usage, it was a verb and adjective rather than a noun. We can enter into its meaning by investigating this etymology. In its basic structure, the character for *qi* consists of three parallel lines, just like the Chinese character for the number three. It might be grounded in the observation of morning dew transforming into lines of steam under the sun. As an image, it may also be meant to capture the appearance of flowing clouds or the steam from cooking rice, which are how the *Shuowen Jiezi* describes it.

Regarding its sound, *qi* has the same sound as *qi*, 乞, which means praying or seeking alms. These interpretations indicate that the term *qi*, on one hand, portrays phenomena in nature based on observation, whereas on the other hand, it also involves religious and ritual activity in human life.

Qi refers to the material that constitutes reality, however, it is fundamentally dynamic. Because all of reality is conceived in terms of dynamic processes, the movements of *qi* have gained an explanatory power over all known phenomena, from natural events to political systems, from

---

[49] C. Tang, "Chang Tsai's Theory of Mind and Its Metaphysical Basis," *Philosophy East and West*, 6 (1956), p. 120.

military battles to medical diagnoses. *Qi* even appears in analyzing literary compositions and poetic imagery. In art, the movement of *qi* is what weaves together the painter, the painting, and the viewer into a single unified experience. The particular fluidity of movement from an idea into the work of art is the momentum of *qi* and should be accomplished in one swoop without interruption or pause.

Qi is the very force of life. As the *Zhuangzi* puts it, "Human life is all about generating *qi*. When *qi* is gathered there will be life; when *qi* is dispersed there will be death."[50] When *qi* declines, one will become sick; when *qi* is lost, one will die. On further analysis, *qi* is a complex of different energies, each animating and controlling various aspects of human life and the human body. We read from the *Huainanzi*:

> Human beings can see clearly and hear acutely; they are able to protect their own body and bend and stretch their one hundred joints. In their discrimination they are capable of distinguishing white from black, beautiful from ugly. In their intelligence they are capable of distinguishing similarity from difference and clarifying right from wrong. How can human beings do so? This is because the *qi* infuses these activities and the spirit (*shen* 神) regulates them.[51]

This primacy of *qi* lies in its self-generating and self-operating power. In this aspect, it can be seen as a more concrete approach to the *Dao*. *Qi* is the *Dao* in its sense of the origin of the myriad things and the basic materials of universe. *Dao* is materialized in *qi* and, thus, in space and time. In fact, in parts of the *Guanzi*, the *Zhuangzi*, and many Neo-Confucian texts, *Dao* and *qi* are practically interchangeable.

Qi is the fundamental stuff of the universe, however, how are the functions of *qi* manifested and organized? How does *qi* generate diversity? Although the diversity of *qi* is discussed in terms of movement and of quantity, it also is said to take on different forms or qualities, so that one can speak of different kinds of *qi*. The classification of kinds (*lei* 類) of *qi* explicates the most basic elements in the universe from which all existence is formed. In a passage mentioned earlier, one of the earliest such uses, the *Zuozhuan* analyzes *qi* as having six forms: yin, yang, wind, rain, dark, and bright. *Qi* is one among many observable natural phenomena, however, as time goes on, *qi* comes to encompass the entire natural world. Similarly, although this passage lists *qi* of yin and *qi* of yang as two

---

[50] Chen, *Commentaries on Zhuangzi*, p. 559.
[51] Modified translation from Lau and Ames, *Yuan Dao*, p. 26, and Roth, *The Huainanzi*, p. 75.

of six forms, in texts from the Han Dynasty and later, the concept of *qi* is inseparable from yinyang. To speak of *qi* is to speak of yinyang.[52]

This *qi* interpretation conceives yin and yang as dynamic and natural forms of flowing energy and manifestation of the primordial potency of the universe. The discussion of *qi* thus offers a context in which yinyang functions. Yin and yang are the two main features of *qi*. They make clear the transformation of *qi* from one form into another, as well as the patterns, regularities, and effects of *qi*. By giving the concept of *qi* actual content, yinyang presents the foundations for the intellectual codification of *qi* and for systematic metaphysics, especially later in Song Neo-Confucianism.

Yinyang as *qi* is not only an explanation for the fabric of the world, but also for the origin of the universe. In cosmogenesis, *yangqi* and *yinqi* have different roles to play, however, they work together to bring out interrelated results: *yinqi* becomes more concentrated whereas the *yangqi* becomes more diffuse. The *Huainanzi* describes this process of cosmogenesis:

> When heaven and earth were not yet formed, all was ascending and flying, diving and delving. Thus it was called ultimate manifestation (*taizhao* 天兆). The *Dao* began in the nebulous void. The nebulous void generates time-space (*yuzhou* 宇宙); time-space generates *qi*. *Qi* moves within the border. The light and bright *qi* spreads and ascends to form *tian* (heaven) and the heavy and turbid *qi* congeals and descends to form *di* (earth). It is easier for the light and subtle *qi* to converge and it is harder for heavy and turbid *qi* to congeal. That is why the heaven was completed first and earth was formed later. The merged essence of heaven and earth yields yinyang. The focused essence of yinyang manufactures the four seasons. The scattered essence of the four seasons produces the myriad things. The accumulated hot yang*qi* generates fire; the essence of fiery *qi* is the sun. The accumulated cold yin*qi* generates water; the essence of watery *qi* is the moon. The essence of the overflowing *qi* of the sun and moon forms stars and planets. Heaven contains the sun, moon, stars and planets; earth contains water, floods, dust and soil.[53]

This passage illustrates what was called the great inception or primal beginning. In the beginning, there is a void, an absence of heaven or

---

[52] For example, Wang Yanxiang (1474–1544) states: "Outside yinyang, there will be no *qi*…When heaven, earth, and everything take the forms, there are the images of clear and turbid, male and female, soft and hard, coming and going – this is called yinyang." Y. Wang, *The Collection of Wang Yanxiang* 王延相集 (Beijing: Zhonghua Press 中華書局, 2009), vol. XXXIII, p. 597.

[53] Modified translation from Roth, *The Huainanzi*, p. 143.

earth, no yin and yang, no four seasons or anything. It is vast, infinite, and peaceful. The *Dao* begins in this nebulous void. Time and space (*yuzhou*) are not abstract systems, however, they are a specific moment in a place, like the north or south, or a moment of time, such as a particular day in spring or a night in autumn. *Yangqi* rises up, diffusing from the beginning of spring and culminating during the summer; the cold *yinqi* descends, concentrating itself from the beginning of autumn and culminating in the winter. The alternation of yin and yang are most closely associated with the movement of *qi* in forming the seasons and thus the basic cycles of existence. Another passage from the *Huainanzi* says: "When heaven and earth were formed, they divided yin and yang. Yang is generated (*sheng* 生) from yin and yin is generated from yang. Yin and yang mutually alternate which makes four fields (celestial circles) penetrating. There is life and there is death; that brings the myriad things to completion."[54]

The connection between *qi* and yinyang indicates that yin and yang are the pulse and rhythm of *qi* that give rise to all things. Through *qi*, yin and yang are theorized as forces embedded in nature – guiding, shaping, or directing natural processes from within. This connection also suggests that the core of *qi* is the proper interplay between different elements. The yin and yang must be harmonized; if not, many problems will arise. We can again use a passage from the *Huainanzi*:

> Emitted *qi* endows, retained *qi* is transformed. Thus yang endows and yin is transformed. The unbalanced *qi* of Heaven, becoming perturbed, causes wind; the harmonious *qi* of Earth, becoming calm, causes rain. When yin and yang gather their interaction produces thunder. Aroused, they produce thunderclaps; disordered, they produce mist. When the yang *qi* prevails, it scatters to make dew; when yin *qi* prevails, it freezes to make frost and snow.[55]

The need to bring about harmony and efficacy through the management of yin and yang will be discussed more in later chapters.

Yinyang and Modes of Change (the *Yijing*)

The *Yijing* or *Zhouyi*, known in English as *The Book of Changes*, is one of the oldest Chinese written texts. The word *yi* 易 itself had three meanings

---

[54] Ibid., pp. 115–116.
[55] J. S. Major, *Heaven and Earth in Early Han Thought* (Albany: SUNY Press, 1993), p. 65.

in pre-Qin times: "change," "simple" or "easy," and "constancy." The focus of the text is on change; by following its guidance, however, one can accomplish things simply and easily. This guidance is possible because of constancy; not only the fact that things always change, but also because change follows regular patterns. The character for *yi* has two parts: on top is the sun, *ri* 日, and on the bottom is the moon, *yue* 月. The combination of sun and moon, with the extended meaning of yang (sun) and yin (moon), points to cyclical change, as we saw in the last section, as well as to the completion of a cycle. In the *Shuowen Jiezi*, *yi* is taken as referring to the lizard, gecko, and dragonfly. They share a common property: change. It was said that these animals could change their skin color twelve times within a single day. Association with the lizard also suggests fertility because the lizard, along with birds and the calabash (plant), symbolized the penis in ancient fertility worship.[56]

In the Warring States Period, the word *yi* also referred to divination techniques, called the "three *yi*": *Lianshan* 連山, *Guichang* 歸藏, and *Zhouyi* 周易. Of these three, the *Zhouyi* is the only one that has survived. The core of the text consists of sixty-four hexagrams (*gua* 卦), each of which is composed of six parallel line segments (*yao* 爻), which can be either solid or broken. Each hexagram has a name, which forms a special vocabulary largely intelligible only within the system of the *Zhouyi*, as well as an image (*xiang* 象). The lines also have their own associated images, and there are explanations of each hexagram (*guaci* 卦辭) and of each individual line (*yaoci* 爻辭).

It was originally a text for divination purposes. Later, commentaries (*zhuan* 傳) were added to these hexagrams and compiled into ten parts, called "ten wings" (*shiyi* 十翼). The commentary is mainly in three areas: an understanding of the *yi* as a whole, explanations of the images and numbers of the *yi* (*xiangshu* 象數), and instructions for divination using the *yi* (*zhan* 占). The commentaries shift focus toward philosophical explanations, and thus, the *Yijing* can be taken as having two sets of vocabularies: one of divination and one of philosophy.[57] As is customary, we can call the core part of the text the *Yi* or *Zhouyi* ("the *Yi* of the Zhou Dynasty"), the commentaries on it the *Yizhuan* ("*Yi* Commentaries"), and the two together the *Yijing* (the *Classic of Yi* or *The Book of Changes*).

---

[56] D. Liu and H. Hu, *The Selection of Sex Antiques Collected by China Sex Museum* (Hong Kong: Wenhui Press, 2000), p. 12.

[57] B. Zhu 朱伯昆, *The Philosophical History of Yi Studies* 易學哲學史, (Beijing: Huaxia Press 華夏出版社, 1995).

According to legend, the *Yijing* was made over time by four sages: Fu Xi 伏羲 drew eight trigrams, King Wen 文王 authored the explanations of hexagrams (*guaci*), the Duke of Zhou 周公 wrote the clarification of the lines (*yaoci*), and Confucius collected the commentaries (*yizhuan*).[58] Most contemporary scholars believe that the hexagrams go back at least to the early Western Zhou period, whereas the commentaries appear in the late Warring States Period (well after Confucius). In any case, the making of the *Yijing* took shape gradually over a span of 700 to 800 years.

Although linked with divination, the *Yijing* became a classic text for intellectual guidance as well. There is a long history of so-called *Yi* studies, or in recent Chinese translations, Yiology (*yixue* 易學). From the Han Dynasty on, it became a necessary part of an education for scholarly achievement as well for personal sagehood. Almost every literati had carefully studied the *Yijing*, and many offered their own commentary on it, especially the Neo-Confucians. According to the Neo-Confucian Zhu Xi 朱熹 (1130–1200), for example, the *Zhouyi* ranks first among the Five Classics (*Wujing* 五經). Zhu Xi describes the name of the book: *Zhou* refers to the name of the *Zhou* Dynasty, whereas *Yi* refers to a specific way of thinking.[59]

Although there is no explicit usage of the term yinyang in the *Zhouyi*, it contains the most systemic utilization of yinyang thought of any early text. One chapter of the *Zhuangzi* offers a summary of the core ideas of the classics. Along with describing the other five classics (*Poetry, Documents, Ritual, Music*, the *Spring and Autumn Annals*), it claims that "The *Yi* confers yinyang" (易道陰陽).[60]

A list of classics in an excavated text called the "Collected Sayings I" describes the role of the text: "the *Yi* is that by which one gathers together the way of heaven and the way of human beings" (易所以會天道人道, strip 36).[61] We have already seen how yinyang thought draws cosmological and natural patterns (the way of heaven) together with the way for human beings to act effectively (the way of human beings). The "Xici Zhuan" ("Commentary on the Attached Verbalizations") in the *Yijing* connects them explicitly, saying, "The conjunction and alteration of yin and yang is called *Dao*" (一陰一陽謂之道).[62] More literally, it says

---

[58] Among Mawangdui unearthed materials ten interpretations of *Yijing* are discovered. It shows the links between these interpretations and Daoist and Huanglao thought. It also supports the objection that *Yizhuan* was written by Confucius.

[59] X. Zhu 朱熹, *The Essential Meanings of the Zhouyi* 周易本義 (Beijing: Chinese Press, 2009), p. 29.

[60] Modification from Ziporyn (trans.), *Zhuangzi*, p. 118.

[61] Liu Zhao (ed.) *Guodian Chujian Jiaoyi*, p. 181.

[62] Gao, Heng 高亨, *Commentary on Zhouyi* 周易大傳今注 (Jinan: Qilu Press, 1998), p. 387.

simply, "One yin and one yang are called *Dao*," a phrase Zhu Xi later clarifies as "The constant interaction of yinyang is the *Dao*."[63] According to Granet, here yin and yang are dominated by the idea of rhythm.[64] In this phrase, *Dao* refers both to the *Dao* as origin of the world as well as to *Dao* as the way of living effectively in the world.

The *Yijing* points to a significant metaphysical development of the concept of yinyang. There are two ways in which to exhibit the role of yinyang in the *Yijing*. One is the yinyang structure of hexagrams and lines; the other is the reconfiguration of these hexagrams as the function and movement of yinyang. In terms of structure, all the hexagrams (*gua*) or symbols are made up of living yinyang configurations. Zhu Xi puts it plainly: "Changes (*yi*) is the way of yinyang; *gua* (hexagrams) are the matters of yinyang; *yao* (lines) are the movement of yinyang."[65] The structural lines that compose them have two modalities, with unbroken lines as yang and broken lines as yin. These yin lines and yang lines, when grouped in threes, multiply to form eight possible trigrams, representing eight natural phenomena: heaven (☰), earth (☷), thunder (☳), wind (☴), water (☵), fire (☲), mountains (☶), and marshes (☱). These eight trigrams can then be combined to form sixty-four possible hexagrams. The yin and yang are the smallest units for this massive combinatory system. In addition, each hexagram as a whole can be classed as yin or yang, so that there are thirty-two yang hexagrams, and there are thirty-two yin hexagrams. The function of this categorization is clearest in the first two hexagrams, *qian* 乾, which consists entirely of yang lines, and *kun* 坤, which consists of all yin lines. The "Xici Zhuan" explains that *qian* is identified with heaven and yang, the principle of power and creativity; *kun* is identified with earth and yin, the principle of receptivity and preservation. Together, the two generate all the myriad things through their interaction.

Here, we see that the *Yijing* not only employs yinyang as a conceptual tool to categorize phenomena, but also posits yinyang as an actual element in the structures, forces, and movements of reality. Yang interacts with yin to generate four heavenly images; hardness (*gang* 剛) interacts with softness (*rou* 柔) to generate the four earthly images. Therefore, eight images or forms emerge and establish the trigrams. Through the interaction of these eight trigrams, the myriad things are

[63] Zhu Xi, *The Essential Meanings of the Zhouyi*, p. 30.
[64] M. Granet, *La pensée chinoise* (*Chinese Thought*) (Paris: Editions Albin Michel, 1968), pp. 72–90.
[65] Zhu, *The Essential Meanings of the Zhouyi*, p. 1.

generated. This is called one dividing into two, two dividing into four, four dividing into eight, eight dividing into sixteen, sixteen dividing into thirty-two, and thirty-two dividing into sixty-four. This is also called dividing yin and dividing yang, the interaction of hardness and softness. This connection between yinyang and generation, which has already appeared in the *Daodejing*, takes a different form in the *Yijing*. *Yi*, through division, generates two then four, eight, sixteen, thirty-two, and sixty-four. This is similar to the composition of a tree: it has a trunk, then branches, then leaves, and so on. It is a linkage between a whole and its parts.[66]

To better comprehend the complex cosmological role of yinyang, we can follow a distinction made in the "Xici," which says that what is above tangible forms (*xingershang* 形而上) is called *Dao*, and what is below tangible forms (*xingerxia* 形而下) is called utensils, instruments, or vessels (*qi* 器) (not to be confused with the *qi* that means vital force or energy, an entirely different word). Yan Fu 嚴複 (1854–1921), the first generation of Chinese translators of European texts, used the expression *xinger shang* to translate Aristotle's metaphysics. Since then, the phrase *xingershang* has gained a particular meaning in the academic discipline – the study of *xingershang* is the study of metaphysics. Metaphysics is understood in reference to becoming and cosmology in the sense that it emerges from the cosmic changes that originate beings. In this sense, the invisible *Dao* that is above the forms and the visible material that are below forms are inherently indivisible.[67]

We have seen that the *Dao*, taken as above forms, is still characterized by the alternation and interaction of yinyang. On this level, yinyang participates in the very origination of being. At the same time, yinyang is used to categorize particular things and as the way to transform, develop, and refine the things that have forms. We see this link in the "Xici," which says, "Opening and closing is called change (*bian* 變), but going back and forth without limit is called penetrating (*tong* 通)."[68] *Bian* and *tong* are aspects of both concrete things and the *Dao*. Both are experienced and embodied in myriad things as tools or utensils (*qi*) and in the oneness that is above form as their source or the "Great Ultimate," *Taiji*. This unity is captured in the term for concrete things, *qi*. The term *qi* refers

---

[66] Pang Pu 庞朴, *On Oneness Divided into Threeness* 浅说一分为三, (Beijing: Xinhua Press, 2004), pp. 223–224.

[67] *Dao* and *qi* are often paired with another set: *ti* and *yong*. *Ti* is the basic structure, whereas *yong* is the function. In this case, *dao* is the *ti*, *qi* is the *yong*.

[68] Gao, *Commentary on Zhouyi*, p. 403.

most specifically to vessels, containers with different shapes for holding water or other daily usages. However, vessels were also a sacrificial tool to be used in worship and divination. *Qi* have forms and shapes but carry the shapeless and formless, representing the *Dao*. We experience *Dao* through *qi*.

The role of yinyang in the generation of concrete things echoes what we have seen from the *Daodejing*, although in a more explicit and developed form. We might say that how concrete things are shaped, connected, and transformed is the focus of the *Yijing*. Nonetheless, the *Yijing*'s yinyang is different than *Daodejing*'s yinyang.[69] The *Yijing*'s yinyang is like a key used to open a world of symbols. In the West, reality has tended to be analyzed through abstract symbol systems such as algebra, geometry, and calculus, which affect human life as mediated through applications and technology, not as a direct confrontation with lived reality.[70]

The *Yijing*'s symbol system represents unbroken wholeness in the flowing movement of reality. It is the unfolding and enfolding of the perceived world from and to a much vaster and more subtly integrated whole order. All things in the universe are interconnected and directly affect our way of thinking, being, and doing. From another perspective, we might say that European thought has tended toward analysis, the breaking into increasingly smaller parts.[71] While the basis of the *Yijing* in the two elements of yin and yang has some resemblances to this approach, *Yi* thinking strives for an adequate synthetic reflection of functional wholes, examining how patterns appear, move, and transform. It puts events into a framework or grid and then investigates their implications. It serves as a form of inductive reasoning, which pays particular attention to configurational forces, as we will see in the next chapter. It seeks something that can be described using Brook Ziporyn's terms: "internal coherence, or hidden coherence, as opposed to explicitly manifest intelligibility."[72]

---

[69] Liu Xiaogan states that "Yin and yang are generalizations. If one summarizes Laozi's dialectics from the point of view of yinyang, this will not sufficiently reflect the characteristics of Laozi's thought. This is because a yinyang view relates to different ancient Chinese teachings and schools. It more accurately reflects Zhouyi's dialectics of the Zhouyi. Therefore it is not helpful to use yinyang to describe Laozi's dialectics." Liu, *Laozi, Past and Present*, p. 671.

[70] C. Cheng, "Paradigm of Change (Yi) in Classical Chinese Philosophy," *Journal of Chinese Philosophy*, 36 (2009), 519.

[71] Martin Schonfeld, "Climate Philosophy and Cognitive Evolution," in R. Irwin (ed.) *Climate Change and Philosophy* (London/New York: Continuum, 2009), p. 7.

[72] B. Ziporyn, *Ironies of Oneness and Difference: Coherence in Early Chinese Thought – Prolegomena to the Study of Li* (Albany: State University of New York Press, Forthcoming).

All existence, including events, phenomena, and affairs, takes some kind of shape or form. The sixty-four hexagrams of the *Yijing* were designed to cover all structures of being and to apply to all possibilities of change in the natural and human world. They illuminate the intelligibility of the coherence of the world.

Before considering a specific example, two related points about the hexagrams must still be addressed – the role of the individual lines and the importance of change. Each hexagram has six lines, which are read from the bottom up. The positions of the lines have great significance. For example, lines one and two associate with earth; lines three and four, with human beings; and lines five and six, with heaven. Each of the lines contains a specific meaning. Moreover, each hexagram is dynamic, tending toward change, which comes through the configuration, transformation, and alternation of the specific lines. Once a line changes, the hexagram will change accordingly, and different interpretations or meanings will emerge. The line change is from yin to yang or yang to yin. Thus, changes arise from yin and yang mutually pushing, pulling, and generating.

As is evident, the *Yijing* is an extremely complicated text. Here we can use one example to illustrate how yinyang thought operates more specifically. The *jiji* 既濟 hexagram (63) is considered as "perfection complete" or "all things perfectly realized."[73] It takes on great importance in the Chinese tradition, and we will encounter it again, first in Zhou Dunyi's *Taijitu* discussed later and then in approaches to bodily cultivation, where it plays an important role in the *Zhouyi Cantongqi*. The name of the hexagram, *jiji*, has been translated as "After Completion,"[74] "Ferrying Completes,"[75] and "Already Fording."[76] In general, the first *ji* 既 means "already," and the second *ji* 濟 stands for "cross the river" or "completed," "done," or "occurred." Put together, the two terms convey that one has embarked on a course of action and that a perfect result has been reached. We can focus on the images and numbers of the *jiji* hexagram and then on its philosophical meaning.

We read from the "judgment" of the *jiji* hexagram: "'Ferrying Complete'" is such that even the small enjoy prevalence. It is fitting to practice constancy, for although in the beginning good fortune prevails, things might end in chaos."[77]

[73] R. J. Lynn (trans.), *The Classic of Changes: A New Translation of the I Ching* (New York: Columbia University Press, 1994), p. 543.
[74] R. Wilhelm and C. F. Baynes (trans.), *The I Ching or Book of Changes* (New Jersey: Princeton University Press, 1950), p. 245.
[75] Lynn (trans.), *The Classic of Changes*, p. 338.
[76] J. Wu, *I Ching* (Washington, DC: The Taoist Center, 1991), p. 213–215.
[77] Lynn (trans.), *The Classic of Changes*, p. 338.

☲ 離 *li* (fire) ☵ 坎 *kan* (water)

既濟 *Jiji* hexagram

2.1. The *Jiji* hexagram.

The configuration of the yin lines or yang lines in any given hexagram involves position, direction, and movement. Each line has a structural "ought" in the sense of what leads to better fortune – that is, a yin line should be in the yin position (*yinwei* 陰位), which are the lines 1, 3, 5, counting up to down, and a yang line should be in the yang position (*yangwei* 陽位), which are lines 2, 4, 6. In the *Jiji* hexagram, both the hard/strong and firm (yang/*gang* 剛) and the soft/weak and yielding (yin/*rou* 柔) behave correctly and, thus, stay in their proper positions. Wang Bi 王弼 (226–249 C.E.) explains that "if both the hard and strong and the soft and weak behave correctly and thus stay in their rightful positions, evil will have no chance to occur. Thus, only when such rectitude prevails, it is fitting to practice constancy."[78] The proper positions are expected to bring success and efficacy. Position (*wei* 位) is one of most important ways to appreciate the *Yi*. As with yinyang, position is not just a means by which things in the world are represented or expressed in the images of the hexagrams; position plays a key role in the world itself and in the evaluation of events. Position also supplies an explanatory framework for social structures, as we will see in later chapters. For example, ruler and subject, male and female, parents and children, old and young, all take positions in certain social contexts. These positions define their proper functions and guide their actions. Such positions are structured and constituted by yinyang configurations.

We have seen that each six-line hexagram is made up of two three-line trigrams. The *jiji* hexagram contains water and fire, with water on top and fire on the bottom (see Figure 2.1).

Water's nature is downward flowing, and fire's nature is upward burning. Thus, we might expect this configuration to be unfortunate or dangerous, but movement is most central to the hexagrams. When water is above, it can follow its natural tendency to go down, and when fire is below, it can naturally move upward. More importantly, water above and fire below will naturally come into interaction. The

---

[78] Ibid.

hexagram gives an image of freedom from blockage and the flow of natural propensities and tendencies. There is no obstacle between fire and water. This is the stage of *tong*, of penetration, communication, or flowing together.

The value of *tong* can be seen in two directions. The focal point is the claim that following a thing's nature is *tong* (*shunxingertong* 順性而通). Everything has its own internal patterns and tendencies, a way in which it flows. As the *Zhongyong* 中庸 claims in its opening statement, "What leads according to its nature is the *Dao*."[79] When a thing flows according to its nature, it is *tong*. In this hexagram, water and fire follow their inherent natures to *tong*. This expresses the privileged value of change and interaction. Following the nature of things will lead to change and transformation; *tong* is the result of *shun* 順 (following or flowing along with), and *shun* is the condition for *tong*.

From another direction, there is the claim that all things are inter-penetrating (*wuwuxiangtong* 物物相通).[80] Thus, the movement of the two trigrams toward interaction with each other is also *tong*. If *tong* is broken down or blocked by other things, then there will be misfortune. This view of *tong* carries great weight in health and in body cultivation. Body cultivation is about promoting *tong*: sickness comes from its obstruction. *Tong* is the best state of being. If there is *tong*, then there is interaction, growth, and prosperity.

The hexagrams assume a dynamic world with multiple dimensions tightly enfolded into the intricate fabric of reality. Instead of celebrating and relaxing at the successful completion of a journey, the *jiji* hexagram cautions others to be aware and to envision possible disasters in the future. This vision is a logical consequence of *tong*. Because *tong* is constantly rooted in interaction, change is inevitable. The commentary on the judgment states:

> If one were to misconstrue Ferrying Complete to mean perfect security, its *Dao* would come to an end, and no progress would occur, so that in the end only chaos would ensue. This is why the text says: "Although in the beginning good fortune prevails, things might end in chaos." That things end in chaos is not due to their becoming so on their own, but happens because of one ceasing to do as one should. Thus the text says: "if

---

[79] Roger T. Ames and David L. Hall, *Focusing the Familiar: A Translation and Philosophical Interpretation of the Zhongyong* (Honolulu: University of Hawai'i Press, 2001), p. 89.

[80] Luoshu 洛書 and Han Pengjie 韓鵬杰 (eds.), *The Complete Works of Zhouyi*, 周易全書 (Beijing: Tuanjie Press 團結出版社, 1990), p. 2184.

one ends up ceasing to practice constancy and to follow the mean, chaos will ensue."[81]

In sequence, all yin lines are above the yang lines. That indicates that yin is rising, whereas bringing things to completion also reveals the seeds of disorder. This specifies a condition of climax. Because change is inevitable, any movement of climax may revert from order to disorder. The sense that things reverse when they reach an extreme is quite common in early Chinese thought. Thus, completion necessitates the utmost caution.

> The image.
> Water over fire the image of the condition
> In after completion.
> Thus the superior man
> Takes thought of misfortune
> And arms himself against it in advance[82]

Yin is the hidden variable that decides which outcome actually occurs. The line text indicates that yin is small and contains possible danger. As a task is completed, the germ of change is already in the making. One must be aware of these things to come. This is called *youhuan yishi* 憂患意識. *Youhuan* can mean anxiety and tribulation, both to encounter troubles and to be troubled by events in the world; *yishi* literally refers to consciousness, awareness, or a mindset. Put together, these terms could be translated as "concerned awareness" or "awareness of concern."

There are two points at the center of this concern. First, uncertainty is a fundamental principle of the universe, as even contemporary science has come to recognize. Our knowledge necessarily is limited by this uncertainty. This principle is captured in the concept of *shen* 神. We can begin by examining in more detail the multilayered word *shen*. The most concrete meaning of *shen* is a spirit, ghost, or deity. By extension, it comes to refer to what happens in a magical, mysterious, or inscrutable way. Sandor P. Szabo brings out the broader sense of the term: "In the second part of the Warring States Period, the word *shen* often meant the group of those existents which could not be experienced by humans, which did not appear for humans in a way that could be sensed."[83] Graham

---

[81] Lynn (trans.), *The Classic of Changes*, pp. 338–339.

[82] Wilhelm and Baynes (trans.), *The I Ching*, p. 245.

[83] S. P. Szabo, "The Term Shenming – Its Meaning in the Ancient Chinese Thought and in a Recently Discovered Manuscript," *Acta Orientalia Academiae Scientiarum Hungaricae*, 56 (2003), 263.

translates the word *shen* 神 with wide a range of meanings, such as spirit, daemon/daemonic, numinous, and the locus of more prosaic aspects of awareness.[84] Willard J. Peterson treats *shen* as an adjective in the "Xici" in *The Book of Changes* and translates it as "numinous," which derives from the Latin *numen* (divinity).

The yinyang governing the process of production and transformation is inscrutable; therefore it is *shen*. The "Xici" claims that, "Being incommensurate with yin and yang is what is meant by numinous (*shen*)" 陰陽 不測謂之神.[85] The term translated as "incommensurate" is *buce* 不測 – *bu* means "no," and *ce* originally refers to measuring the depths of water. Thus, *shen* is what our measurements cannot quite reach. *Shen* is a necessary result of the process of changing lines (*bianyao* 變爻). Any given hexagram must go through changes (*bian*), however, these changes are not entirely predictable or determined.

In a much later time, Zhang Zai 張載 in the Song Dynasty uses *shen* in this sense to emphasize the inscrutable, wondrous aspect of the process of generation. Yinyang is the way of *shen* and is the spontaneous principle of the universe. Zhang Zai writes:

> The generation of things is transformation (*hua* 化); the transformation reaching its limit is called change (*bian* 變); the unpredictability of yinyang is called *shen*. Those who can apply *shen* without restrictions are called sages. Now, the function of transformation and change in heaven is the profound and dark (*xuan* 玄), among human beings is the *Dao*, and in the earth is transformation. Transforming generates the five tastes, *Dao* generates wisdom, and the profound and dark generates *shen*.[86]

> 故物生謂之化, 物極謂之變, 陰陽不測謂之神, 神用無方謂之聖. 夫變化之為 用也, 在天為玄, 在人為道, 在地為化, 化生五味, 道生智, 玄生神.

Shen is intrinsically connected with yinyang and with what cannot be directly grasped through our present cognitive ability.

In part, yinyang is *shen* because the yin and yang lines interact to form unpredictable emergent properties. The *Yijing* reflects a strong acceptance of chance – yinyang will always change and have different configurations.

---

[84] A. C. Graham (trans.), *Chuang-tzu, The Inner Chapters* (Indianapolis: Hackett Publishing Company, INC. 2001), p. 58.

[85] W. J. Peterson, "Making Connections: 'Commentary on the Attached Verbalizations' of the Book of Change," *Harvard Journal of Asiatic Studies*, 42 (1982), p. 104.

[86] Zhang Zai, *The Complete Collection of Zhang Zai's Work* 張載集, (Beijing: Chinese Press, 1976), Z. p. 17.

Shen is not just in the unpredictability of change, but also in the fact that the origin of those changes cannot be fully grasped. Yinyang plays a mediating role in addressing the origination of the myriad things. This yinyang function is *shen*. Yinyang is easier to identify, however, *shen* is difficult to see. Therefore, it can be taken to express an otherness or thirdness. Zhang Zhan, a scholar from the Jin Dynasty, explains this claim in a commentary on the *Liezi*:

> The generation of transformation has a form, but the generator of generation (*shengsheng* 生生) has no image (*xiang* 象). The beings with form can be called things; being with no image is called *shen*. The trace of *shen* is its function and it belongs to the class of yinyang. Talking of its true existence, it is unpredictability of yinyang. That's why the *Yi* states that the unpredictability of yinyang is called *shen*.[87]

Shen can also illustrate the actions of a sage or one capable of utilizing yinyang as Zhang Zai states: "The *shen* of a person is the manifestation of sageliness. Harmonizing yinyang with unity, going forward and backward, living and dying at the right time, these are natural heavenly principle. Human beings have to apply movement and rest, hardness and softness, humanity and righteousness to measure it. This is the *shen* of a sage."[88]

Second, this *youhuan yishi* assumes a certain conception of the role of human action in the world. According to the twentieth-century Chinese scholar Xu Fuguan 徐復觀 (1904–1982), this sense of concern differs from fear or hopelessness, as it comes from a vision that is the result of reflection on fortune and misfortune, success and failure. In this account, one finds the connection between these events and one's action, leading to a sense of responsibility. *Youhuan* is the manifestation of consciousness of one's responsibility toward events and a manifestation of an emerging humanistic spirit.[89] This concept of *youhuan yishi* originates from the transitional period between the Shang and the Zhou, in which people realized they had control over their own lives and fate. This followed from the emergence of a view of *tian* (heaven) as being responsive to human virtue. Because of this broader context, one must still be cautious when placing trust in one's ability alone. This realization has three interrelated elements: (1) the proper place of human effort, that one's action makes a

---

[87] Yang Bojun, 杨伯峻 (ed.) *Liezi Jishi*, 列子集釋, *Commentaries on Master Lie*, (Beijing: Chinese Press, 1979) p. 1.

[88] Zhang, *The Complete Collection of Zhang Zai's Work*, p. 151.

[89] F. Xu, *History of Chinese Discussions on Human Nature* (Shanghai: Huadong Normal University Press, 1982), p. 14.

difference in determining success and failure; (2) a future-oriented vision or reflection on future events, how one can sustain success and avoid failure; (3) a sense of one's responsibility to bring about the best outcome in the future, how one will contribute to future success or failure.

The need for caution and diligence rests on an epistemic assumption: any given point of knowledge is only one single and small knot in a giant coherent web. Knowing contains infinite unknowing because the known is only part of what is unknown. There is a holographic nature to reality: every event is part of a continuum. For example, confronting one hexagram, its information or meaning is at hand, however, it also contains the information from the other sixty-three hexagrams hidden within it. The hexagram can be seen as one thing, however, it implicates the myriad things in the world. The difference is that at a particular moment in time and space, the information is known or seen in connection with the unknown and unseen, or we might say, with what does not yet appear. The *jiji* hexagram is followed by *weiji* 未濟 (the sixty-fourth hexagram), whose name means "what is not yet finished." It is the inverse of the *jiji* hexagram, meaning that every line position is wrong – however, it is an auspicious hexagram, because good fortune follows after disaster.

Yinyang and the Development of Systematic Cosmology

Although the *Daodejing* and the *Yijing* articulate reality from different angles, there are common threads in all of the accounts we have seen, centering on the spontaneous generation of complexity from simplicity and the emergence of patterns and order. In all of these accounts, yinyang is woven into the very fabric of a generative reality, and it is the notion of yinyang that makes these patterns coherent and, ultimately, manageable. Yinyang can simplify, exemplify, and expand various relationships. It underpins all beings by shaping and directing natural processes from within and across boundaries, interfaces permeable to information, energies, and influences.

We have already seen what is probably the most central problem – what is the relationship between the spontaneous, unified, undifferentiated origin and the order and patterns we find among particular things? This is the question of the relationship between presence/being (*you*) and non-presence/nonbeing (*wu*), or between the *Dao* and the myriad things, or between what the "Xici" in the *Book of Changes* designates as "what is above forms" (*xingershang*) and "what is below forms" (*xingerxia*). Under Buddhist influence, the question concerned the status of beings

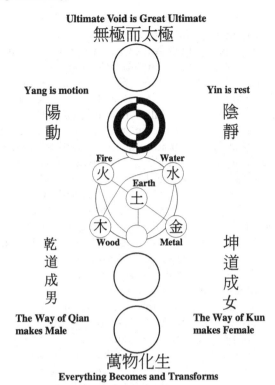

2.2. Zhou Dunyi's *Taijitu*.

and patterns in relation to the nonbeing at the foundations of the world. We have noted yinyang plays a central role both in understanding the relationships between particular things and events (what is below forms) and in the process that generated those things (what is above forms). Thus, as we would expect, yinyang continues to play a crucial role in Chinese metaphysical thought. An examination of the role of yinyang in later Chinese metaphysics is beyond the scope of this book, however, we can briefly consider two examples, beginning with Zhou Dunyi's conception of the "Great Ultimate" (*Taiji* 太極) and then Zhang Zai's discussion of *qi* and "Great Emptiness" (*Taixu* 太虛).

Zhou Dunyi 周敦頤 (1017–1073) is considered the forerunner of Neo-Confucianism and founder of *Daoxue* 道學 in the Song Dynasty. He published a "Diagram of the Great Ultimate" (*Taijitu* 太極圖 see Figure 2.2) and wrote a concise 256-word philosophical account of it (*Taijitu Shuo*太極圖說). Zhou's influence set the parameters according to which yinyang theory was assimilated metaphysically and systematically into later Confucian thought and practice.

Zhou Dunyi's *Taijitu* consists of five images, along with six line inscriptions. The first image is a circle placed directly under the inscription "Ultimate Void (*Wuji*) is Great Ultimate (*Taiji*)."[90] The second image consists of interlocking empty and shaded areas forming six semicircles with a smaller empty circle in the middle. This image is of the *Jiji* hexagram of the *Yijing*, which we have just discussed. A correct reading of it should start from the middle and divide this image into two parts. The left part is *li* 離 (fire), one of the eight trigrams turned on its side, with two light (yang) lines outside and one dark (yin) line inside. The right part is *kan* 坎 (water), another *gua* turned on its side, with two dark (yin) lines outside and one light (yang) line inside. On either side of these images are inscribed the words *Yangdong* 陽動 "Yang is motion" (on the left) and *Yinjing* 陰靜 "Yin is rest" (on the right). These words acknowledge the crucial role of yinyang and its cosmic significance.

The third image of the *Taijitu* is the flow of five phases or elements (*wuxing* 五行): fire, water, earth, wood, and metal. One of Zhou Dunyi's efforts is to integrate the five elements into the rhythmic pattern of yinyang. The last images, four and five, both contain a circle equal in size to those featured in the first image. On either side of image four is an inscription: on the left, "The Way of *Qian* makes male"; on the right, "The Way of *Kun* makes female." *Qian* and *Kun* refer to the first two hexagrams, with *Qian* composed of all yang lines, and *Kun*, all yin lines. The *Taijitu* is completed with an inscription centered under the last circle: "Everything becomes and transforms."

The overall philosophical interpretation hinges on the first inscription, which links *Taiji* and *Wuji*. The term *ji* 極 here means extremely, utmost, or pole.[91] *Tai* means "great" or "ultimate." We have already discussed *wu*, meaning to lack or be without. The concept of *Wuji* first appears in the *Zhuangzi*. *Ji* refers to the highest boundary of space. It is

[90] For more discussion on this statement see R. Wang, "Zhou Dunyi's Diagram of the Supreme Ultimate Explained (*Taijitu shuo* 太极圖說): A Construction of the Confucian Metaphysics," *Journal of the History of Ideas*, Vol. 66, No.3, (July 2005), 307–23.

[91] W. T. de Bary and Bloom translation of *taiji* as "Supreme Polarity" is consistent with their translation of the same term in the *Taijitu shuo*. They argue for the superiority of their translation over other possibilities, including "Great Ultimate," because "*taiji* is the yin-yang principle of bipolarity, which is the most fundamental ordering principle, the cosmic "first principle." Their translation of *wuji* as "Non-Polar" follows from this translation of *taiji*, which they claim is consistent with Daoist usages likely to be familiar to Zhou Dunyi. William Theodore De Bary and Irene Bloom. *Source Book of Chinese Tradition*, (New York: Columbia University Press, 2000), p. 677.

used with the term of *liu ji* 六極 (six extremes or directions). "Tang asks Li, 'There are limits (*ji*) in up, down, and four directions?' Li responds, 'There is *wuji* outside of *wuji*.'"[92] In the "Xici," *Wuji* suggests the state of beings where there are no numerical distinctions. The origin of the hexagrams comes from this stage of non-distinction. When it comes to Zhou Dunyi, the *Taiji* is the *Dao*. This leads to Zhou Dunyi's argument that there is no metaphysics of being separated from the cosmology of origination, becoming, and evolution, thus his identification of *Taiji* with transformation and yinyang. The concepts of the numinous or divine (*shen*) and transformation (*hua*) are both the function and manifestation of the changes of yin and yang. *Taiji* is a self-contained notion. Zhou Dunyi's *Taijitu Shuo* explains how this can be the case.

Zhou Dunyi declares that the movement and rest of the yinyang inter-action generate the five phases (water, fire, wood, metal, and soil) as the five constituents of the myriad things and, ultimately, human beings. Zhou Dunyi directly and clearly identifies yinyang with *dongjing* 動靜 (movement and rest) as critical to the generation of the universe. By characterizing yinyang in terms of the polarity of movement (*dong*) and rest (*jing*), or activity and stillness, Zhou Dunyi opens a line of inquiry that remains philosophically promising to this day. As representative of yinyang interactions generally, rest and movement occur in fluctuating or alternating patterns, even though they are encompassed within *Taiji* itself. As Fung Yu-lan remarks, "It is possible for both of these phases to be concurrently present."[93] In other words, neither yin nor yang is abso-lutely prior to the other, or more powerful, or more dominant; their con-currence is logically and metaphysically necessary. Here is Zhou Dunyi's more detailed articulation from the *Tongshu* 通書, chapter 16:

> Activity as the absence of stillness and stillness as the absence of activity characterize things (*wu*). Activity that is not [empirically] active and still-ness that is not [empirically] still characterize spirit (*shen*). Being active and yet not active, still and yet not still, does not mean that [spirit] is nei-ther active nor still. For while things do not [inter] penetrate (*tong*), spirit subtly [pervades] the myriad things.

> The yin of water is based in yang; the yang of fire is based in yin. The Five Phases are yin and yang; yin and yang are the Supreme Polarity [*Taiji*]. The Four Seasons revolve: the myriad things end and begin [again]. How undifferentiated! How extensive! And how inexhaustible! [5:33b–34b][94]

---

[92] Chen, *Commentaries on Zhuangzi*, p. 11.

[93] Fung Yu-lan, *A History of Chinese Philosophy* (trans.) Derek Bodde (New Jersey: Princeton University Press, 1983), p. 443.

[94] Bary and Bloom, *Source Book of Chinese Tradition*, p. 678.

What is unique about yin and yang interactions in the dimension of *shen* (spirit) is that they are not restricted by the law of logical noncontradiction ("something cannot simultaneously be and not be in the same time and place, and in the same aspects"). The formulation of the metaphysical paradox of yinyang as *dongjing* (movement and rest) in the Great Ultimate, however, is carefully distinguished from the realm of the myriad things and the human beings who are generated by yinyang interactions.

Everything begins from one source, in which the Great Ultimate (*Taiji*) as Ultimate Void (*Wuji*) is itself unlimited, undifferentiated, uncaused, and beyond the ontological dynamics of movement (yang) and rest (yin) apparent in the myriad things and human beings. Zhou Dunyi thus uses movement and rest to define the ontological significance of yang and yin. In his account, the metaphysical unity of all things is primary; their differentiation into a multiplicity of things is secondary. Within this assumption of primordial unity, the task of metaphysics is to give a coherent account of the patterned interrelations of all things. The patterned polarities apparent in the myriad things as well as in human relations are neither ultimate, nor in opposition to one another.

Although later Neo-Confucians, following Zhu Xi, would express critical reservations about Zhou Dunyi's location of the yinyang dynamic within *Taiji* itself, he remains the first to explicate these forces in terms of *dong* and *jing*. This is one of Zhou Dunyi's major philosophical contributions to yinyang theory. As we have seen, the concept of yinyang had been employed to construct a justification for the structure of the universe at least since the *Yijing*. These classics would argue that yinyang is the main force penetrating all beings in the universe. However, they fall short of disclosing how and in what ways yin and yang perform their functions or undertakings. Zhou Dunyi correlates *dong* and *jing* with yang and yin and, thus, confers a specific framework on yinyang thought. The functions of yang and yin are manifested in the form of movement (*dong*) and rest (*jing*); in other words, *dong* and *jing* are modes of yinyang activity. Following Zhou Dunyi, Zhu Xi identifies yin and yang with his concepts of *ti* 體 (structure) and *yong* 用 (function).

Underlying Zhou Dunyi's theory of the Great Ultimate is a concern with the relationship between differentiation and the primordial origin of the world. The Neo-Confucian philosopher Zhang Zai can be seen as taking up the same concern from a different angle, concentrating more on nonbeing or emptiness as the ultimate. This concern can be traced most directly to Guo Xiang 郭象 (?–312 C.E.), the famous commentator on the *Zhuangzi* and one of the thinkers most representative of the *Xuan* School

玄學 (Mysterious Learning). Guo Xiang inherited Wang Bi's concern for the problem between nothingness (*wu*) and being (*you*) and developed it into a more coherent and detailed argument. For Guo Xiang, the question is, if something comes from nothingness, then where does nothingness come from? He responds that nothingness and being cannot be related in a linear sequence of generation, such that nothingness is first and then gives birth to something. Rather, they must be bound together in a state of transformation. In other words, nothingness and existence are always intertwined in all beings. Guo Xiang makes use of *qi* to establish this knot of nothingness and being. It is because of *qi* that beings exist in myriad forms, however, this *qi* can lead to change, so that beings can become nothing. He states, "There is one *qi* but myriad forms; there is change and transformation but no dying or birthing."[95] Nothingness is not absolute nonbeing because it still contains *qi*. He explains, "Even though the changes and transformations constantly replace each other, their *qi* originally is one."[96] Clearly, *qi* is the reason for the existence of something; nevertheless, *qi* is also the cause for nothingness. In other words, *qi* explains both the coming into and going out of existence of particular beings. *Qi* takes on a clearly ontological function as the ground for all existence, including both being and nothingness. At the core of this view is the belief that *qi* is generation (*sheng*) and transformation (*hua*). We could call this a form of agricultural thinking, modeled on the growth, flourishing, and death of seasonal crops.

When Neo-Confucians contemplated how *qi* could be the ultimate source of the universe and of human minds, they were particularly concerned with the demands of moral cultivation. The understanding of *qi* that resulted was an integration of Qin-Han cosmology and Wei-Jin ontology, developed through the interplay between Confucianism, Daoism, and Buddhism. Zhang Zai's *Theory of Qi* (*Qilun* 氣論) lays out the foundation for this new paradigm for the articulation of *qi*. According to Zhang Zai, "Void is *qi*. It is something and nothing, hidden and manifest, numinous and transforming."[97]

The focal point of this speculation is the "Great Void" or "Great Emptiness," *Taixu* 太虛, which was taken as the ultimate source for all particular beings. By interpreting the "Great Void" so that it contained *qi*, Zhang Zai denied the Daoist and Buddhist equation of *Taixu* with

---

[95] Guo Xiang, commentary on "Ultimate Happiness" in *Zhuangzi Jishi Collections of Zhuangzi's Commentaries* (Beijing: Zhonghua Press, 1961), p. 629.

[96] Guo Xiang, commentary on "Yuyan" in *Zhuangzi Jishi*, p. 951.

[97] Zhang, *The Complete Collection of Zhang Zai's Work*, p. 8.

complete nothingness – an equation that Zhang Zai took as the "hole in the net" of their arguments. The key to understanding Zhang Zai's conception of *Taixu* is through its relationship with *qi*. The question is whether *Taixu* and *qi* have the same fundamental quality or mode of existence (*tongzhi* 同質) or if they were different (*yizhi* 異質). If *Taixu* has the same quality as *qi*, then *Taixu* is only another manifestation of *qi*. If *Taixu* and *qi* are different, then *Taixu* is bound to transcend the realm of *qi*, and, thus, of all being. The central problem for Zhang Zai, then, is that *qi* and *Taixu* can neither be completely identical nor completely different.

Taixu contains *qi*, however, it is not equal to or identical with *qi*. This is a central assumption of Zhang Zai's ontology and moral teaching, and it enables him to explain the ontological status of the myriad things. When *qi* condenses, the myriad things begin to exist; when *qi* disperses, the myriad things disappear. This is similar to the way water freezes when it is cold but evaporates into air when heated. These physical changes for Zhang Zai convey a metaphysical necessity: "Ultimate void cannot exist without *qi*; *qi* must condense to form the myriad things; the myriad things must disperse to return to the ultimate void."[98]

The fundamental claim is that *Taixu* is in both the dispersion and the condensing of *qi*. Zhang Zai verifies the interlocking of *Taixu* and *qi* by again using the comparison with water and ice. Ice is solid or condensed water just as *Taixu* is condensed *qi*.[99] On a conceptual level, this bond exemplifies one existence in two forms (一物兩體). *Taixu* necessarily permeates *qi*, however, it is not equal or identical to *qi*. From a naturalistic point of view, *Taixu* and *qi* are the same because they both can explain the existence of concrete things. *Qi* is the source for diversity and transformation in the universe. The interdependence of *Taixu* and *qi* is an interface between the ultimate absolute being and the multitude of concrete phenomena. This position enables Zhang Zai to resist the Buddhist view that concrete things are only illusions.

Zhang Zai identifies *Dao* with *qi*, *qi* with void (*xu*), and void with yinyang. Yinyang makes Zhang Zai's *qi* theory complete and coherent. Zhang Zai justifies this connection through a detailed and interesting interpretation of the properties of yinyang. *Qi* has two forms of existence: yin and yang. Yin and yang have three properties: motion and rest (*dongjing* 動靜), bending and expanding (*qushen* 屈伸), condensing and dispersing (*jusan* 聚散). We can consider the property of condensing and dispersing

[98] Ibid., p. 7.
[99] Ibid., p. 8.

as an example: the nature of yin is *ju* (condensing or concentrating), and the nature of yang is *san* (dispersing and expending). These two are in a constant motion of interaction. What forms depends on the proportion and forces of these two. Yang wants to spread and disperse; yin wants to condense and concentrate. When *qi* condenses, things begin to exist; when *qi* diffuses, things disappear.

Although the numinous (*shen*) has several meanings in Zhang Zai's thought, its conception is intrinsically connected with transformation (*hua*). More importantly, *shen* and *hua* both rely on the following presuppositions:

- The myriad things are different (*shu* 殊);
- These differences are bound to generate radiation/resonance (*gan* 感) between things;
- The resonance between things leads to uniting (*he* 合);
- The unity is possible because all things come from a single source, "Ultimate Void" (*Taixu*).

Yinyang relations are crucial in understanding these presuppositions. Zhang Zai says, "Although there are myriad things that are known, in fact, there is only one thing that must be known: there is nothing without yinyang. If one wants to know the changes of heaven and earth, one must know these two aspects."[100]

Furthermore, there is the necessity of resonance (*gan*) between different things and the necessity of uniting (*he*) as a result of this *gan*. These come together to exhibit a concurrence between the one and the many, planting the seeds of Zhuxi's later phrase, "there is one principle yet multiple manifestations" (理一分殊).

We have already examined the link between *qi* and yinyang, however, through Zhang Zai's developments, we can conclude with two general points. First, taking *qi* as a foundation resists any dualistic formulation of yin and yang, as if the one could be abstracted from the other, regarded as superior, or be considered metaphysically separate and distinct. Yin and yang represent opposite but complementary qualities of *qi*. They are the rhythm and harmony within *qi*, the condensation and development, or the withdrawing into the depths and the surging to the exterior. The fabric of *qi* reality allows us a glimpse of the extensive underlying unity of the universe. Synchronicities in heaven, earth, and human beings in Chinese texts unveil the absence of division between the physical world and our inner psychological reality.

---

[100] Ibid., p. 8.

Further, the ultimate – as *Dao*, *Taiji*, or *Taixu* – contains *qi* within itself so that it has an intrinsic system of generation and transformation. Yinyang interaction makes obvious the power of self-organization as a source of order. Order emerges from an enormous, contingently assembled network. *Qi*'s quantities and contents (descending and ascending, condensing or dispersing) elucidate the formation of heaven and earth and the patterns of the world, from the changing seasons to family relations to the health of bodily organs. The underlying assumption is that the interaction of yinyang forces spontaneously and naturally generates order and patterns. This kind of emergent order is different from laws that would be absolute, necessary, and externally imposed.

3   Yinyang Matrix: Organizing the World

When a sage is acting, he must set the root in heaven and earth and have yinyang as the core.

Liji (Record of Rituals)

The categories of yinyang bring the interaction and completion of all things.

Hanshu (The Book of Han)

The origin of the myriad things, the structure of the universe, the source of change, and the beginning of life are all fundamental problems requiring explanation. Yinyang thought weaves a coherent fabric of understanding that integrates these issues with what is imminent in one's own situation. In the previous chapter, we examined how yinyang explains the basic structure of the world, in particular how the genesis of concrete things from a simple undifferentiated origin to the more complex forms, involves the interplay between the forces of yin and yang. One of the most important functions of yinyang is as a matrix to describe, guide, and structure concrete phenomena. Historically, in the third and second centuries B.C.E., yinyang classifications of spatial orientations and temporal cycles emerged and developed as an attempt to give a rational description of the world that went beyond shamanistic and magical operations. As Paul Unschuld writes, "The yinyang and Five Agents doctrines focused on the classifications and relations of the myriad things, but they conveyed the same general message as science in ancient Europe: there are laws that persist irrespective of time, space, and human or numinous beings."[1]

---

[1] Paul Unschuld, *Medicine in China, A History of Ideas*, 25th edition (Berkeley: University of California Press, 2010), p. xxii.

Yinyang explanation functioned as analogous to scientific accounts, although extending more broadly to encompass ethics, politics, and aesthetics, as well.

Yinyang thought arranges knowledge into a simple, integrated, and flexible pattern, which can be applied to an extremely wide range of phenomena. As the *Huangdi Neijing* states:

> As for yinyang, it has a name but no form, thus if you count it, it can be ten; if you separate it, it can be a hundred; if you disperse it, it can be a thousand; and if you extrapolate from it, it can be ten-thousand.[2]

> 且夫陰陽者, 有名而無形, 故數之可十, 離之可百, 散之可千, 推之可萬, 此之謂也.

Human experience is infused with multifarious connections to our surroundings. These relationships require organization brought about by comprehension, and yinyang was the main tool for that comprehension. This chapter will explore the yinyang matrix as a way of linking and amplifying particular phenomena. The yinyang matrix is a logical structure and method that classifies all things and reveals yinyang as something like a vital information-bearing hologram, in the sense that a hologram "is a multidimensional entity where even the smallest part of the entity contains, in condensed form, all of the information necessary for a detailed and complete expression."[3] Many aspects of Chinese thought and culture are encrypted in this yinyang holographic matrix: an unfolding continuum, a net of relationships, and a paradigm.

The yinyang matrix found its basis in the fundamental relationship between *tian* (heaven) and *ren* (human being) in ancient China. One aim of writing classical texts was to reveal this relationship. The "Wuxing" chapter of the *Hanshu* 漢書 (*The Book of Han*) describes the origins of the classics:

> In the past in the Yin Dynasty, Dao was lost, so King of Wen created the *Zhouyi* (*The Book of Changes*). In the Zhou Dynasty, the Dao was ruined so Confucius wrote the *Chunqiu* (*Spring and Autumn Annals*). They followed the yinyang of heaven and earth and modeled the "Hongfan's"[4] rewards and punishments, and thus the Dao of heaven and human beings was known and clarified.[5]

---

[2] Niu Bingzhan 牛兵占, (ed.), *Huangdi Neijing*, 黃帝內經 (Shijiazhuang: Hebei Science and Technology Press 1993), p. 105.

[3] D. Parrish M.D., *Nothing I See Means Anything: Quantum Questions, Quantum Answers*, (Boulder: Sentient Publications, 2006), p. 15.

[4] Hongfan is the title of the chapter in *Shangshu* (*The Book of History*).

[5] Ban Gu 班固, *Hanshu* 漢書 (*The Book of Han*), commentary by Yan Shigu 顏師古 (Beijing: Chinese Press, 1962), p. 1316.

This concern with the relationship between heaven and human is evident on many levels. The *Zhuangzi*, in the "Great Teacher" chapter, claims that the ultimate knowing is to know what are the works of *tian* (heaven) and what are the works of *ren* (human beings).[6] Historical works also maintain a concern for this relationship. For example, it was said that the ultimate goal of the *Shiji* (*The Records of the Historians*) by Sima Qian is to "understand the relationship between *tian* and *ren*; to grasp the changes of past and present, and to establish specific schools of thought."[7] The relationship between heaven and human also extends to a concern for agriculture and growth: the *Lüshi Chunqiu* tells that crops are planted by human beings, germinated by earth, and nourished by heaven.[8] We have already seen the *Yijing* considered as uniting the way of heaven and the way of humans. Yinyang has played a crucial role in providing a commonality for explaining the relationship between heaven and human.

The direct way to approach the yinyang matrix is through the concept of *lei* 類 (category or kind; or as a verb, to place into categories or kinds). The notion and method of *lei* is the underlying logical structure of the yinyang matrix. In contemporary usage, *lei* literally refers to a group of things with shared features or qualities and, thus, placed under the same category. This categorization has enjoyed a privileged position in Chinese thought. The Han Confucian Dong Zhongshu asserts, "if one uses *lei* to unite them, then heaven and human are one" (以類合之, 天人一也).[9] He also says, "Looking at the oneness of human rituals, it is high beyond all things and is of a kind [*lei*] with heaven"[10] (觀人之禮一, 何高物之甚, 而類於天也). The integration of heaven and human was taken as a connection through *lei*. The *He Guanzi* makes the same point: "There is nothing which does not belong to a *lei*" 物無非類者.[11] All things under heaven are unified or differentiated through *lei*. We see the important role of *lei* as logic in the "Xiaoqu" chapter of the *Mohist Canon*, which

[6] Chen Guying, 陳鼓應, 莊子今注今譯, *Commentaries on Zhuangzi*, (Beijing: Chinese Press, 1983), p. 168.
[7] Z. T. Fang, "The Cultural Principle of Unity between Heaven and Human Beings," in Luoshu 洛書 and Han Pengjie 韓鵬杰 (eds.) *The Complete Works of Zhouyi* 周易全書 (Beijing: Tuanjie Press 團結出版社), p. 2072.
[8] Knoblock and Riegel, (trans.) *The Annals of Lü Buwei: A Complete Translation and Study* (Stanford: Stanford University Press, 2000), p. 662.
[9] Dong Zhongshu. *Chunqiu Fanlu* 春秋繁露義證 *(Luxuriant Dew of the Spring and Autumn Annals)*, Si Yu (ed.), (Beijing: Chinese Press, 1996) p. 341.
[10] Ibid., p. 355.
[11] Wang Xinzhan 王心湛 (ed.). *Collected Interpretations of He Guanzi* 鶡冠子集解, (Shanghai: Guangyi Press, 1936), p. 26.

says, "use kinds [*lei*] to accept, use kinds to propose [以類取, 以類予]."[12]
The *lei* method rests on the reasoning that everything can be categorized
and classified into a kind, or a group based on its definition, function,
and movement. Derk Bodde names this feature of Chinese thought as
"categorical thinking," which "reduces all phenomena under sets of
orderly, all-inclusive schemata."[13]

The origin of the term *lei* can be traced back to early ritual sacrifices
in the Yin and Zhou dynasties. *Lei* was the one of five procedures used
to select materials for sacrifice in rituals.[14] *Bilei* 比類 (comparing categories) was used to arrange the offerings by dividing them into different
groups for different kinds of ceremonies. The character for *lei* itself has
different parts, pointing toward its etymological meaning. According to
Yuan Jinmei:

> The left part of *lei* 類 is "𥝖." It is a combination of "米, *mi*, vegetables" and
> "犬, *quan*, dogs." The right part of *lei* 類 is "頁 *ye*." The classical writing of
> "頁 *ye*" is "𩑋." The meaning of "頁 *ye*" is often restricted to the head. It has
> "𦣻," a human face at the top and "儿," a son at the bottom.[15]

The complex role of *lei* in Chinese logic is comparable to the role of categorical propositions in the West, more specifically in Aristotelian logic.[16]
Categorical propositions are a hierarchical system of classes forming a
tree like structure of genus and species. There is a predictable relationship between genus and species, which allows for various kinds of inferences. Although similar in some ways, the *lei* or kind is more like a net of
associations that locates things in a changing world.[17] It lacks the fixed
predicate syllogism, however, it "separates things according to the way
one looks at them and locates them according to different associations."[18]
In this sense, *lei* cannot be freed from context or perspective. There are
many *lei* one can use to separate things, however, the easiest way to sort
them is through the *lei* of yin and the *lei* of yang.

---

[12] I here follow the translation in Dan Robins, "The Later Mohists and Logic," in *History and Philosophy of Logic*, Volume 31, Issue 3, 2010, pp. 247–85.
[13] Derk Bodde, "Types of Chinese Categorical Thinking," in C. Le Blanc & D. Bore (eds. and int.) *Essays on Chinese Civilization* (Princeton University Press, 1981), p. 341.
[14] Wang, Mengou, 王夢鷗 (ed.) *Liji*, 禮記今註今譯 (*Record of Rituals*), (Taipei: Taiwan Commercial Press, 台灣商務印書館, 1981), p. 289.
[15] Yuan Jinmei, "'Kinds, Lei?' in Chinese Logic – A Comparison to 'Categories' in Aristotelian Logic," *History of Philosophy Quarterly* **22** no. 3 (July 2005), p. 186.
[16] Ibid., 188.
[17] Ibid.
[18] Ibid.

To see how *lei* categorizing works, we can take an example: the word "mother." It is a predicate for a woman who has given birth or has a child. If one were to follow deductive logic, one could go by this: all mothers have a child; Mary is a mother, therefore, Mary has a child. According to *lei* logic, mother belongs to the *lei* (category) of yin, things with giving and nurturing functions, and thus can be grouped with earth, moon, and water. Anything perceived as yin or nurturing fits into this image of giving and nurturing. Mary is a mother, therefore, she has the yin properties of x, y, and z. A similar thought pattern is evoked in the Christian phrase, "God is our Father," which suggests authority and kindness. Such *lei* is linked or associated with a sense of scope. A. C. Graham elucidates this logic in the *Mozi*: "For us, oxen and horses are 'classes,' for the Mohists they are *lei*, but it does not follow that we can translate *lei* by 'class.' In English X and Y are or are not members of the class Z, in Chinese X and Y are 'the same in *lei*' or are 'not *lei*'類同, 不類]"[19]

The basis of *lei*'s flexibility is in its application on different levels and with different scopes. Two things can be in the same *lei* in one sense, however, in different *lei* on another level; for example, the sun and ginger belong to the same *lei* of yang because they both have properties of being hot and warm. Snow and watermelon belong to the *lei* of yin because they have properties of being cool. They are also different *lei*, however, because sun and snow belong in a group in heaven, and ginger and watermelon belong to the group in earth. We have seen this also in the multiplicity of yin and yang relationships. Given this complexity, skill in grouping and distinguishing *lei* is fundamental to good reasoning: "The validity of an argument in Chinese logic is not guaranteed by deductive rules but by how to effectively distinguish different kinds."[20] As the Mohists say, "The difficulty in extrapolating *lei* is in their being large or small [in scope]."[21] These require a particular skill in knowing how to connect things and recognize similarities and differences. Yinyang is one of the most popular and important criterion for such categorizing.

The fundamental importance of the use of *lei* appears across a variety of texts from the late Warring States and Han. The greatest learning is to learn these *lei*. The *Liji* 禮記 (*Record of Rituals*) says that after seven years of schooling, one only has a small accomplishment. In contrast, "Learning

---

[19] A. C. Graham, *Later Mohist Logic, Ethics and Science* (Hong Kong & London: SOAS, 1978), p. 169.

[20] J. Yuan, "*Kinds, Lei* 類 *in Chinese Logic*," p. 196.

[21] Sun Yirang 孫詒讓. *Mozi Xiangu* 墨子閒詁 (Shanghai: Shanghai Books 上海書店, 1935), p. 195.

the *lei* is the highest accomplishment after nine years of learning. It is the highest accomplishment (*da cheng* 大成)." [22] To learn is to learn about *lei*, as *lei* is bound up with culture (*wen*) itself. To be cultured is to master the application of *lei*. The idea of meaning is inherent in an ability to categorize all things based on similarities, with yinyang as its foothold.

The ability to use *lei* is also particularly associated with sageliness. For example, *Xunzi* distinguishes sages from gentlemen and petty people because of the sage's relation to *lei*: "Therefore, a sage, though he speaks often, always observes the *lei;* a gentleman, though he speaks but seldom, always accords with the model. The petty man speaks frequently without model, his thought drowning even if discriminating." [23]

The difference between a sage and a gentleman is that, although gentlemen follow established models with caution, sages go beyond these models through the use of *lei*, or the logical categories appropriate to the discussion. This association between sages and *lei* appears also in the *Guanzi*, which says, "The sage who wishes to see clearly the nature of things/must consider the category [*lei*] from which they have come. Therefore the virtuous prince is careful to heed what he puts first." [24]

The *Gui Guzi* also characterizes sages as knowing through *lei*: "The person of perfection is united with heaven; the one who knows through inner cultivation is a sage. Sageliness is knowing through *lei*." [25]

Dividing phenomena according to yin and yang constitutes *lei* at the broadest level, ultimately explaining all things. We find such claims across a range of texts: "Due to the interaction of yinyang, the *lei* of things resonate; this is the reason of the ten thousand events" (夫陰陽之感, 物類相應, 萬事盡然). [26]

Yinyang as the classificatory matrix for the world has many dimensions. Consider how the *Huainanzi* classifies animals:

> Hairy and feathered creatures make up the *lei* of flying and walking things and are subject to yang. Creatures with scales and shells make up the *lei* of creeping and hiding things and are subject to yin. The sun is the ruler of yang. Therefore, in spring and summer, animals shed their fur.... The moon

[22] Wang (ed.), *Liji*, p. 595.

[23] Modified translation from Knoblock (trans.), *Xunzi: A Translation and Study of the Complete Works*, 3 vols. (Stanford: Stanford University Press, 1988–1994), p. 133.

[24] Allyn Rickett, Allyn. (trans.). *Guanzi, Political, Economic, and Philosophical Essays from Early China*, (New Jersey: Princeton University Press, 1998), p. 214.

[25] Xu (ed.), *The Guiguzi jixiaojizhu*, p. 202.

[26] Ban Gu 班固 *Hanshu* 漢書 (*The Book of Han*), Commentary by Yan Shigu 颜师古, (Beijing: Chinese Press, 1962), chapter 24, p. 1140.

is the fundamental of yin. Therefore when the moon wanes, the brains of
fish shrink....Things within the same *lei* mutually move one another.[27]

This yinyang matrix is built on structures of relationships and dynamic
tendencies rather than on individual characteristics of things. It functions primarily through analogies and correlations. All things categorized
as yang share common tendencies in dynamic relation to other elements,
just as phenomena that are more yin will also share commonalities.[28]

Categorizing requires a complex process of interweaving objects and
their properties, individuals and collectives, time, space, causality, events,
agency, and social situations into a totality. The *lei* possesses an explanatory
capacity within which all things are linked in a coherent whole. We will
examine the application of yinyang categorization in specific areas in later
sections of this chapter, however, for now, following Dong Zhongshu, we
will turn to the four seasons. Just as the four seasons have four different
functions, the king should have four policies in connection with these
seasonal functions, such as congratulations in spring, rewards in summer, penalties in fall, and punishments in winter.[29] These analogies run
on many levels. For example, regulations for managing forests require
attending to the seasons: "In winter cut down yang trees and in summer
cut down the yin trees...the cutting should follow the season."[30]

For the categorization of emotions, Dong Zhonshu writes, "The *qi* of
yinyang inhabits the celestial as well as the human world. For human
beings, it is loving, hating, being pleased, and being angry; in heaven, it
is warm, clear, cold, and hot."[31] This shows the changes of the emotions
through the analogy with changes in weather (and vice versa), while also
claiming an inherent link between these two realms. They are more than
analogous; they are actually composed of the same basic materials – *qi* as
configured through yinyang. The *Huainanzi* also uses *lei* to characterize
human emotions. The relation between human's happiness and anger is
likened to the categories of dawn and dusk, cold and heat.[32]

---

[27] Harold Roth (trans. and ed.), *The Huainanzi: A Guide to the Theory and Practice of
Government in Early China* (New York: Columbia University Press, 2010), p. 116.

[28] Here, we should recall the point from the first chapter, that yin and yang themselves are
relational terms, so that the same thing could simultaneously be yang in one relationship
and yin in another.

[29] Dong, *Chunqiu Fanlu*, p. 353.

[30] Wang Yunwu (ed.), 王雲五，*Zhouli Jinzhujinyi* 周禮今注今譯，(*The Commentaries on
Ritual of Zhou*,), (Taibei: Taiwan Commercial Press, 1972), p. 171.

[31] Dong, *Chunqiu Fanlu*, p. 463.

[32] Harold. Roth (trans.), *The Huainanzi*, p. 852.

Although yin and yang are pervasive categories extending to any phenomena, a classificatory system based on only two classes would lack the specificity needed to make much sense of concrete experience. Greater specificity comes through the concept of *xiang*, as in the phrase *juxiang guilei* 据象歸類 (using images to define categories).[33] The term *xiang* 象 is of special philosophical interest for it affords us an appreciation of the distinctive features of a Chinese way of thinking.[34] The concept of *xiang* came from early divination procedures in the Shang Dynasty. People carved lines on turtle bones and then burned them. The bone would crack and form different images, patterns, or figures called *xiang*. We read from the *Zuozhuan* (Xigong 15): "Turtles are *xiang* (images) while yarrow stalks are *shu* (numbers). When things are generated, they will have *xiang*; when *xiang* grow, they will have *shu* (numbers)."[35]

These *xiang* conveyed information, and by reading these *xiang*, one could infer good fortune (*ji* 吉) or bad fortune (*xiong* 凶). These *xiang* lie somewhere in nature between pictures and numbers, containing elements of both. Reading, organizing, and analyzing *xiang* evolved as a tradition of thinking with two centers. One focuses more on the patterns of the symbols or signs themselves, a tradition known as *xiangshu* 象數 (images and numbers). Each configuration of symbols serves as a basis for some kind of mental activity: reasoning, predicting, and diagnosing. The second approach focuses on the principles behind these symbols, which are seen only as mediating the rules or meanings shared by a tradition. This is called *yili* 義理 (meanings and principles). The paradigmatic systematization of *xiang* is in the *Yijing*, where each hexagram can be taken as a *xiang*.[36]

For example, the *qian* hexagram (made of all yang lines) is sky, sun, fire, male, and so on. The *kun* hexagram (made of all yin lines) is earth, moon, water, female, and so on. This is the identification of images. From this

---

[33] Although *xiang* can be taken as a form of *lei*, they were sometimes distinguished. For example, the "Tiangua Shu" chapter of the *Shiji* associates *xiang* with heaven, and indeed one of the paradigms for *xiang* is in connection with the changes of constellations, calendars, and cyclic movement of seasons and planets. It then associates *lei* with earth (*di*), taking yinyang as the main form of *lei*. Sima Qian 司馬遷, *Shiji* 史記 (*Records of the Historian*) (Beijing: Chinese Press, 2003), chapter 27, p. 1342.

[34] Hu Shi has given the explanation for the etymological origin of the word. See S. Liu, "The Use of Analogy and Symbolism in Traditional Chinese Philosophy," *Journal of Chinese Philosophy*, 1 (1974), 316.

[35] Li Mengsheng, 李夢生 (ed.) *Zuozhuan Yizhu* 左傳譯注 (Shanghai: Shanghai Guji Press 上海古籍出版社, 1998), p. 238.

[36] Gao Heng 高亨, *Commentary on Zhouyi* 周易大傳今注 (Jinan: Qilu Press, 1998) pp. 433–34.

identification, we can infer specific properties: the sky is active, the sun is bright, the male is dominant, the earth is nourishing, the moon is dark, and the female is passive. These entities are classified in terms of function. That is why a successful ruler can "look up and observe the *xiang* in heaven; look down and model the *lei* of earth."[37] Thus, *xiang* evoke the functions of yinyang and are the benchmarks for classification.

The use of *xiang* as diagrams or figures will be discussed more in Chapter 6. Here we can focus on *xiang* as a basis for classifications, for *lei*. *Xiang* can be taken in three ways: (1) as human symbols involving, for example, yin lines or yang lines; (2) as real patterns in nature itself; and (3) as unseen tendencies, directions, and structures. *Xiang* can be a particular image one confronts now and also has the power of representing and, thus, this image enables projecting forward by analogy. The latter aspect is largely open to interpretations based on one's experience, knowledge, and intentions. The reading of *xiang* is a dynamic process.

In this use of *xiang*, we can see the second key aspect of the use of yinyang as *lei* – the categorization of phenomena allows the derivation of inferences: *bilei xiangtui* 比類相推, which translates literally as "comparing kinds to infer to each other." *Bi* refers to putting together things that are similar and analogous. By examining things of the same kind or having the same function, one can derive certain properties, and by placing new experiences into *lei*, one knows how to approach them. All things in the world can be organized into yang *lei* or yin *lei*, and from these, inferences can be derived.[38] One then has some sense of how things should be treated and approached. As Dong Zhongshu puts it, "Reasoning from the *lei* of things is using the easy to see into what is difficult. The actuality can be attained."[39]

The *Yijing* is the best example for this reasoning mode. It suggests that *lei* thinking takes a small thing (a concrete thing) and extends its application to a big thing (general concept) through a process that is called *qu lei* 取類 (getting the *lei*). One takes natural phenomena or an arrangement of hexagrams and then infers the characteristics of other things or events, "taking the image to elucidate the meaning, the small can refer to the big."[40] There are intrinsic links among all things; yinyang is a rhythmic

---

[37] Zhou Zhenfu 周振甫, *Book of Songs Annotation* 詩經譯注 (Beijing: Chinese Press, 2002), p. 1342.

[38] One example would be the interpretation of dreams, as *Zhouli* and *Liezi* interpret six different kinds of dreams. There are yang dreams and yin dreams according to the intensity and the function of yinyang. B. Yang (ed.), *Liezi Jishi*, pp. 102–103.

[39] Dong, *Chunqiu Fanlu*, p. 467.

[40] Gao, *Commentary on Zhouyi*, p. 417.

pathway through these links. Once an entity or event is defined in yinyang terms, the way of managing them can be derived.

The basic *xiang* are contained in the trigrams of the *Yijing*. With different configurations and combinations, the three yin or yang lines form eight trigrams, each of which represents a certain image derived from human experiences. The "Xici" of The *Book of Changes* claims that, "When the eight trigrams were completed in their proper order, the *xiang* were present there within them" (八卦成列, 象在其中矣). [41] *Xiang* is a way to focus on what is familiar in our everyday experience. The drawings and natural phenomena are intrinsically intertwined. This method is also developed in the *Huangdi Neijing* for healing practices. If one does not know how to *bilei* 比類 (compare categories), then situations will not be clarified, leading to internal disruptions. [42]

"Comparing kinds to infer to each other" (*bilei xiangtui*) holds that each person belongs to the same class – human beings. Therefore, any individual is bound to function like others. This is called *leitui*: using the same group to make an inference. The *Mengzi* offers a similar argument – Yao is a human being, and I am a human being, but Yao became a great sage, while I am just a common person. That is why gentlemen are always anxious to become like Yao. [43]

Beyond classifying and grounding inferences, the third important element of the yinyang matrix is in explaining influence and causality. We have seen that categories primarily name dynamic situations, tendencies, and patterns rather than static things. They are, thus, oriented toward change and specifically toward how to act effectively in relation to the world. The patterned bond of human beings to heaven and earth exemplifies a deeply rooted orientation toward practice. Areas of involving human effort, such as astrology, alchemy, calendrics, and medicine, should not be pursued in their own right, but because of their practical utility for guiding human action. We see this shift toward practice in the use of *lei* when Dong Zhongshu says, "One must extrapolate from the refined essence of heaven and earth and move from the *lei* of yinyang in order to distinguish the principle of following and going against." [44] The *lei* of yinyang lets us determine what follows smoothly and what goes against the grain. In the ability to respond to situations smoothly, *lei* resembles timing, *shi*. The

[41] Ibid., p. 417.
[42] Zhang Yingan 張隱庵 (ed.), *Huangdi Neijing Commentaries* 黃帝內經素問集注 (Beijing: Xueyuan Press 學苑出版社, 2002), p. 783.
[43] Bryan Van Norden, (trans.). *Mengzi, with Selections from Traditional Commentaries,* (Indianapolis: Hackett Publishing, 2008), 4B28, p. 112.
[44] Dong, *Chunqiu Fanlu,* p. 326.

"Yueli" chapter of the *Liji* explains: "In commencing great undertakings, there should be no opposition to the great periods. They must follow the timing (*shi*) and pay special attention to its *lei*."[45] Attending to *lei* has the same importance as following the demands of the time.

Lei functions partly to clarify how things change and, thus, how human beings should react. We read from the *Liji*: "The reason for the ten thousand things is that they have their own *lei* and move according to their *lei*. Therefore, gentlemen use *qing* 情 (real nature) to harmonize the will and use *bilei* (comparing categories) to complete their actions."[46] The myriad things move based on their *lei*, and this is the principle of all things. Sages complete their actions through comparing *lei*. *Lei* is a way to grasp the underlying patterns of the ten thousand things and complete them through action. This rationale can realize the *Yijing*'s aspiration: "Penetrate the power of spirit and classify (*lei*) the real nature (*qing*) of the ten thousand things" (以通神明之德, 以類萬物之情).[47]

The fact that the tendencies and movements of things are located in complex systems of correlation suggests that things of the same kind can influence each other. This influence proceeds because there are mutual intrinsic links between things, since entities are mutually interconnected. The unity of heaven, earth, and human beings lies in their sharing structures, patterns, and movements. Moreover, heavenly movements have implications for the human world. Consider again the example of the seasons. The rhythm of the seasons provides the rhythm of life: spring is *fa* 發 (emergence); summer is *zhang* 長 (growing); autumn is *shou* 收 (harvesting); winter is *sha* 殺 (death). In terms of human activity, autumn is also the time to collect and harvest, and winter is for *cang* 藏 (storing). This is the cycle of seasons, conceptualized through a complex relationship between yin and yang. Spring gives rise to life, followed by the yin part of the yang season, summer, which is responsible for growth. Autumn is yang within the yin season, and it is the beginning movement of yin, collecting. Winter is the accomplishment of this movement, the yin within yin. The winter stores, which gives the foundation for the spring. Essences are stored to later germinate.

Dong Zhongshu makes use of *lei* to justify two basic understandings of the relationship of influence between heaven and human beings. First, human beings and heaven are of the same kind (*tonglei* 同類), therefore, *renfu tianshu* (人副天数), a phrase that can be loosely translated as

---

45 Wang (ed.), *Liji*, p. 291.
46 Ibid., p. 629.
47 Gao, *Commentary on Zhouyi*, p. 419.

"human beings embody heavenly numbers" or "human beings have the same structure as heaven." For example, human physiology is modeled on nature. Dong Zhongshu explains:

> Human beings have 360 joints, matching with heaven's number; human beings have physical form, bones and flesh matching with earth's soil. Human beings have ears, eyes, and brightness above that are the images of the sun and moon; human beings have organs and vessels within that are images of hills and valleys; human beings have a heart of sadness, happiness, delight, and anger that belong to the *lei* of spirit and *qi*. Looking at human beings from the oneness of rituals, they are the highest beyond all other things. They are *lei* of heaven.[48]

The second point Dong Zhongshu emphasizes is *tianren ganying* (天人感應) – the resonance between heaven and humanity. This view holds the mutual responsiveness between human actions and their environment. According to Dong Zhongshu, it is a case of "getting one and responding with ten thousand," which is "order through *lei*."[49] As the *Liezi* puts it, "One body's being full and empty, rising and falling, all of these interact with heaven and earth and respond to the *lei* of things" (一體之盈虛消息, 皆通于天地, 應于物類).[50]

The interconnection and resonance between things of the same kind has important consequences for action. It first implies that we can gain insight into human affairs by examining analogous realms of nature. For example, in the "Jiushou" chapter of the *Wenzi* 文子 (the *Master Wen*), also known as the *Tongxuan Zhenjing* 通玄真經 (the *Authentic Scripture of Pervading Mystery*),[51] human beings and heaven are the same *lei*. So what happens in nature predicts what happens in the human world:

> Heaven has wind, rain, cold, and hot; human beings have taking and giving, pleasure and anger. Gallbladder is like clouds, lung is *qi*, spleen is wind, kidney is rain, liver is thunder. Human beings have the same *lei* as heaven. The heart is the master. Ears and eyes are sun and moon; blood and *qi* are wind and rain. If the sun and moon lose their way, there will be

[48] Dong, *Chunqiu Fanlu*, p. 354.
[49] Ibid., p. 469.
[50] Yang Bojun, 杨伯峻 (ed.) *Liezi Jishi*, 列子集釋, *Commentaries on Master Lie*, (Beijing: Chinese Press, 1979), p. 102.
[51] This is a debatable Daoist early text after *Daodejing*. Its bamboo strips were excavated in a 55 B.C.E. from tomb number 40 in Ding Count Hebei in 1973. It was canonized with *Daodejing*, *Zhuangzi*, and *Liezi* as Daoist classical scriptures by Emperor Xuangzang of Tang in 742 C.E.

no lights; if the wind and rain come untimely, there will be disasters; if the
five stars lose their way, all districts and states will have suffering.[52]

This line of reasoning runs through Chinese divination practices, as well
as things such as the process of diagnosis in Chinese traditional medicine, which will be discussed in later chapters.

The second practical consequence is that we can influence one realm
of nature by controlling structures that are analogous to it. One of the
clearest examples is facing natural disasters. There were three main
kinds of natural disasters in ancient China: droughts, floods, and insect
infestations (*huangchong*). Dealing with disasters was one of the central
responsibilities of the emperor. This suggests that natural disasters are
the result of human actions. Can certain types of human actions affect
the natural world? Dong Zhongshu discussed this resonance between the
natural world and the human world, and he articulated many practices
to promote and guide this interaction. He projected a seasonal form of
governance that revolved around reward and punishment. In the spring,
the government should give the order for the cultivation of goodness
and benevolence; in the fall, the government should withdraw forces and
revise the law.

Seeking rain and stopping floods were important parts of governmen-
tal affairs. Many emperors engaged in rain-seeking rituals by means of
the correlation between *lei*, grounded in yinyang.[53] Dong Zhongshu pro-
posed such a method for controlling floods and droughts. He claims that
a spring drought indicates an excess of yang and a lack of yin in the
world. So, humans should engage in activities that can "open yin and
close yang."[54] He advises the government to order the south gate, which
is the direction of yang, to be closed. Men, yang, should remain in seclu-
sion. Women, yin, should appear in public. All married couples should
copulate (*ouchu*) to secure more yinyang intercourse. It is also particularly important during this time to make women happy.[55] In chapter 75,
"Stopping the Rain," Dong alleges that floods prove there is too much
yin *qi*, so one should "open yang and close yin."[56] The north gate, the

[52] D. Li, *Wenzi Yizhu* 文子譯注 (Harbin: Heilongjiang People's Press, 2003), p. 62.
[53] There are four kinds of methods for seeking rain (Li Sheng, p. 643). Dong Zhongshu
put forward methods to increase or decrease yinyang interaction in world. See R. Wang,
"Dong Zhongshu's Transformation", pp. 209–31.
[54] Dong, *Chunqiu Fanlu*, p. 432.
[55] Ibid., p. 436.
[56] Ibid., p. 438.

direction of yin, should be open. Women should be concealed, and men should be visible. Officers in the city should send their wives to their countryside homes to ensure that yin will not conquer the yang. Derk Bodde calls such practices "sexual sympathetic magic."[57] Another practice was to hit a drum as yin on earth so that it will generate yang in the sky. Heaven would then stop the floods.

The *Shuoyuan*, a text from Western Han dynasty compiled by Liu Xiang 劉向, also identifies causes of floods and droughts with relations of yinyang and suggests one way to deal with them:

> Floods and droughts are all the actions of yinyang. If there is a drought, one should conduct ritual sacrifices to seek rain; if there is a flood, one should sound a drum to compel the spirits. Why it is so? Droughts are the result of excess yang *qi* overbearing the yin. Yin is suppressed by yang. Yang is filled up and yin cannot rise. Therefore, ritual sacrifices invite [yin/rain] to come. Floods are the result of excess yin *qi* taking away from yang. The low overrides the high and the base rises up to noble. This is not proper, so sound a drum to compel them.[58]

> 夫水旱俱天下陰陽所為也。大旱則雩祭而請雨, 大水則鳴鼓而劫社. 何也?
> 。。。 今大旱者, 陽氣太盛以厭於陰, 陰厭陽固, 陽其填也, 惟填厭之太甚,
> 使陰不能起也, 亦雩際拜請而已, 無敢加也. 至於大水及日蝕者, 皆陰氣太盛
> 而上減陽精, 以賤乘貴, 以卑陵尊, 大逆不義, 故鳴鼓而懾之...

By grouping things according to *lei*, everything is patterned on yinyang. The political structure is patterned on the yinyang distinctions; familial relationships are modeled on yinyang positions; the human residence is constructed according to yinyang interaction such as *fengshui*; cities are built on a yinyang blueprint; musical instruments, such as the *guqin* 古琴, are made of yinyang materials. All of these also directly relate to the moral universe of human beings, "in which human actions resonated along the celestial axis to create – literally – good or bad vibrations both in the heaven and on earth."[59]

Yinyang in Political Structure

Insofar as the matrix of yinyang classifications guides our actions, it also has a normative dimension. Structures created by human

---

[57] Bodde, "Types of Chinese Categorical," pp. 373–374.
[58] Liu Xiang 劉向. *Shuo Yuan Yin De*, Harvard-Yenching Institute Sinological Index Series No. 1., (Beijing: Harvard-Yenching Institute, 1931),.Vol. 18, *Bianwu*, 辨物.
[59] John Major, *Heaven and Earth in Early Han Thought*, (Albany: SUNY Press, 1993), p. 67.

beings – institutions, cultural forms, and artistic products – can and should fit within the broader correlations that organize the rest of nature. One must abide by *lei* in all things.[60] We can begin with an example of political order, including both government institutions and ritual, which was one of the main forces guiding social and political life. We have already seen several passages that emphasize the importance for sages to master yinyang and *lei*. Sages, like Yao and Shun, were also rulers, and thus, the association between sages and the mastery of *lei* points to the importance of *lei* for communal life. *Lei* embodies a kind of cultivated ability. The "Ruxiao" chapter of the *Xunzi* portrays the great sages. "Only sages can articulate *lei* in their words as they perform ritual actions."[61] Yinyang is the way of managing political structures.

Given the link between ritual and the stability of the social order, ritual texts should be considered political texts. There are three classical ritual texts in early Chinese history: the *Zhouli* 周禮 (the *Rites of Zhou*) also known as the *Zhouguan*; the *Yili* 儀禮 (the *Etiquette and Rites*); and the *Liji* 禮記 (the *Record of Rituals*).[62] The *Zhouli* focuses on political structures; the *Yili* contains specific descriptions of rituals; and the *Liji* provides explanations and justifications for the rituals.

The *Zhouli* is one of the Thirteen Classics 十三經 (*shisan jing*). It has had political relevance throughout Chinese history, and it was of great importance for the Northern Song reform leader Wang Anshi (1021–1086).[63] Although its date is uncertain, the latest research suggests that it is most likely a work from the beginning of the Western Han Dynasty (206 B.C.E. to 24 C.E.). The text integrates Confucianism, Legalism, and the school of Yinyang and *Wuxing*.[64]

The *Zhouli* offers a detailed account of political structures and the chief mission of government. This arrangement is based on the yinyang matrix in several ways.[65] For example, yinyang is a guide for forming and dividing responsibilities. Government positions and titles are created in correspondence with the positions of heaven and earth. There are two

---

[60] Ban Gu, *Hanshu* 漢書, p. 132.

[61] Knoblock (trans.), *Xunzi*, p. 190.

[62] These books have had a lasting influence on Chinese thought and culture. For example, in contemporary China, the motto of universities is often expressed in eight words, and many university mottos come from the *Liji*. See Q. Guo (ed.), "Five Lectures on Liji," in *Research on Confucian Culture*, 3rd edition (Beijing: Sanliang Shudian, 2010), p. 279.

[63] F. Li, *Bureaucracy and the State in Early China: Governing the Western Zhou* (Cambridge University Press, 2008).

[64] Peng Lin, *A Study of the Main Thought and the Date of the Zhouli* (Beijing: China Renmin University Press 2009), p. 21.

[65] Ibid., p. 20.

central roles in the governing bureaucracy: the emperor and the empress. The emperor has six *qing* ministers located in the South Palace, which is a yang position. The empress has six *gong* (wives) located in the North Palace, which is a yin position. The emperor and empress further carve up their own divisions and responsibilities according to yin and yang.

There are six sets of offices, which are organized as heaven, earth, spring, summer, autumn, and winter offices. Each office contains sixty positions that add up to a total of 360 positions to form the Chinese bureaucracy. The Offices of Heaven (*Tianguan Zhongzai*, 天官冢) concern government in general; Offices of Earth (*Diguan Situ*, 地官司土) oversee education; Offices of Spring (*Chunguan Zongbo*, 春官宗伯) cover social and religious institutions; Offices of Summer (*Xiaguan Sima*, 夏官司馬) manage the army; Offices of Autumn (*Qiuguan Sikou*, 秋官司寇) enact justice; and Offices of Winter (*Dongguan Kaogongji*, 冬官考工記) supervise population, territory, and agriculture. The particular function of each office correlates to its seasonal specialty: heaven for regulating (order); earth for teaching (nourishment); spring for ritual (beginning growth); summer for political events (activeness); autumn for punishment (coldness); and winter for resting.

The entire universe and all of human life are arranged into yang *lei* and yin *lei*. There is yang political order and yin political order, there is yang sound and yin sound, and so on. Every practice is built on yin or yang. For example, there is yang teaching, and there is yin teaching: "use yin ritual to teach the six *gong* (wives) and yin ritual to teach the nine *bing* (imperial concubines)" (以陰禮教六宮, 以陰禮教九嬪).[66] The "Digua" chapter of the *Zhouli* explains what one should do:

> On the first says use rituals of worship to teach respect and the people will not be frightened; on the second says use yang rituals to teach yielding and the people will not compete; on the third says use yin rituals to teach familial affection and the people will have no resentment; on the fourth says use music rituals to teach harmony and the people will not fight[67] (一曰以祀禮教敬, 則民不苟. 二曰以陽禮教讓, 則民不爭. 三曰以陰禮教親, 則民不怨. 四曰以樂禮教和, 則民不乖).

The use of yinyang in social and political structures is most apparent in theories of ritual. Worship divided into yin type and yang type was not seen before the Warring States Period, and it might have started with the first Qin emperor's worship of the eight immortals. Heaven

[66] Wang (ed.), *Zhouli*, p. 71.
[67] Ibid., pp. 97–98.

and earth, yin and yang, and sun and moon are all parts of worship.[68]
Dong Zhongshu promotes "ritual as the manifestation of heaven and
earth and the embodiment of yinyang." (禮者, 繼天地, 體陰陽) [69] Ritual
links heaven, earth, and human beings, and thus it must fit into the overall matrix of correspondences. On a broad level, worship was classified
into two *lei* (kinds): yang sacrifices and yin sacrifices. The *Liji* states,
"Sacrificial ceremony is looking for the meaning of yinyang. The people
in the Yin Dynasty first sought it in yang; the people in the Zhou Dynasty
first sought it in yin." (故祭, 求諸陰陽之義, 殷人先求諸陽, 周人先求諸
陰). [70] The distinction between yang rituals and yin rituals appears in the
Zhouli as well.[71]

The performances of ritual actions were also coordinated according to
yinyang. For example, at worship, the altars of grain and soil (*sheji*) for earth
should be on the right, because the right is yin; the ancestral temple (*zong-
miao*) should be on the left, because the left is yang. Wang Anshi applied
this principle to set up his political reforms. Finally, whether a ritual was
yin or yang then determined the content of the ritual itself. For example,
the *Zhouli* gives a detailed account of which kinds of furry animals should
be used for yang sacrifices and which kind for yin sacrifices.[72]

The relationship between *de* (virtue) and *xing* (use of punishments)
was another important political debate among earlier thinkers that
became linked to yinyang. Confucius praised the use of virtue and dis-
couraged punishment. In contrast, Legalists like the *Hanfeizi* thought
virtue was useless and that order must rely on punishments and rewards.
The *Guanzi* first connected yinyang with the *xingde* pair, through a focus
on harmony and balance:

> Yinyang is the primary organizational principle of Heaven and Earth, and
> the four seasons are the primary patterns of yinyang. Punishment (*xing*)
> and virtue (*de*) should correspond to the four seasons. The sun controls
> the yang and the moon controls the yin. The yearly cycle (*sui*) controls the
> harmony. The yang is for *de* (virtue) the yin is for *xing* (punishment), and
> the harmony is for conducting matters of state.[73]

Dong Zhongshu elaborates this brief statement into a full chapter. Dong
correlates punishment and virtue with yin and yang. Yang constitutes

---

[68] Peng Lin, *A Study of the Main Thought*, p. 22.
[69] Dong, *Chunqiu Fanlu*, p. 275.
[70] Wang (ed.), *Liji*, p. 436.
[71] Wang (ed.), *Zhouli*, p. 193.
[72] Ibid., p. 29.
[73] Rickett (trans.), *Guanzi*, pp. 111–116.

virtue (*de*), and yin constitutes punishment (*xing*). In many places, Dong gives a straightforward definition of yin and yang in terms of *xing* and *de*: "Heaven and earth are constant and there is one yin and one yang. Yang is heaven's virtue (*de*) and yin is heaven's use of punishments (*xing*)."[74]

In such passages, Dong Zhongshu thus takes up the first part of Guanzi's idea, however, he leaves out the focus on harmony, emphasizing instead the dominance of yang (virtue) over yin (punishment).

Yinyang in Gender Relationships

The yinyang matrix was utilized to justify and structure all forms of human relationships, from that between ruler and minister to that between husband and wife. Given the close association between yin and the feminine, and yang and the masculine, the role of yinyang in organizing human relations appears most clearly in gender relations. By examining gender relations, we can also see the complex intersection of claims that yin and yang are equal and mutually dependent with a claim that yin is subordinated to yang.

The close connection between yinyang and female and male appears in many early texts. The *Taipingjing* says simply: "male and female are the root of yinyang."[75] The "Following Dao" chapter by Dong Zhongshu identifies yinyang and gender explicitly: "The yinyang of heaven and earth should be man and woman; man and woman should be yinyang. Therefore, yinyang can be called man and woman, and man and woman can be called yinyang."[76] The "Distinction of Things" chapter of the *Shuoyuan* plays out the same connection in terms of gender as the way of heaven.[77]

The generation of life through the unity of male and female is just one version of how the interactions of yinyang bring about the myriad things. The mutual dependence of male/female in the linkage of yinyang appears most prominently in Daoist thought. As Despeaux and Kohn put it, "Cosmologically, Daoism sees women as expressions of the pure cosmic force of yin, necessary for the working of the universe, equal and, for some schools, even superior to yang."[78] In Daoism, gender differences are cosmological, physiological, and social. These differences are

---

[74] Dong, *Chunqiu Fanlu*, p. 341.

[75] *Taipingjing*, p. 94.

[76] Dong, *Chunqiu Fanlu*, p. 446.

[77] X. Liu, *Shuoyuan*, p. 619.

[78] C. Despeaux and L. Kohn, *Women in Daoism* (Cambridge: Three Pines Press, 2003), p. 1.

identified within three categories: innate nature (*benxing* 本性), which includes yin and yang, yielding and unyielding, stillness and motion, the moon and the sun, and impurity and purity; physical structure (*xingti* 形體), distinguishing bodily features, sexual attributes, fluids like blood and semen, and different kinds of energy; and practice (*gongfu* 功夫) a wider range of bodily cultivation and meditation.[79]

We can glimpse this gender interplay initially through mythology. The complementary relationship of male and female appears in depictions of the mythical figures of Nüwa and Fuxi. There are many legendary stories about each. Nüwa restored order to heaven and earth after a horrible catastrophe caused heaven to tilt to the north so that it no longer covered everything. This may refer to the first observation of the oblique elliptic and the angle of the pole star. Fuxi became the first emperor of law and order, which also implies the establishment of government. On a more practical level, he is said to have invented axes for splitting wood and to have created the eight trigrams of the *Yijing*. In the underground tomb of Fan Yanshi (d. 689 C.E.), two painted silk veils show the snakelike interlocked body of Nüwa and Fuxi intimating several aspects of gender differences (Figure 3.1).[80]

The image contains many symbolic gestures and linking categories. In addition to ropes for hunting and nets for fishing, Fu Xi holds the set-square as he rules the four-cornered earth, whereas Nüwa holds the compass, the instrument related to heavenly observations, as she rules the circling heavens.[81] In the Warring States Period (475–221 B.C.E.), the compass and square "symbolized fixed standards and rules that impose order on unruly matter."[82] The compass was associated with bringing "ordered space out of the chaos of the flood," whereas the square was "credited with the invention of kingship."[83] The two characters were paired to form one term, *guiju* 規矩, which denotes a standard, rule, or custom, as well as the possibility of establishing and keeping order. The *Hanshu* explains the two and identifies them with yinyang: "The compass

[79] L. Kohn and R. Wang (eds.), *Internal Alchemy* (Dunedin, FL: Three Pines Press, 2009), p. 152.

[80] There were many similar images in Chinese cosmogonic art from the Eastern Han dynasty (206–220 C.E.). For more information see: Liu Wensuo 刘文锁, "Examination of Images of Fuxi and Nüwa" 伏羲女娲图考 in *Research on the Art History* 艺术史研究, vol. 8, (Guangzhou: Zhongshan University Press, 2006), p.147. Thanks to Prof. Mou Fasong 牟发松 for this reference.

[81] A. Schinz, *The Magic Square: Cities in Ancient China* (London: Edition Axel Menges, 1990).

[82] Y. Bonnefoy (comp.), *Asian Mythologies* (University of Chicago Press, 1993), pp. 234–235.

[83] M. E. Lewis, *The Flood Myths of Early China* (Albany: State University of New York Press, 2006), pp. 125–127.

3.1. Image of Fuxi and Nüwa from Xinjiang Turfan Tang Dynasty tomb 新疆吐鲁番唐代墓葬 unearthed 1967.

is used to standardize circles so they attain their *lei*; the square is used to standardize squares so that they do not lose their form. The compass and square are mutually dependent. When yinyang are in order and position, the circle and square will be completed."[84] The carpenter's square is the symbol of the earth, whereas the compass represents the circle, the

---

[84] Ban Gu, *Hanshu*, p. 955.

symbol of heaven. Fuxi, the male (yang), binds with a symbol of earth to give order to the earth (yin), whereas Nüwa, the female (yin), binds with the symbol of heaven to give order to the heaven (yang). The intertwining of yinyang occurs at every level.

Nüwa and Fuxi are considered the ancestors of the Chinese people, making them figures of generation and productivity. In this image, they are not two separate and independent entities but one unitary body that consists of two necessary and interrelated parts: male and female.[85] Nüwa and Fuxi are entwined bodies rotating around an invisible vertical axis. This spiral movement is the ultimate source of order and transformation.

We can see the significance of circular intertwining of male and female by way of a contrasting example. For the ancient Greeks, the circle is a perfect shape. "No matter how much or how little a perfect circle is rotated about its center, it maintains its original appearance: its appearance is constant. It is important to note that perfection is identified with constancy – something that is perfect cannot be improved, so it must remain constant."[86] This perfect form itself, however, is equated with men. In contrast, for the Chinese, if there is no woman, then the man will not be a perfect circle. The circle forms only through man and woman together. This spiral-like movement is the ideal vision of the world.

The proper functioning of the universe depends on the correct balance of both yin and yang. In the *Taipingjing*, we witness this idea:

> If *Dao* is lost today, there will be disorder. Therefore, if yang is at peace, the myriad things will self generate; if yin is at peace, the myriad things will self complete. Yinyang orders *Dao*. Teaching ministers; transforming the people; embodying life from heaven, receiving forms from earth; learning from masters: this is the core of *Dao*.[87]

---

[85] The division into men and women can be seen in some sense as already falling away from the perfect union of yinyang symbolized here. Thus, the pre-sexual infant is sometimes taken as expressing this union most fully. In a claim that seems to develop a passage from the *Daodejing*, the *Taipingjing* says, "human beings contain yinyang at birth. Movement, stillness, anger and delight all have a timing. An infant has no sexual activity but has the potential for sexual ability. This is evidence of yinyang functioning for the generation of life.... *Dao* is heaven, yang, controlling generation; *de* is earth, yin, controlling cultivation" *Taipingjing* (p. 513).

[86] N. Spielberg and B. D. Anderson, *Seven Ideas that Shook the Universe* (John Wiley & Sons, Inc. 1987), p. 17.

[87] *Taipingjing*, p. 55.

The balance of yinyang as a cosmic force requires an equal balance
between men and women. The *Taipingjing* discusses the two hands of the
divine "master" (*zhu*):

> Heaven and earth are two hands to make great all of existence; the four
> seasons are the master's two hands for nourishing the myriad things; the
> five elements are the master's two hands for the generation of all things;
> male and female and husband and wife are the master's two hands for
> covering yin and yang; masters and disciples are two hands for passing on
> literati and classical texts; sovereigns and ministers are the master's two
> hands for people's affairs. These six things are the cores of events. One can
> see the order of them, but they cannot be learned from books. All things
> have to have the two hands in order to be completed.[88]

The teaching of "two hands" is about the complementarity of things,
particularly the need for both male and female. This connection could
be used to emphasize the importance of women, as in the *Huainanzi*,
which states:

> The extreme yin brings cold wind, the extreme yang brings bright light.
> They are in intercourse and connection, which completes the stage of har-
> mony and then myriad things are generated. If there are so many males but
> no females, how can anything be transformed and be able to produce? This
> is the argument without words and the way without saying.[89]

The *Taipingjing* even applies the idea of yinyang to oppose female
infanticide:

> Since losing the *Dao*, there are many killings of girls. This results in fewer
> girls than boys. This damages the yin *qi* and does not correspond to the
> law of heaven and earth. The law of heaven and earth are if yang has no
> partner, it will cause droughts. The sky will not have timely rain. Female
> reflects earth and if the female is harmed then the world is harming the
> earth, killing the *qi* of earth and causing the *qi* of earth to not regenerate.
> When the earth is angry, disasters will be plentiful. The world will not be
> at peace.[90]

This interconnection with distinction runs through yinyang thinking
and categorizations. As is well known, however, women were more or
less socially subordinated to men throughout Chinese history. Although
this subordination seems to contradict original yinyang thought, we have
seen its basis already. Consider the common associations around yin

---

[88] Ibid., pp. 1161–1162.
[89] Roth, *The Huainanzi*, p. 190.
[90] *Taipingjing*, p. 81.

and yang: yang is heaven, male, ruler, father, elder, master; yin is earth, female, minister, child, the common people. Even in the *Daodejing*, the masculine is associated with power, control, and dominance, whereas the female is associated with yielding, flexibility, and submissiveness. The *Daodejing* inverts these values, pointing out the power of the feminine, however, that inversion went against mainstream views, particularly those of the Confucians who dominated social and political institutions.

The more specific basis for the subordination of yin to yang (and, thus, women to men) has appeared in our discussion of the *Zhouyi*, in the concept of position, *wei*. We have seen that the meaning and favorability of a hexagram was not so much in the quantity of yin and yang but rather in their positions within the hexagram. Moreover, some positions are meant to be occupied by yin lines and some by yang lines, setting a normative matrix. The family was conceived on the same model, with each person in the family having a proper position. In family relations, the female is inside (*nei* 內), and the male is outside (*wai* 外). In the *Liji*, social roles based on proper position become a moralization of the male and female relationship: "Male is at outside; wife is at home. The great sun starts in the east and the moon starts in the west; this is the distinction of yin and yang, the position of husband and wife." [91]

These male and female positions are set in a matrix of correspondences, as for example, the male corresponds to heaven, and the female, to earth.

The *Lüshi Chunqiu* similarly emphasizes the connection between order and position. For order to exist, one must first rectify social divisions. Ruler, minister, father, son, husband, wife: these six positions must be in their proper place. Such correspondences structure many dimensions of male-female interaction and division. For example, the male position is on the left, and the female is on the right, so women cross a threshold with the right leg first, and men use the left leg. Where do these requirements come from? It follows the rhythm of the movement of the sun. When you face south, the sun rises to your left, which is yang, and on the right is the sunset, representing the transition from yang to yin. Therefore, the male is on the left, and female is on the right.

The correspondence between proper positions of male and female extended to all aspects of life, such as selecting the proper timing for a marriage. The *Baihutong* 白虎通 (the *Comprehensive Discussions in the White Tiger Hall*) suggests that marriage must take place in spring,

---

[91] Wang, (ed.), *Liji*, p. 406.

because in spring time heaven and earth interact and the myriad things begin to generate: "It is the time of yin and yang interchanges."[92]

Through the concept of position, male and female had to retain the proper order. This can be seen as a version of what Confucius praises as *zhengming* 正名 (rectifying names) in the *Lunyu* (*Analects*). If a name is not correct or a distinction is not recognized, there will be no proper function and disorder will ensue. The *Huangdi Neijing* connects this order to the *Dao*: "If one can distinguish left and right, one has the way; there are different positions for male and female, which is called yinyang."[93]

Given the way that things of the same *lei* have mutual influence, disorder between the sexes disrupts nature itself. Male as yang should be cultivated or else the day will suffer; female as yin should be cultivated, too, or else it will affect the moon. The *Liji* states:

> If the changes are not timely, there will be no generation; if there is no distinction between male and female, there will be disorderly movement. This is the real character [*qing*] of heaven and earth.[94]

化不時則不生, 男女無辨則亂升; 天地之情也.

This type of classification would become the dominant voice for inequality between male and female. That this order requires the submission of yin to yang also appears in *Yijing*'s famous statement: "Heaven is honored, earth is lowly" (天尊地卑).[95] Although both heaven and earth are necessary and inseparable, heaven is elevated. This view puts male and female on a different scale; male is higher and weightier than female. Why is yang elevated and yin lowly? Here is the *Taipingjing*'s explanation:

> Why is yang considered lofty, and therefore valued; why is yin named lowly and disvalued? Yang is lofty, therefore valued, because it is often full (*ying* 盈) and substantial (*shi* 實); yin is seen as low, therefore disvalued, because it is empty and not substantial. Heaven names yinyang and males/females originate in primordial *qi*. Yinyang is the beginning of the gate. Male is embodied with a full and constant plenty [i.e., sperm]. Also male has the "substance" of left and right testicles. Up it responds to heaven and has the ability to transform; down it can generate. Left corresponds to human beings; right corresponds to the myriad things. They are all substantial. This *shi* makes male valuable. Yin is female. It is low because of her place at the beginning of life. It is a void (*kong* 空) and empty (*xu* 虛). No extras and no substances. So she is low and devalued.[96]

[92] *Baihutong*, p. 466.
[93] Niu (ed.), *Huangdi Neijing*, p. 122.
[94] Wang (ed.), *Liji*, p. 621–23.
[95] Gao, *Commentary on Zhouyi*, p. 381.
[96] *Taipingjing*, p. 902.

Here, the high (*zun*) and low (*bei*) distinction is based on male and female reproductive organs. Male body parts are visibly apparent; female body parts are hidden and mysterious. Males' reproductive body parts are substantial and full. This valuation is the opposite of Laozi's valuing of emptiness (*xu*) and void (*kong*).

Although we can see some earlier basis for using yinyang to justify subordination of yin/women, that view achieved systematic and stable form only through the philosophy of Dong Zhongshu. As the founder of imperial Confucianism, Dong Zhongshu was the first prominent Confucian to integrate yinyang theory into Confucian social and political norms. The state is empowered to codify standards of social and personal conduct that correspond to the ethical dimensions of yinyang, something we have just seen in his correlation between virtue as yang and punishments as yin. Political power is governed by the yang and avoids the yin. This leads to a dualistic value division of yinyang. Anything that is identified with yin is bad, problematic, or in need of reshaping. This lays a rational basis for political authority and sets the tone for the Confucian State for generations to come, integrating appeals to the will of heaven with a more naturalistic system of yinyang. According to Benjamin Schwartz: "Tung Chung-shu [Dong Zhongshu] finds no difficulty in speaking of Heaven's reaction to human misbehavior in language which refers simultaneously to the dislocations of yin and yang and the five elements and the language which refers to 'heavenly intent' (*tianyi*)."[97]

Dong created a novel cosmology, unknown before his time, by incorporating Daoist and Yinyang naturalist cosmology into Confucianism. This synthetic work is described by Schwartz as an "architectonic Confucianized system of corrective cosmology."[98] As a result of Dong's work, yinyang theory lost many of its original meanings, and the construction of the gender identity grounded in yinyang concepts suffered. Most detrimentally, yinyang concepts were used to validate the subordination of women.

Dong Zhongshu construes all natural and human events as the result of yinyang's function. This encompasses all human relations:

> Yang is encompassed in yin, yin is encompassed in yang, husband is encompassed in wife, wife is encompassed in husband, father is encompassed in son, son is encompassed in father, sovereign is encompassed in minister, minister is encompassed in sovereign. The righteousness between sovereign and minister, father and son, and husband and wife all are taken from

---

[97] Schwartz, *The World of Thought*, p. 372.
[98] Ibid., p. 370.

the way of yinyang. The sovereign is yang, the minister is yin; the father is yang, the son is yin; the husband is yang, the wife is yin.[99]

In this passage, we can already see the view that, although male and female (like yin and yang) are mutually dependent, the male yang takes on a dominant position.

The basis for this hierarchy was the link between yinyang, position, and order. Dong Zhongshu suggests there is a struggle between yin and yang, such that one will dominate the other. The goal within this struggle is proper order (*xu* 序). During Dong's time, the newly unified empire would encourage and justify this kind of "urge to organize all knowledge into a coherent whole, filling in with conjecture where necessary."[100] For Dong Zhongshu, achieving the proper order between yin and yang is the highest righteousness: "Keeping the position of heaven and earth, rectifying the order (*xu*) of yin and yang, following the Way straightly and knowing the difficulties, all of these are the highest righteousness."[101] To justify the need for order (*xu*) within human relationships, Dong Zhongshu declares:

> Everything must have *he* 合 (unity).[102] Yin is the *he* of yang, wife is the *he* of husband, son is the *he* of father, minister is the *he* of ruler. There is nothing without *he* yet wherever there is *he*, there is yinyang....The righteousness of ruler and minister, father and son, husband and wife all come from the way of yinyang.[103]

Yinyang interaction as a natural process has been transformed into a description of social relationships. As a result, it not only changed the meaning of the yinyang theory itself but also transformed early Confucian teachings into a fixed state ideology.

This hierarchy of yang over yin as developed in the thought of Dong Zhongshu had many detrimental effects on the social position of women over the course of Chinese history. Bret Hinsch states:

> The cosmological turn in elite thought had profound consequences for gender discourse. Most early Chinese discussed the relations of woman

---

[99] Dong, *Chunqiu Fanlu*, p. 350.

[100] T. Woo, "Confucianism and Feminism" in A. Sharama and K. K. Young (eds.) *Feminism and World Religions* (Albany: Sate University Press, 1999), p. 121.

[101] Dong, *Chunqiu Fanlu*, p. 87.

[102] The term of *he* has multiple meanings: close, shut, join, combine, the whole, total and corresponding, fitting, and not contrary to. According to the commentary, Dong uses *he* in the sense of *ou*, in pairs.

[103] Dong, *Chunqiu Fanlu*, p. 350.

and man in terms of gendered social roles. Debates about gender relations tended to be arguments about which social roles are appropriated for each sex, and what sort of ideal behavior ought to append each role....But cosmologists understood gender in an entirely different light. Instead of viewing gender as interlocking sets of dynamic roles, they believed that we should see gender as a static fact....Gender became something increasingly simple, clear cut, and unequal.[104]

One of the profound consequences of this change was the development of female capacities and virtues into limitations and role-based restrictions in later dynasties. Women were trained to conform and be ordered. In classical Confucian texts, no virtue was singled out as more important than the others. However, in the Sui (81–618 C.E.) and Tang (618–907 C.E.) dynasties, female chastity emerged as the most crucial of all womanly virtues, with harsh punishments meted out to those judged unchaste. Even more horrific practices were justified in the name of Confucianism during the Song Dynasty. The later Confucian defenses of the denigration of women appear clearly in the genre of "stories of women martyrs" [*lienuzhuan* 烈女傳], which developed from the Song Dynasty and went so far as to endorse self-mutilation and suicide.

All yinyang thought requires some differentiation between male and female, however, it does not necessarily entail or demand an evaluative standard of good and bad. Heaven and earth are different, however, this difference does not justify the normative claim that heaven is good and earth is bad. At this point, we can see the importance of gaining a better awareness of yinyang interplay to prevent its misuses in social, political, and cultural situations.

Fengshui 風水: Placing the Living and the Dead

Fengshui (geomancy) is a well-known practice in Asia that has begun to gain popularity in the fields of architecture and interior design around the world, including in the United States. Its primary concern is arranging human space in accordance with natural patterns, structured most fundamentally around yinyang. The origins of *fengshui* are in burial practices. Mourning and funerals were one of the central elements of Confucian rituals. The *Xunzi* puts it simply:

---

[104] B. Hinsch, *Women in Early Imperial China* (New York: Rowman & Littlefield Publishers, 2002), p. 13.

Ritual is sedulous in giving order to matters of birth and death, for birth is the beginning of human beings and death his end. When both the beginning and end are good, the Way of Man is complete.[105]

The importance of *fengshui* to burial practices can be traced back to the theory of the division of the soul or life forces into *hun* 魂 and *po* 魄 as early as the Zhou dynasty. *Hun* and *po* are two important terms in Daoist body transformation and will be discussed in more detail in Chapter 5. *Hun* is a kind of *qi* that belongs to yang; it comes from heaven and will ascend to heaven; *po* is a kind of *qi* that belongs to yin, which has a specific form and will go down to earth, the ground. According to popular belief, *hun* will come out of a dead body (*linghun chuqiao* 靈魂出竅) and ascend to the sky to become a spirit (*shen* 神), whereas the bodily *po* (*routi luopo* 肉體落魄) will enter the ground to become a ghost (*gui* 鬼). The "Jiaotexing" chapter of the *Liji* offers this view: "The *hun* of *qi* return to heaven and the physical form and the *po* return to earth. Thus, in sacrifices, one seeks in the rightness of yinyang."[106] 魂氣歸于天, 形魄歸于地. 故祭, 求諸陰陽之義也.

A key part of ancestor worship and rituals of reverence was to build a proper tomb for the body and the *po* soul. Given its associations with *po*, the earth, and darkness, the tomb was called "the house of yin."

The methods of searching for and arranging a proper "yin house" gradually developed into a comprehensive architectural system. In the Jin Dynasty, Guo Yi（276–324 C.E.), the father of this practice, first used the term *fengshui* to convey this method in his *Zangjing* 葬經 (The *Classic for Burials*). The *Jin Shu* 晉書 (The *Book of Jin*) has a record of his family and his extraordinary abilities, which included divining to choose a proper burial site, as well as selecting the site for the city of Wenzhou in Fujian Province.[107] The story of his choice for his mother's tomb tells that he selected a burial site that was only one hundred steps from water. People worried that this was too close and that the water would cover it, but he predicted that the water would eventually be gone and the burial site would be surrounded by crops. His prediction turned out to be correct.

His *Classic for Burials* has only about two thousand characters and covers basic ideas for burial.[108] Its main contribution was for the first time to categorize what had already been developed through a long history of practice. The opening line declares: "Burying is all about riding with generating *qi*."

[105] Knoblock (trans.), *Xunzi* 荀子, p. 617.
[106] Wang (ed.), *Liji*, p. 436.
[107] X. He and J. Luo, *History of Chinese Fengshui* (Beijing: Jiuzhou Press, 2007), p. 86.
[108] Ibid., pp. 88–91.

In Chapter 2, we read, "*Qi* will disperse when it meets wind and *qi* will congregate when it meets with water....Ancient people gather it to not let it disperse and find a way to stop it. This is called *fengshui*."[109]

Here, *fengshui* contains three basic elements: *qi*, wind (*feng*), and water (*shui*). *Fengshui* is the art of generating *qi*. The association between wind and water is found in the *Yijing* in hexagram 59, *huan*. The *huan* image is about dispersing (*san*) and departing (*li*), however, the point is to use human effort to keep the *qi* together. The flow of *qi* will change when it encounters wind and water. *Qi* will be dispersed when it meets wind, and *qi* will gather, be concentrated, and reside when it meets water. So in selecting a burial site, one must find a place that avoids wind and generates water. This is the original meaning of *fengshui*, which literally means "wind-water." Its ultimate goals are to create a smooth flow of *qi*, therefore leading to good fortune and averting ill fortune. *Fengshui* hunts for a flourishing life by using patterns of yinyang to locate a specific place or arrangement for the sake of having *qi* flow properly.

On a broader level, finding the proper place for the living and the dead lies largely in configuring the relationship between heaven, earth, and human beings. One has to pay close attention to three interrelated aspects, bringing together heavenly timing (*tianshi*), earthly benefit (*dili*), and human harmony (*renhe*). This requires the investigation of astrology, terrain, weather, and so on.

Just as the places for the dead were called "yin homes," places for the living were designated as "yang homes." Each had different rules determining the optimal location. The factors for a yin house for the dead, a tomb, involved many elements, including the timing for choosing an auspicious day. Most important was the selection of a location.[110] This concern is seen in a description of Confucius's burial of his parents. In the *Liji*, there is a story in which Confucius finds his father's tomb and buries his mother within it. He also builds it up four *chi* 尺 (feet) above the ground. In the "Tangong I" chapter of the *Liji*, Confucius explains why:

---

[109] 葬經 *Classic for Burials* reprinted by the Daoist Association and circulated in Daoist temples with no publisher or dates. However, this reference is also in *The History of Yinyang School*," p. 188.

[110] In the Han dynasty this skill was called 堪與 (*kan yu*). In the *Shouwen jiezi*, the *kan* 堪 refers to the way of heaven and *yu* means a the way of earth. With extension, *kan* means a higher place like a little hill of dirt on the ground. It might originally be related to the idea of *fen*, which was a burial mound or house for the dead. Yu is a lower geographical place. The term appears in Roth, *The Huainanzi*, p. 142 (太陰所居辰為厭日, 厭日不可以舉百事, 堪輿徐行, 雄以音知雌, 故為奇辰).

> When Confucius had succeeded in burying (his mother) in the same grave
> (with his father) at Fang, he said, "I have heard that the ancients made
> graves (*mu*) only, and raised no mound (*fen*) over them. But I am a man
> who will be (traveling) east, west, south, and north. I cannot do without
> something by which I can remember." On this, he raised a mound four
> feet high.[111]

This passage implicitly conveys that the "house of yin" (the tomb) has a
proper position (*wei*), such as south, north, east, or west. It also reveals
one practical purpose of the burial mounds, which was to help locate the
tomb for ritual purposes. Regarding *fengshui*, one of the main concerns
for selecting the location for a tomb would be how *qi* flows and generates in a particular location. It also requires a concern for the quality
of the soil, which should be such that the coffin will not degenerate too
quickly.

For the yang house of the living, proper geographic location was
identified through three phrases: backing mountains (*beishan* 背山),
fronting water (*bangshui* 傍水), and facing the sun (*xiangyang* 向陽). All
three are interrelated and embody yinyang principles. The mountain
will give support to the house and stop *qi* from flowing away. Water will
gather the *qi* and make the *qi* stay at the house instead of dispersing.
Relying on a mountain, one can block the chill from the north in the
winter, whereas by facing the sun one can have enough sunlight and
warmth. Fronting water can bring a breeze from the south in summer.
This configuration recalls the *Daodejing*, chapter 42, which states that
everything bears yin on its back and embraces yang in front. Sun and
water are the two most important considerations. Aside from these factors, one might point to something more vague that we could describe
as an aesthetic feeling. This aesthetic sentiment arises from many different aspects, such as the interaction of mountain and water, whether
a home is open and bright, and how it flourishes as a harmonious part
of its surroundings.

From an emperor's palace to the homes of common people, from
Daoist temples to Buddhist monasteries, from capital cities to town centers, all take this basic approach to finding an ideal place or position.
Throughout Chinese history, some made their living by determining the
best place for the living or dead. These professionals were called "Master
Fengshui," however, because they so thoroughly applied yinyang terminology, they were also called "Master Yinyang." Their skills included the

---

[111] Wang (ed.), *Liji*, p. 83.

determining of locations, but often encompassed various forms of fortune telling, particularly the closely related field of physiognomy.[112] In physiognomy, there is a saying: "Look at the forehead in southern people; look at the chin in northern people." The south is yang, and what is higher is yang, so for southerners one looks at the forehead; the north is yin, and the lower is yin, so for northerners one looks at the chin. Similarly, the head is yang, and the male is yang, so one concentrates on the head in men; the feet are yin, and the female is yin, so one focuses on the feet for women. Here again we see categorizations according to yin and yang used to derive conclusions. This practice of using facial structure, voice, and bones to make predictions about one's fortune, life expectancy, health, and wealth remains popular in China to this day.

Returning to *fengshui* more specifically, although there are regional and lineage differences in the method, *fengshui* can be found everywhere, from the arrangement of furniture in a room to the rhythmic layout of city streets. We can take the city of Beijing as an example, because Beijing is one of the earliest examples of a planned city. It has a Beijing *fengshui zhen* 風水陣 (arrangement of wind and water). We see the role of *fengshui* and yinyang in a few ways (Figure 3.2). First is the position and shape of the inner and outer city. In Beijing, the streets are built along north-to-south and east-to-west axes. The outer city is on the south side, representing heaven and yang, and is shaped like a circle; the inner city is located on the north side, representing earth and yin, and is shaped like a square. This design reflects the image of heaven as a circle and earth as a square.

There are four temples for different sacrificial offerings. There is the temple of heaven (*tiantan* 天壇) for worshipping heaven, built to the south of the Forbidden City because heaven is yang and yang is south. The temple of earth (*ditan* 地壇) is to the north of the Forbidden City, because the earth is yin and yin is north. The materials and structures, such as the stones, steps, and columns of the temple of earth were all of odd numbers because odd numbers are yin; the temple of heaven used materials of even numbers because even numbers are yang. The temple of the moon (*yuetan* 月壇) is in the east, and the temple of the sun (*ritan* 日壇) in the west. Jingshan park is in the center, following natural

---

[112] One famous example is when the well-known physiognomist Bu Zixing (布子卿) reportedly described Confucius: Confucius has the physiognomy of an emperor: Yao's forehead, Ji's eyes, Yu's chin, Futao's mouth. But if you look at him from the back, he has high shoulders and a narrow spine, similar to a lost dog. *Shiji*, p. 1921.

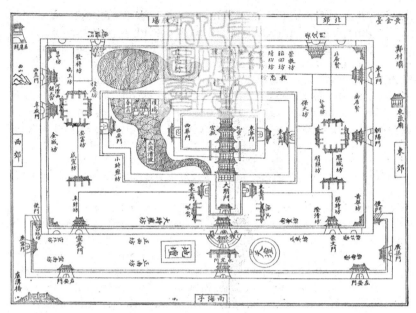

3.2. Map of Beijing City in 1562. Jingshi Wuchengfangxianghutongji
京師五城坊巷衚衕集, by Zhang Jue 張爵.

terrain, to align itself with the north-south direction. Also, the city is
structured with four directions and based on the five elements. On this
point, it is different from the city of Xi'an, which is an ancient capital
with clear directional points, however, not much consideration of the five
elements.

Music and Art

As we have seen in other areas, categorization through yinyang both con-
figures practices internally and situates them externally in the broader
matrix of nature. Music, *yue* 樂, represents the harmony (*he*) of heaven
and earth, and it stands with ritual as part of the order of nature, integrated
through yinyang. The *Liji* says: "Music comes from the yang aspect, ritual comes from the yin aspect. When yin and yang unite together, the ten
thousand things will be attained" (樂由陽來者也, 禮由陰作者也, 陰陽和
而萬物得).[113] The *Lushi Chunqiu* also connects music with yinyang: "As a

---

[113] Wang, (ed.), *Liji*, p. 416.

general principle, music is the harmony between Heaven and Earth and the perfect blend of yin and yang" (凡樂, 天地之和, 陰陽之調也).[114]

Because of the correspondences between yinyang relations within musical practice and the same relations in the rest of the world, music can influence not only human beings but also the natural world. The "Lu Lizhi" chapter of the *Hanshu* concludes:

"Therefore, yinyang carries out transformations, the myriad things have a beginning and ending, and the classifications extend to the twelve notes of the scale and also go through the cycles of day and night. Thus, the actual nature of changes can be seen. (故陰陽之施化, 萬物之終始, 既類旅於律呂, 又經歷於日辰, 而變化之情可見矣)"[115]

The characters translated here as "twelve notes of the scale" are *lülü* 律 呂, the first referring to the six yin notes and the second to the six yang notes. The *Liezi* gives details on how the ancient Chinese ruled the world through the institution of music. An overabundance of wind caused the yang *qi* of things to disperse and scatter, and fruits and nuts not to ripen. So they invented a five-string zither to attract yin *qi* and to arrange the survival of the myriad things.[116] This reveals the importance of yin and yang, and that a musical instrument is created for the sake of generating yin *qi*. Following this story comes another case: water was too much, people were depressed, and there was too much yin, so they invented dancing to guide yin, perhaps to produce yang to balance yin. Dancing is yang; music is yin to accompany dancing.

Music was frequently paired with ritual (*liyue* 禮樂) and had a very similar status. Both were crucial social functions and central to the Confucian project of self-cultivation. Although fundamentally aesthetic, artistic training is also a part of the cultivation process through which human actions and emotions are regulated. As people are cultivated in the six arts, their hearts are connected with the patterns of heaven that are exhibited in cultural patterns (*wen* 文), so that eventually the people become works of art reflecting heaven. The aesthetic functions within Confucian teachings are means of education and transmission, as a means to comprehend heaven (and through heaven, one's innermost nature), and as a means for displaying these patterns in the world.

Music shows yinyang at work. In the "Luli Zhi" chapter of the *Hanshu*, musical notes are divided into yin and yang. The *lu* (rhythm) are the twelve pitches formed by the Pythagorean method, which builds the

[114] Knoblock and Riegel, *The Annals of Lü Buwei*, p. 138.
[115] Ban Gu, *Hanshu*, p. 965.
[116] Yang (ed.), *Liezi Jishi*, p. 146.

A Part of the Structure of the Guqin

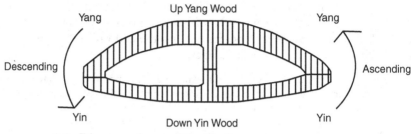

3.3. Diagram of part of the Guqin.

notes using the ratio 3:2. These twelve pitches are divided into six yang notes and six yin notes.[117] The yang notes integrate (*tong*) *qi* and classify (*lei*) things. They are the basis of the five sounds. Six yin notes function as sending out yang and distributing *qi*. The yinyang interface represents the sound of the musical spheres, the harmonic proportions of the movements of the heavenly bodies, and they directly transmit this resonance to the *qi* to effect a positive change.

Yinyang theory penetrates all aspects of music, including the selection of materials and design of the instruments themselves. We can take the *guqin* 古琴, a seven-stringed zither-like musical instrument, as an example. The *guqin* is among the oldest of musical instruments, according to legend originating at the time of the sage kings Yao and Shun. It was already very popular by the time of Confucius. The design of the *guqin* embodies yinyang principles. It is made of yang-type wood and yin-type wood. Because of the seasons and other natural influences, some parts of a tree will be hard and strong, and some parts of tree will be soft and weak. Therefore, there is an art to picking the parts of the tree that make an instrument. One should select the yin portions that are soft and yielding to build the yin sections of the *guqin*, and one should select the hard/strong portions to construct the yang sections (see Figure 3.3). The surface board is round and represents heaven, or yang. The bottom board is flat to represent the earth, or yin. The entire length of the *guqin* (in Chinese measurement) is 3 *chi*, 6 *cun*, and 5 *fen*, representing the 365 days of the year. Each part of the *guqin* has meaning, some more

---

[117] The yang notes are 黃鐘 *huang zhong*, 太族 *tai zu*, 姑洗 *gu xi*, 蕤賓 *rui bin*, 夷則 *yi ze*, and 亡射 *wang she*. The yin notes are 林鐘 *lin zhong*, 南呂 *nan lü*, 應鐘 *ying zhong*, 大呂 *da lü*, 夾鐘 *jia zhong*, and 中呂 *zhong lü*.

obvious, like the "dragon pool" as the yang pool, and the "phoenix pond" as yin pool. The *guqin* imitates the human body, divided into head, chin, shoulder, waist, leg, and foot. This *guqin* body forms a circulation of *qi* movement such that, when played, the *guqin* transmits sound from yin to yang: from the supporter (yin), then to the peg pool (yang), and finally to the forehead (yin). This path of sound migration in the *guqin* reflects the fact that yinyang is the pathway to all movements.

Another area where yinyang is a deep-seated structure of composition is in painting and calligraphy, where there is a dynamic relationship between painter and painting. Often, the yang represents the artist who is doing the movement, whereas the yin represents the subject to be presented. Yang is the movement of the artist, whereas yin is the silence and stillness of the subject. The principal aesthetic values and standards manifested in Chinese paintings are based on yinyang: *yanggang* 陽剛 (strength of yang) and *yinrou* 陰柔 (softness of yin). These appear in many Chinese landscape paintings as complementary pairs: light/dark; full/empty; movement/stillness; heavy/light; straight/curl; manifest/hidden. The beauty of yang strength and yin softness is different in two aspects from Western aesthetic values of the beautiful and the sublime.[118] First, in Chinese landscape paintings, yang strength and yin softness always take up different forms, creating some kind contrast, and promoting variance and dynamic movement. Thus, Chinese paintings always involve some tension. Second, yang strength and yin softness are mutual opposites, however, united together they form a dynamic whole. The painting always converges on oneness.[119]

Unlike some European painting traditions, many Chinese landscape paintings did not try to portray an exact likeness or replica of reality, but rather to accentuate the hidden nature and spirit of the subject. A painting presents a wholeness of all its constituents. Whereas European styles often concentrate more on perspective and shading elements, Chinese landscapes highlight brush strokes, which could be variegated in thickness and tone. These features reflect a yinyang interplay. This connection between visual art and yinyang goes far back in Chinese history. For example, the Eastern Han artist Cai Yong 蔡邕 (132~192 C.E.) used a yinyang matrix to formulate nine positions (*Jiushi* 九勢) in calligraphy. These positions derive from the movement in calligraphy of up and down, left and right, in and out, vertical and horizontal, head and tail,

---

[118] Q. Zhang, *The Meaning Beyond Images: Zhouyi's Meanings and Images and Chinese Aesthetics of Calligraphy and Paintings*, (Beijing: Chinese Bookstore, 2006), p. 73.
[119] Ibid.

3.4. "Mountain Scene in the Spring Mist" by contemporary artist
Dai Bole 戴伯樂.

and beginning and ending. Cai Yong writes, "My calligraphy is rooted
in nature. Yinyang is generated in nature. The positions come from the
generation of yinyang."[120] One of the most systematic statements linking yinyang to aesthetics is the *Yinyang Xushilun* 陰陽虛實論 (the *On
Yinyang Emptiness and Fullness*), written in the eighteenth century by the
well-known artist Ding Gao (?–1761). Ding Gao makes clear that every
aspect of painting – from composition to the use of ink to the relationship between the artist's mental state and the painting itself – all need to
follow the patterns of yinyang. He writes:

[120] Ibid.

Everything under heaven is about yinyang. When considering light, bright is yang, dark is yin. When considering a house, outside is yang and inside yin. When considering things, high is yang and low yin. When considering a hill and valley, convex is yang and concave yin. Everything that artists perceive has yin and yang. Therefore painting has emptiness (*xu* 虛) and fullness (*shi* 實). There is yin within yang and yang within yin – such a painting should have fullness in emptiness and emptiness in fullness. Emptiness is moving from having to lacking, that is, diluting (*xuanran* 渲染); fullness is seeing traces and marks, that is, filling (*shiran* 實染). Emptiness is the exterior of yang and fullness is the interior of yin. Therefore high and low and convex and concave all rely on emptiness and fullness. Yinyang develops from emptiness to fullness as high is the result of low. All flat is pure yang and it is not the method of coloring. There is high then there is coloring (*ran* 染); there is low then there is a painting (*hua* 畫). Although the level area is low, yang makes it bright; although a convex curve is high it must have a background to reveal the highness.[121]

We can see many of these features in the "Mountain Scene in the Spring Mist" painting by the contemporary artist Dai Bole (Figure 3.4). The entire composition appears through the interplay of dark and light, which is to say, spaces that are empty or full. These are conceptualized in term of yin softness and yang hardness. This interplay works on the broadest level, in which the fullness of the center is surrounded by emptiness at the periphery in a swirling pattern that might remind us of the yinyang symbol, but also within what is full, there is emptiness, and within what is empty, there are marks that are filled in. In describing his work, Dai Bole says that he uses the contrast between light and dark and the composition of angles to make manifest the movement of yinyang *qi*.

[121] Y. Wang and Lu Chunyan 王宜文 路春豔, *The Collections of Chinese Classic Aesthetic Concepts* 美苑咀華 – 中國古典美學範疇集粹 (Beijing: Beijing Normal University Press, 北京師範大學出版社, 2000), p. 412.

4   Yinyang Strategy: Efficacy in the World

However acute one's intelligence may be, it is better to rely on the potential inherent in the situation.

Mengzi

Of the ways to achieve success, expanding and contracting in accordance with the Yin and the Yang is the most precious.

Guanzi

The previous two chapters concern the role of yinyang first in the realm of heaven and earth (*tiandi* 天地) and then in the realm of "all below heaven" (*tianxia* 天下), the human world. This chapter will focus on the specific ways in which yinyang thinking is applied as a behavioral model. In spite of common assumptions about yinyang, its main function is not in describing the world or its origins, but rather in enabling one to live well in it. In a tale contained in the *Liezi* (列子), a very poor Mr. Xiang from the state of Song asks a rich man from the state of Qi for his technique (*shu* 術) for gaining wealth.[1] The rich man answers simply, "I'm good at stealing [*dao* 盜]."[2] Mr. Xiang is excited and thinks he has found the secret to gaining wealth, so he goes out to commit a robbery. Unfortunately, he is caught and punished. Later, he goes back to ask the rich man why he tricked him. The rich man clarifies "the way of stealing": "Heaven has its seasons, earth has its benefits. I rob heaven and earth of their seasonal benefits, the clouds and rains of their irrigating floods, the mountains and marches of their products, in order to grow my crops, plant my seeds, raise my walls, build my house."[3]

---

[1] Yang Bojun, 杨伯峻 (ed.) *Liezi Jishi*, 列子集釋, *Commentaries on Master Lie*, (Beijing: Chinese Press, 1979), p. 35.

[2] Ibid.

[3] A. C. Graham (trans.), *The Book of Lieh-tzu, A Classic of Tao* (New York: Columbia University Press, 1990), p. 30.

Mr. Xiang was still perplexed and thought this rich man was trapping him again. So he came to Master Dongguo for clarification. Master Dongguo answered: "Is not your very body stolen? When you must steal the Yin and Yang energies in harmonious proportions even to achieve your life and sustain your body, how can you take the things outside you without stealing them?"[4]

The *shu* (technique) for becoming rich is to "steal" yinyang. The comparison between yinyang and stealing will sound strange to those who assume that yinyang is purely about harmony. Here, yinyang serves to achieve specific accomplishments in the world. The character used here for steal or rob, *dao* 盜, has complex sense. Its pronunciation is the same as the *Dao* 道 that means "the way." The meaning of the character itself has a double sense: in one definition, it denotes "to steal," however, in another it means "to be secretive." This link to stealing and secrecy appears in other texts, as well. For example, in the "Shuogua" commentary in the *Yijing*, the hexagram that corresponds to yin, *kan* (坎) is given roughly twenty-five manifestations. Some of these are what we would expect, such as water and the moon, however, the last one is *dao*, stealing or being secretive. The use of stealing points to an underlying assumption about yinyang as a strategy: it involves having great achievements without appearing to exert effort, doing so by taking advantage of unseen factors and hidden beings. The *Liezi* passage suggests another key aspect of yinyang, which is the importance of aligning one's self with heaven's timing and terrain's placement – that is, with skillfully taking advantage of the available context.

The *Huangdi Yinfujing* 黃帝陰符經 (*The Yellow Emperor's Book of Secret Correspondence*), a text that probably originated in the Han Dynasty but may go back to the Warring States Period, is one of the most popular texts in contemporary Daoist temples, after the *Daodejing* and the *Zhuangzi*.[5] Li Quan 李筌, a Tang dynasty commentator, explains the title – that yin is *an* 暗 dark, hidden and *fu* 符 is to join, combine, or follow. The *Yinfujing* literally means the classic of joining obscure or dark forces. It directs one to seek, understand, and align with the hidden forces of the universe. This text explicitly affirms the role of stealing:

---

[4] Ibid., p. 31.

[5] The text is commonly chanted daily in the morning and evening in Daoist temples across China today. Although this text has only about 400 characters, there are more than twenty commentaries and versions of the text collected in the *Daozang* 道藏 (*Daoist Canon*). The most popular version is from Li Quan 李筌, a Tang Dynasty commentary. The original date for the text itself is uncertain.

The myriad things are thieves (*dao*) of heaven and earth; human beings are thieves of the myriad things; the myriad things are thieves of human beings. When the three thieves are appropriate, the three resources are in equilibrium.[6]

天地, 萬物之盜; 萬物, 人之盜; 人, 萬物之盜. 三盜既宜, 三才既安.

The use of *dao* to refer to stealing or robbing in this passage first of all shows dependence – the myriad things need the resources of heaven and earth, and human beings and the myriad things need each other. The use of *dao*, however, also suggests a more agonistic relationship, that each side must *take* from the other. Li Quan explains that although heaven and earth generate the myriad things, they can also harm them, as when natural disasters occur that destroy crops. Thus, to live a good life, one must skillfully take what is beneficial while avoiding what is harmful. When each thing does this in proper measure, all the elements of the world will be in a sustainable relationship.[7]

Yinyang brings all things into oneness. As an explanatory matrix, this oneness is built on shared structures and functions as well as on interactions and causal connections. The earth is the fundamental root of human beings. Soil is the base, and water is essential to what terrain can engender. Terrain, however, cannot be separated from heaven, as it relies on heavenly timing or seasonal changes. The peace of the human world depends on these seasonal and terrestrial conditions. The relationship between heaven, earth, and human beings exists as a great unity with distinctions: heaven concerns *shi*, timing or seasons; earth determines the place or location; human beings embody this harmony in time and space.

This harmony, however, is not something pursued for its own sake, but rather a way of becoming successful and prosperous. Yinyang is a strategy for success in the world. Another passage, in the *Huainanzi*, says simply: "No brigand [*kou* 寇] is as strong as yinyang."[8]

Yinyang strategy concerns utilizing resources, evaluating situations, and bringing about success. The *Liezi* says, "Things have imperfections. That is why in ancient times Nüwa [媧] smelted stones of five colours to patch up their flaws, and cut off the feet of the turtle to support the four corners."[9] In an interpretation of the *Liezi*, Zhang Zhan in the Jin

---

[6] *Yellow Emperor's Book of Secret Correspondence* in Daozang 道藏 (*Daoist Canon*), vol. 4, p. 2467.

[7] Ibid.

[8] Harold Roth (trans.), *The Huainanzi: A Guide to the Theory and Practice of Government in Early China* (New York: Columbia University Press, 2010), p. 303.

[9] Graham (trans.), *The Book of Lieh-tzu*, p. 96.

Dynasty explains that imperfection throws off the balance of yinyang. Nüwa, the mythological female figure encountered already in Chapter 3, was able to cultivate the essences of the five constancies to harmonize yinyang and to bring things into order.[10] If things have imperfections in them, as this passage says, then human beings cannot simply align with things, but rather must bring them into proper or beneficial order.

Yinyang is a multilayered strategy that requires cultivated ability, allowing one to blend multiple factors into a coherent whole. As François Jullien explains, "According to the ancient treatises, the key to Chinese strategy is to rely on the inherent potential of the situation and to be carried along by it as it evolves."[11] Contrary to common assumptions, yinyang does not solely concern perfect symmetry but rather a kind of intelligence that is, in the words of Jullien, "manifestly, eminently *strategic*."[12] There is a constant breaking of symmetry where yin and yang are not in perfect harmony or balance, however, this leads to a state of *huanliu* (the flowing of circularity 環流), a spiral motion. Yinyang as a strategy depends on the propensity of things and never limits itself to a single level, allowing things to transform and exchange.

Yinyang is a *shu* 術, a strategy or technique that enables one to function effectively in any given circumstance. The word *shu* in oracle bones refers originally to a road, thus connected to the way, *dao*. According to the *Shuowen Jiezi*, the original meaning is a way [*dao*] through a town [術, 邑中道也]. Discussions of *shu* became increasingly important as classical Chinese thought developed, marking a shift in how the world was approached. According to Donald Harper:

> By the third century B.C., the belief that all knowledge and action could be formulated as a technique was widespread, and philosophers also used the vocabulary of "recipes" and "arts" [*shu*] to designate the techniques of statecraft, rhetoric, mind cultivation – virtually any significant activity [that] had a skill particular to it.[13]

Yinyang became central to most of these *shu* and, in fact, could itself be considered a *shu*. We will consider this use of yinyang as a strategy or method in this chapter.

---

[10] Yang (ed.), *Liezi Jishi*, p. 150.

[11] F. Jullien, *A Treatise on Efficacy: Between Western and Chinese Thinking*, J. Lloyd (trans.) (Honolulu: University of Hawai'i Press, 2004), p. 20.

[12] Ibid., p. 24.

[13] Harper (trans.), *The Mawangdui Medical Manuscripts* (London and New York: Kegan Paul International, 1998), p. 46.

On the most basic level, *shu* are methods or tactics. These *shu* are necessary elements of human life and must be constructed and practiced. We see this view across a broad spectrum of texts. For example, the "The Ruler's *Shu*" chapter of the *Huainanzi*, warns, "If one has *shu*, one can rule others; if one has no *shu*, then one is ruled by others."[14] The *Hanfeizi* says, "If speech and argument are not in accordance with law, the heart and intelligence have no *shu*, and if one has many abilities but cannot follow laws and measures in managing affairs, then they are doomed to fail."[15]

Shu were often conceived in the context of skill. The *Hanfeizi* compares *shu* to the skills of craftsmen: "If the craftsman has not mastered his skill and technique the house will collapse or the bow will break. If the leader does not know the techniques [*fang* 方] and *shu*, the state will be disordered and endangered."[16] Another passage explains further:

> Having virtue for human beings is just like having a *shu* for riding a horse-drawn chariot. The state represents the leader's chariot. The power of the leader's influence is the horse. Without a *shu* for steering it, even if one works hard they cannot avoid disorder; if there is a *shu* for steering it, one can be relaxed and joyful and will still have success like that of the great emperors and kings.[17]

Everything has a *shu*. The *Mengzi* (7A24) even announces, "there is a *shu* for the contemplation of water. It is necessary to look at it as the foam in waves [觀水有術, 必觀其瀾]."[18] *Shu* were particularly associated with wisdom. For example, the *Hanshu* (*The Book of Han*) analyzes the four virtues of benevolence (*ren* 仁), righteousness (*yi* 義), ritual propriety (*li* 禮), and wisdom (*zhi* 智). It claims that wisdom is originated in *shu*. Wisdom is then described as "taking the handle of life and death, the paths that connect or are blocked, seeing the measurement of what is

---

[14] Modified translation from Roth, *The Huainanzi*, p. 323.

[15] Chen Qiyou 陳奇猷. *New Annotation of Hanfeizi* 韓非子 (Shanghai: Shanghai Guji Press, 2000), p. 64.

[16] Ibid., p. 156.

[17] Ibid., p. 199. Another passage builds on the same metaphor: "If one rides with a *shu*, he can sit in the court with the look of a virgin girl and there will be no danger but rather order; if one has no *shu* for riding, even if one puts all his or her labor into it, there will be no benefit." Chen (ed.), *Hanfeizi*, p. 155.

[18] Van Norden, Bryan (trans.). *Mengzi, with Selections from Traditional Commentaries*, (Indianapolis: Hackett Publishing, 2008), p. 177.

light or heavy, analyzing the way of gain or loss, and making what is near or distant, genuine or fake appear to those above. All of these are called *shu*."[19]

Shu, techniques, stand halfway between the spontaneity of the *Dao* and the use of coercion. *Shu* is coercive in a sense of being active and directed toward a goal; however, it attempts to bring about results through what is easiest and smoothest, instead of relying on something like skill. *Shu* are also more specific and technical, as we see in another passage contrasting *Dao* and *shu*, from the *Hanshu*: "*Dao* mixes to take form spontaneously; the *shu* have the same origin but different branches."[20]

The meaning of *shu* also extends to a profession or even a way of life. We read from the *Mengzi*:

> Is the arrow-maker less benevolent than the armor-maker? Yet the arrow-maker only fears that he may not harm people; the armor-maker only fears that he may harm people. The shaman-healer and the coffin-maker are the same way, respectively. Hence, one may not fail to be careful about one's choice of craft [*shu*].[21]

There is a *shu* of medicine and a *shu* of divination. Martial arts are *wu shu* (武術), literally the *shu* of combat or what is martial (*wu*). In modern usage, academia is referred to as *xue shu* (學術), which means the *shu* of study or learning. Any school of thought could be described as a kind of *shu*. For example, the *Xunzi* comments that if the Mohist *shu* 墨術 is carried out, the world will have ever-increasing poverty, hardship, conflicts, sadness, and disharmony.[22] On the contrary, the *Ru shu* 儒術 (the Confucian method) will bring greater wealth and success, such as the harmonious music of bells and drums.[23] More specifically, the Confucian way is described as *ren shu* (仁術), the *shu* of benevolence or humaneness (*Mengzi* 2A7). Hanfeizi has a law (*fa*) *shu* (法術); Laozi and Zhuangzi have *dao shu* (道術). On this account, *shu* is the particular kind of *zhi* 智 (wisdom) endorsed by any school. As Harper puts it, "All philosophy is assumed to be an art [*shu*]."[24] Characterizing a school of thought as a *shu*, however, has decisive implications. It reveals how even

---

[19] Ban Gu 班固, *Hanshu* 漢書 (*The Book of Han*), commentary by Yan Shigu 颜师古, (Beijing: Chinese Press, 1962), p. 2616.

[20] Ibid., p. 2711. 敘傳上道混成而自然兮,術同原而分流.

[21] Van Norden (trans.), *Mengzi*, (2A7), p. 47.

[22] Knoblock, John (trans.). *Xunzi: A Translation and Study of the Complete Works*, 3 vols. (Stanford: Stanford University Press, 1988–1994), p. 290.

[23] Ibid.

[24] Harper (trans.), *The Mawangdui Medical Manuscripts*, p. 47.

philosophical systems were intended to be practical ways of living, to be methods or techniques.

One final sense of *shu* is as a pattern or model, which is how one of the earliest Chinese dictionaries, the *Guang Ya* (third century C.E.), defines it, "*Shu* is pattern [*fa* 法]."[25] Because human thought is patterned on nature, *shu* can be derived from nature and can even exist in the natural world itself. Thus, for example, the "*Lüli*" (律曆) chapter of the *Houhanshu* claims that "the *shu* of the sun and moon thus has the winter and has the summer, and between winter and summer there is the spring and there is autumn"[26] [日月之術, 則有冬有夏; 冬夏之間, 則有春有秋]. Here *shu* is a recurring or specific pattern, although we might also take it as the way that the sun and moon operate. It is probably in this sense of *shu* as part of nature that Laozi 老子 is described as the "one who respects its *shu*."[27]

The aspect of *shu* as a part of nature comes out perhaps most clearly in an explanation given by the well-known strategist Fan Li 范蠡 (517 B.C.E.–?) when explaining *shu* to Goujian 勾踐 (497–465 B.C.E.), the famous king of the state of Yue (越). The dialogue appears in an early history of the state of Yue, the *Yuejueshu* (越絕書). The king begins by asking, what should be on the left and what on the right, what should be abandoned and what should be taken? Fan Li responds:

> On the left is *Dao* and on the right is *shu*; abandon the insignificant and take the substantial....The *Dao* is before the heaven and earth, never getting old; completing all myriad things without names or craft. Thus it is called the *Dao*. *Dao* generates *qi*, *qi* generates yin, yin generates yang, yang generates heaven and earth. After heaven and earth are established, there is cold and hot, dry and wet, the sun and moon, stars and galaxies, and the four seasons, and then the myriad things are completed. *Shu* is the will of heaven. At the peak of summer, the myriad things grow. Sages rely on the heart of heaven, helping what delights heaven and finding joy in the growth of the myriad things.[28]

---

[25] 術, 法也. (廣雅).

[26] H. Fan, (ed.), *Houhanshu* 後漢書, *The Book of Later Han* (Beijing: Chinese Press, 1965) p. 3055.

[27] Zhenpu Zhou 周振甫, *Commentary on Shijing* 詩經 (*The Book of Odes*) (Beijing: Chinese Press, 2002), p. 1975.

[28] The date and authorship of this historical text is uncertain. The earliest suggested time is the Spring and Autumn Period, but it could be as late as the end of the Eastern *Han*. The authorship is also unclear. There are five different names associated with it, three of whom were disciples of Confucius. In any case, it is regarded as the one of the most important texts for the study of early Chinese history. In chapter 13, "Goujian," the

左道右術, 去末取實. ”越王曰: “何謂道? 何謂術? 何謂末? 何謂實? ”范子對:
“道者, 天地先生, 不知老; 曲成萬物, 不名巧. 故謂之道. 道生氣, 氣生陰, 陰
生陽, 陽生天地. 天地立, 然後有寒暑、燥濕、日月、星辰、四時, 而萬物
備. 術者, 天意也. 盛夏之時, 萬物遂長. 聖人緣天心, 助天喜, 樂萬物之長.

We have already seen the contrast between *Dao* and *shu* earlier, where
Dao was primary and more spontaneous. One should call to mind that,
like *shu*, *Dao* can refer both to a way of acting and to the way of nature
itself. In this passage, *shu* is the will of heaven and propensity of things,
which is produced from the *Dao* through yin and yang. It is, therefore,
more concrete and specific than the *Dao* itself. In this passage, the work
of sages is continuous with this *shu* of nature.

Although there are an infinite variety of *shu*, two are particularly significant in early texts: *Daoshu* 道術 (the method/techniques of the *Dao/
way*) and *xinshu* 心術 (the method of the heart/mind). These *shu* focus
on living efficaciously and frequently draw their practices from yinyang
thought.

Daoshu: Techniques of the Way

We have already seen the contrast between *Dao* and *shu*. Their combination as *Daoshu* mainly refers to the *shu* of Daoism, which, as we have
seen in the *Daodejing*, is based on softness, emptiness, nonaction, and
spontaneity. According to the *Hanshu*:

> The Daoist School is about not doing [*wuwei*] 無為, but leaving nothing
> undone. Its substance is easy to practice but its expression in words is hard
> to know. Its *shu* takes emptiness and nonexistence as its root and takes fol-
> lowing along as its function [道家無為, 又曰無不為, 其實易行, 其辭難知.
> 其術以虛無為本, 以因循為用].[29]

The *Huainanzi* also takes the foundation of *Daoshu* as nonaction, saying, "non-action (*wuwei*) controlling deliberate action (*youwei*) is the
shu"[30] (無為制有為, 術也).

The *Zhuangzi* describes the *Daoshu* by comparing the relationship of a
fish to water with the relationship between human beings and the *Dao*:

> Confucius said, "Fish come together in water, and human beings come
> together in the *Dao*. ... Thus it is said, fish forget one another in the rivers

king of *Yue*, asks his minister Fan Li how ancient sages govern, which leads into this
discussion (*Yue jue*, chapter 13 and 16, p. 65).
[29] Ban Gu, *Hanshu*, p. 2713.
[30] Modified translation from Roth, *The Huainanzi*, p. 565.

and lakes, and human beings forget one another in the *shu* of the *Dao* (道術)."[31]

Here, the *shu* of the *Dao* is in fitting one's environment so well that one forgets it is even there. Another passage from the *Zhuangzi* contrasts the *daoshu* with the specific *shu* of each of the schools: "The *shu* employed in the regulation of the world are many; and they all think that the efficiency of their own method leaves nothing to be added. But what has become of what the ancients called the *Daoshu*? We must reply, 'It is everywhere.'"[32]

The *Dao* is again taken as more fundamental and comprehensive than any particular *shu*. Taking the *Dao* itself as a *shu* is in some ways a rejection of *shu* in the more usual sense.

The *Daoshu* commonly has three distinctive qualities. All three of these elements were central parts of yinyang methods, as we will see. The first concerns the ability to deal with multiplicity or complexity through unity or simplicity. We read from the *Wenzi* (*Master Wen*), "look at the root to know the branches and focus on the one to respond to the ten thousand – this is called *shu*" (見本而知末, 執一而應萬, 謂之術).[33] We have already seen yinyang described in similar ways, both as the source of diverse things and as the most basic *lei*, category, that encompasses all things.

The second is in following along with circumstances, or we might say, in nonaction. This aspect of *Daoshu* is manifested in the story in the *Zhuangzi* and the *Liezi* of a man playing in the water. The waterfall is more than 200 feet high, the whirlpool covers ninety miles; fish and turtles cannot swim there, and crocodiles cannot live there. However, this man goes in and out of the water with playful ease. Confucius asks him if he has a *daoshu*. The man responds, "I enter by being loyal and trusting to the water and I come out following this loyalty and trust. This loyalty and trust lead me to throw my body in the current and I do not dare to act selfishly."[34] In this sense, one has to trust and follow the flow; this is the *shu* of *Dao* (cf. *Daodejing*, chapter 51).

A third aspect of the *Daoshu* is concentration on the internal. The *Wenzi* says:

[31] Modified translation from Ziporyn (trans.), *Zhuangzi, The Essential Writings with Selections from Traditional Commentaries* (Indianapolis/Cambridge: Hackett Publishing Company Inc., 2009), p. 47.

[32] Chen Guying, 陳鼓應, 莊子今注今譯, *Commentaries on Zhuangzi*, (Beijing: Chinese Press, 1983), p. 856.

[33] D. Li, (ed.), *Wenzi* 文子 (Haer Bing: Heilongjiang People's Press, 2003), p. 177.

[34] B. Yang (ed.), *Liezi Jishi*, p. 248.

"Sages internally cultivate *Daoshu* and do not decorate the outside with benevolence and righteousness. They know the appropriateness of the nine sense openings and the four limbs and they wander with spiritual harmony. This is the wandering of sages."[35]

是故聖人內脩道術而不外飾仁義, 知九竅四支之宜, 而遊乎精神之和, 此聖人之游也.

This focus on the internal overlaps with the *xinshu,* method of the heart/ mind, which will be discussed in the next section.

The idea of *Daoshu* points toward a kind of morality, or perhaps an alternative to morality. One can distinguish two kinds of ethical ideals in early Chinese texts. One is *daode* 道德 (the way and its power); the other is *lunli* 倫理 (the patterns in human kinship and relations). Although the terms *daode* and *lunli* are interchangeable in contemporary usage, both meaning "ethics" or "morality," they have different connotations in the early Chinese language. Following the pattern of the world is *daode,* whereas to keep human relationships orderly is *lunli.* Like Kant's categorical imperative and Mill's principle of utility, *daode* and *lunli* are different ways in which to resolve dilemmas about how to act, using different forms of reasoning and different standards. Yinyang supplies a definitive structure for both approaches.

Ethics as *lunli,* orderly relations, appears mostly in Confucian teachings. *Lun* (倫) refers to human relationships, and *li* (理) is principle or coherent pattern. *Lunli* is, thus, the principle, pattern, or proper arranging of human relationships. The *Mengzi* designates five kinds of relationships: sovereign and minister, father and son, older and younger, husband and wife, and between friends. He then discusses the virtues appropriate to each one (*Mengzi,* 3A4). Confucians take these human relationships as the fundamental fabric of morality. Dong Zhongshu in the Han Dynasty extended yinyang thinking to human relationships based primarily, as we have seen, on position (*wei* 位). From this connection to yinyang, he then derives many moral precepts.[36] We have already examined this in the last chapter.

From the *daode* point of view, however, morality is not about the dichotomy of right versus wrong or good versus bad, but rather aligning one's activities with the forces and propensity of the natural world. The moral person is one with the *Dao. De* (德) – a term often translated as

[35] D. Li (ed.), *Wenzi,* p. 41.
[36] See Robin Wang, "Dong Zhongshu's Transformation of Yin/Yang Theory and Contesting of Gender Identity," *Philosophy East and West,* 55 no. 2 (April 2005), 209–31.

virtue in a Confucian context – is then a kind of power or efficacy that comes from harmonizing with *Dao*. The *Taipingjing* discusses one who has the highest *de* as one who can be with heaven and earth:

> The good person will accord with the work of heaven. They will not lose constant proper order. This is the highest virtue (*shangde* 上德). There is nothing that cannot be completed; there is nothing that cannot be attained; they do not lose the brightness, they do not lose the substance; they do not lose the yinyang, for generations; they do not lose the four seasons for coming and going.[37]

The person of highest virtue will embody primordial *qi* and spontaneity (*ziran* 自然). They become the highest sages.[38]

Dao is heavenly movement; *de* is earthly nourishment. By applying *Dao* and *de*, one will transform along with the great rhythm of the world. This provides an ideal for human behavior.[39] The greatness of *Dao* is in its ability to transform and change. The *Zhuangzi* explains how sages deal with the transformations of the vast world: *de* is "responding by attuning," *Dao* is responding by "pairing or matching."[40] Both require a creative synergy. According to the *Zhuangzi*, when you get the *Dao*, you will be able to penetrate the patterns (*li*), and then you will have a clear head to weigh or balance things (*quan* 權), and then you will also gain bodily powers. Fire, water, birds, and beasts cannot do any harm to this kind of *de* person.[41] The mind becomes clear, and the body transcends physical limits.[42] The *de* 德, usually translated as virtue, is a cognate with the *de* 得 that means to "obtain." Thus, *de* as virtue is linked to *de* as efficiency in attaining one's goals.[43] The result of *daode* is power and skill.

In this context, *shan* (善), goodness or excellence, refers to what "unites with yinyang." In contrast, one who lacks goodness, damaging the source of yinyang, will be the target of the punishments of heaven and earth.[44] Another passage in the *Taipingjing* says, "One who has no *Daode* in their life is not with heaven but is in the same lot with animals."[45] Heaven is the *Dao*, and *de* is the earth. "Like the movement of heaven, only true

---

[37] Yang Jilin 杨寄林 (ed.). *Taipingjing* 太平經 *Classic of Great Peace*, (Shijiazhuang: Hebei People's Press, 2002), p. 1191.
[38] Ibid., p. 1221.
[39] Ibid., p. 1022.
[40] Chen, *Commentaries on Zhuangzi*, p. 250.
[41] Ibid., p. 426.
[42] Ibid., *Xiaoyaoyou* chapter.
[43] Jullien, *A Treatise on Efficacy*, J. Lloyd (trans.), p. 93.
[44] *Taipingjing*, p. 963.
[45] Ibid., p. 994.

Dao can generate; like the earth, only good *de* can nourish. If one has no *Dao* and *de*, one has nothing to do with heaven and earth."[46] A person who has no *Dao* and *de* will be isolated, cut off from the support of heaven and earth.

For perfectly cultivated people:

> Heaven is the model; *de* is the basis of action; *Dao* is progenitor [*zong* 宗]. Thus, they transform and change with things, never reaching an end. Their refined essence [*jing* 精] fills heaven and earth, never depleted. Their spirit [*shen* 神] covers the cosmos [*yuzhou* 宇宙], never having a boundary.[47]

This is a sound explanation of human actions and how one should be in the world. Heaven, *de*, and *Dao* are the guiding forces, however, the core is in change and transformation. Cosmological patterns, such as the waning and waxing of yinyang, provide a permanent and unchanging order of things. Through yinyang, the flux of human conduct can be explained, measured, and validated. Yinyang, thus, grounds correct human actions in the cosmos. As a result, it suggests a strong awareness of one's surroundings and the orders of human emotions.

Xinshu: Techniques of the Heart/Mind

The second important kind of *shu* is *xinshu* (心術), which deals with one's internal landscape. The character *xin* (心) is an image of the heart, but because the heart was considered to be the organ of emotions and thought, it is often translated as heart/mind. *Xinshu*, then, is the method of the heart/mind, the method for thinking and feeling. As thinking about *xinshu* developed, it became closely connected with yinyang thought. In chapter 3, the *Zhuangzi* uses the expression "the troubles of yinyang" (*yinyang zhihuan* 陰陽之患) to refer to a state of emotional and psychological distress and unbalance.[48] In context, it describes someone about to take on an important office, someone who says that if he does not succeed, he will have the troubles of the human world, however, if he does succeed, he will have internal or psychological trouble, described as the trouble of yinyang. The trouble of yinyang points to anxiety and self-doubt.

---

[46] Ibid.

[47] Knoblock and Riegel, (trans.) *The Annals of Lü Buwei: A Complete Translation and Study* (Stanford: Stanford University Press), p. 347.

[48] Chen, *Commentary on Zhuangzi*, p. 122.

The *Lüshi Chunqiu* suggests that the sense organs themselves have desires for sounds, scents, tastes, and so on, however, if one wants to find joy in these, then this must originate in the heart/mind (*xin*). The heart/mind is the real source of joy. This *le* (樂) – delight, joy, pleasure – derives from being one with nature. Being with heaven and earth and flowing with events efficiently is the source of true happiness. This happiness relies on yinyang. *Zhuangzi*'s heavenly joy (*tianle*) 天樂 is thus described: "One who in living moves according to the movements of heaven and who in dying follows the transformations of the myriad things knows heavenly joy. Stillness is uniting with the *de* of yin; movement is synchronizing with the waves of yang. One who knows heavenly joy has no complaints, no troubles."[49]

To have this joy, the heart/mind must be harmonized or balanced, *he*; to reach *he*, the heart/mind must be fitting or appropriate (*shi* 適), and this comes from complying with the order or pattern of things.[50] Compliance with yinyang as the ordering of things enables one to taste, smell, and see things with enjoyment. This is how the heart/mind governs the senses, and how the heart/mind can be a possible source of pleasure.

The *Guanzi* 管子 has a special chapter on *xinshu* (心術), which provides a more detailed explanation. The passage begins by saying, "The art of the mind [*xinshu*] lies in controlling the apertures through nonassertiveness [*wuwei*]." It then explains:

> "Do not attempt to do the running for a horse." "Do not attempt to do the flying for a bird." These two statements mean that you should not try to preempt the ability of others nor compete with your subordinates. […] The ruler of men stands in the Yin. The Yin is quiescent. Therefore the statement says: "if you move, you will lose your position." By occupying the Yin, one is able to control the Yang. By being quiescent, one is able to control activity. Therefore the statement says: "If you remain quiet, you will naturally retain it."[51]

In the *Guanzi*, *xinshu* is identified with six factors: fullness, sincerity, thickness, extension, measure, and reciprocity [實也, 誠也, 厚也, 施也, 度也, 恕也, 謂之心術].

In a Confucian context, *xinshu* is most closely connected to the proper arrangement of emotions and desires. The "Classic of Music" chapter of the *Liji* says:

> Now, the people have dispositions of the blood-and-*qi* and of the mind and knowing, but they do not have constancy in sorry, joy, pleasure, and anger.

[49] Ibid., p. 340.
[50] Knoblock and Riegel, *The Annals of Lü Buwei*, pp. 142–143.
[51] W. A. Rickett (trans.), *Guanzi, Political, Economic, and Philosophical Essays from Early China* (New Jersey: Princeton University Press, 1998), p. 75.

They are stimulated and respond when things arise and then they move. Afterward, the *xinshu* takes form.[52] (夫民有血氣心知之性, 而無哀樂喜怒之常, 應感起物而動, 然後心術形焉).

Chapter 2 of the *Hanshi Waizhuan* 韓詩外傳, compiled by Han Yin 韓嬰 in the Western Han Dynasty (202 B.C.E.–8 C.E.), makes many of the same connections:

> One must follow the mandate of heaven, manage the *xinshu*, coherently order loves and hates, and properly adjust emotions and dispositions, and then managing the *Dao* will be complete. If one follows the mandate of heaven, then one will not be confused by fortune and misfortune, and if one is not confused by fortune and misfortune, stillness and movement will be cultivated. If one manages the *xinshu*, then one will not recklessly love and hate, and if one does not recklessly love and hate, then rewards and punishments are not feared.[53]

> (原天命, 治心術, 理好惡, 適情性, 而治道畢矣. 原天命則不惑禍福, 不惑禍福則動靜脩. 治心術則不妄喜怒, 不妄喜怒則賞罰不阿).

In both passages, *xinshu* is connected with the proper cultivation of emotions and desires (loves and hates).

Xinshu is a focal point in *Xunzi*'s practices for self-cultivation, the way of managing *qi* and cultivating the heart/mind. For the *Xunzi*, this can be only done through the rituals and teachings of masters: "For the *shu* of managing *qi* and nourishing the heart, nothing is more crucial than following rituals, more essential than obtaining good teaching, or more numinous that unifying one's likes. Now that is called the *shu* of managing *qi* and nourishing the heart/mind."[54]

For the *Xunzi*, *xinshu* is a necessary part of sagehood: "When water reaches the utmost balance, neither side tilts. When the *xinshu* is like this, it is the image of a sage."[55] In a passage opposing physiognomy, the *Xunzi* spells out:

> Telling fortune by reading facial features is not as important as discussing the heart/mind, and discussing the heart/mind is not as important as selecting the *shu*. The facial features cannot override the heart/mind, and the heart/mind cannot override *shu*. If *shu* is correct, then the heart/mind

---

[52] Wang, Mengou, 王夢鷗 (ed.) *Liji*, 禮記今註今譯 (*Record of Rituals*), (Taipei: Taiwan Commercial Press, 1981), p. 625.

[53] Z. S. Zhao 趙善飴 (ed.), *Hanshi Waizhuan* 韓詩外傳, (Beijing: Commercial Press, 商務印書館, 1938), p. 69.

[54] Modified translation from by Knoblock (trans.), *Xunzi*, p. 32.

[55] Modified translation from Ibid., p. 799.

will follow it. Even if there is badness in the facial features, the goodness of *xinshu* will not hinder his becoming a gentleman.[56]

In this passage, the *Xunzi* makes it clear that the heart depends on the *shu* it follows. It is, thus, ultimately the *shu* rather than the heart that determines who will become petty and who will become gentlemen or sages.

Dong Zhongshu in the Han Dynasty was the first thinker to interpret human nature itself in terms of yin and yang. He identifies yang with human nature (*xing* 性) and yin with emotions (*qing* 情).[57] Human nature is a composite of yin and yang: yang as the beneficent force of heaven expresses itself as benevolence (*ren* 仁), whereas the yin expresses itself as covetous desire or greed (*tan* 貪). Dong Zhongshu thus resolves the classical dispute between Mengzi's description of human nature as good and *Xunzi*'s description of human nature as bad by concluding that human nature contains not only "rudimentary goodness" (*shanduan* 善端) because it has yang but also the seed of badness (*e* 惡) because it has yin: "The human body has *xing* and *qing* just like heaven has yin and yang. One can not discuss the basic elements (*zhi* 質) without bearing in mind the *qing* – that would be like talking about yang in heaven without considering yin."[58]

Wang Chong elucidates Dong Zhongshu's position in his influential work, the *Lun Heng* 論衡:

> Dong Zhongshu studied the works of Xunzi and Mengzi and established the theory of human nature and emotion (*xing*/*qing*). According to this theory, the primary principle of heaven is the alternation of yin and yang; the primary principle of human being is the alternation of emotion and nature [*yinqing and yangxing*]. *Xing* is born from yang and *qing* is born from yin. *Yinqi* is low and greedy and *yangqi* (陽氣) is high and benevolent (*ren*). The view that human nature (*xing*) is good only catches sight of yang, the view that human nature is bad sets eyes only on yin. According to Dong Zhongshu, Mengzi only perceives yang and Xunzi only notices yin. It is acceptable that these two schools each have their own merit, but also one has to recognize that human nature (*xing*) and emotion (*qing*) have both good and bad.[59]

---

[56] Modified translation from Ibid., p. 96.

[57] For further discussion, see Wang, "Dong Zhongshu's Transformation of Yin/Yang Theory."

[58] Dong Zhongshu. *Chunqiu Fanlu* 春秋繁露義證 *(Luxuriant Dew of the Spring and Autumn Annals)*, Si Yu (ed.), (Beijing: Chinese Press, 1996), p. 296.

[59] Wang Chong 王充, *Lun Heng* 論衡 (Beijing: Chinese Press, 1990), p. 140.

The linking of *xing* and *qing* to yang and yin became widely accepted and has been endorsed by many thinkers and literati. The *Shuowen Jiezi* echoes Dong Zhongshu in its definitions of the words *xing* and *qing*: "*Qing* is human being's yin *qi*, having desires. *Xing* is human being's yang *qi*, having goodness."[60] Here is an excerpt from the special section on *xing* and *qing* in the *Baihutong* 白虎通 (the *Comprehensive Discussions in the White Tiger Hall*):

> What are *xing* 性 and *qing* 情? Yang makes what is *xing*, yin brings what is *qing*. Human life is endowed with yin and yang, therefore it contains within five *xing* and six *qing*.[61] *Qing* is the product of yin; thus there are varying desires. *Xing* is the effect of yang; thus there is the forming of principles. Yang *qi* is benevolence (*ren*); yin *qi* is greed (*tan*); therefore, *qing* has desires and *xing* has benevolence (*ren*).[62]

Here, yinyang is integrated into human nature and used to explain a wide range of emotions. The *Hanshu* similarly claims that "human beings embody the yinyang *qi* of heaven and earth to possess the emotions of happiness, anger, and sadness."[63]

We have already seen that *daoshu* also concerns the internal, so *daoshu* and *xinshu* are interrelated. *Zhuangzi* articulates two levels of the heart/mind (*xin*). One is the heart/mind that knows external objects. It makes distinctions and has a yes or no (*shi-fei* 是非) point of view on the world. In this activity, the heart/mind cannot get the *Dao*. The other heart/mind is no-mind, or the heart of the *Dao*. It transcends all distinctions and dualistic views and is connected with the heart/mind of the universe. The true person with an empty heart/mind can transcend the limits of physical forms and allow his or her mind to wander in complete freedom. We could say that this is a movement from an empirical ego (*ziwo* 自我) to an ontological true self (*zhenwo* 真我).

The *xinshu* associated with *daoshu* concerns the quieting of the heart/mind, or even eliminating its role. For example, several times the *Master*

---

[60] Xu Shen, *Shuowen Jiezi* (Shanghai: Shanghai Guji Press, 1981).

[61] The five *xing* are benevolence 仁 (*ren*), righteousness 義 (*yi*), ritual 禮 (*li*), wisdom 智 (*zhi*), and trust 信 (*xin*). The six *qing* are pleased 喜 (*xi*), angry 怒 (*nu*), sad 哀 (*ai*), joy 樂 (*le*), love 愛 (*ai*), and 貪 greed (*tan*).

[62] L. Chen, (ed.), *Baihutong* 白虎通, *Comprehensive Discussions in the White Tiger Hall*, (Beijing: Chinese Press), p. 374.

[63] Ban Gu, *Hanshu*, p. 1027.

Wen links the techniques of Laozi with the *xinshu*, as in a passage from the "Nine Guards" (*Shoujiu* 守九), which says:

> Laozi says, those who were for the *Dao* among the ancients, coherently ordered 理 (*li*) their emotions and dispositions, managed *xinshu*, nourished it with harmony, supported it with what was fitting, enjoyed the *dao* and forgot lowly position, finding peace in virtue and forgetting poverty.[64]
>
> 老子曰: 古之為道者, 理情性, 治心術, 養以和, 持以適, 樂道而忘賤, 安德而忘貧.

Another passage, from the "Guard Softness" (*Shourou* 守弱) chapter, says:

> Laozi says, sages rest together with yin and move together with yang. They can reach the utmost in being without joy and thus are never without joy. Being never without joy reaches to the ultimate of joy.... They attain to the discussions of the xinshu. Since desires and hates are on the outside, thus there is nothing which pleases them, nothing which angers them, nothing which makes them feel joy and nothing which makes them suffer. They and the myriad things form a profound unity, without negation and without affirmation.[65]

In these passages, we can see the close connection between *daoshu* and *xinshu*. Their focus is on removing the obstacles caused by the emotions and the judgments of the heart/mind and endorsing nonaction and spontaneity.

Yinyang Strategy: The Way of Ways

The preceding discussions expose the conceptual and practical importance of *shu*. The question is, how does yinyang connect with *shu*? We can now examine the key specific ways in which yinyang thought grounds strategies for effective action.

Yinyang Strategy, Factor I: The Timing of Heaven
and the Benefits of Earthly Terrain

We have seen that the origins and functioning of the natural world (heaven and earth) were theorized through yinyang. The most fundamental

---

[64] Li (ed.), *Wenzi*, p. 71.
[65] Ibid., p. 81.

aspect of yinyang strategy is working properly with these conditions. In distinguishing a specifically Chinese conception of efficacy, Francois Jullien concludes that "Chinese thought of human efficacy as a natural transformation. A general made the situation evolve to his advantage in the same way as nature makes a plant to grow or a river continuously hollows out its bed."[66] Yinyang strategy consists in having a situation develop in a certain way so that the outcome flows naturally from the situation and accumulated conditions. Sunlight and water are two basic natural prerequisites for farming. Plentiful sunlight and timely rain will secure a harvest to support human life. Sun and water provide the basis for human actions, captured in the timing (or seasons) of heaven (*tianshi* 天時) and the advantages of earth (*dili* 地利).[67] From the sun, one learns to follow the rhythm of seasons or the changes of yinyang; from irrigation, one investigates how to go along with the rhythm and circumstances of the earth, taking advantage of conditions without coercing things.

The *Xunzi* claims: "Heaven has its seasons; earth its resources, human beings their order. Therefore the three of them can participate together (*can* 參)."[68] Literally, they can "form a triad," using "three" (*san* 三) as a verb. In another passage, the *Xunzi* connects this alignment specifically to yinyang, saying that one must follow the benefits of heaven's timing and the earth's advantages, and one must know the principle of the waxing and waning of yinyang.[69] The *Xunzi* articulates these elements in many passages, sometimes with a clear focus on strategy, as in the "*Yibing* 議兵" (Discussing Amy) chapter on the use of military force: "Above one must attain heaven's timing and below one must utilize the earth's advantages, examining the enemies changes and movements, where the rear issues from and where the front reaches to. This is the essential *shu* for using of the army."[70]

Yinyang strategy develops as the main method, *shu*, for evaluating, aligning with, and using these conditions.

We have already seen the connection between ruling and the mastery of yinyang. The *Huainanzi* delineates kingship as patterned according to yinyang: "The thearch embodies the Grand One; the king emulates yin

---

[66] Jullien, *A Treatise on Efficacy*, p. 59.

[67] The *Mengzi* also articulates three basic things needed for any accomplishment: heavenly timing (*tianshi*, 天時), advantage of terrain (*dili*, 地利) and the harmony of human beings (*renhe*, 人和) (Book 6). The specific example he gives is in relation to defending a town.

[68] Modified translation from by Knoblock (trans.), *Xunzi*, p. 535.

[69] Ibid.

[70] Ibid., p. 453.

and yang.... One who emulates yin and yang has potency (*de*) comparable to Heaven and Earth and brilliance like that of the sun and moon; his essence is as comprehensive as that of ghost and spirits."[71]

The earth offers stable space and strategic location; heaven provides changing time and weather. In earth we see the stability of the mountains as quietness, and in heaven we see the movement of the clouds as circulation of the wind.

The role of heavenly timing and earthly benefit could be extended into more abstract terms of time and space. Time is a sequence and a flow; space is like the roof of a house that covers all things. Space has a sense like *tianxia* 天下, what is under the sky. The *Zhuangzi*, however, has a different way to characterize space and time or the universe. Its understanding of space and time is not from extending what we experience but rather from considering the nature of space and time itself: "What is substantial but located in no position is space. What has duration but no beginning or end is the whole expanse of time."[72] Here, space has a fullness (*shi* 實) such that it has high or low, long or short, big or small, however, it also has no fixed form and, in this sense, is empty (*xu* 虛). Fullness and emptiness in co-existence make space. Time is a constant continuity with no end or beginning. This understanding of time and space opens other perspectives on yinyang.

We can begin with timing, which is most central to early Chinese conceptions of efficacious action, running across all schools of thought. For example, the *Mengzi* (5B1) says that Confucius is the sage of timeliness and compares him to a full symphony.[73] Sagely action consists of knowing when to respond properly to each moment. The *Liezi* states this simply: "Pick the right time and flourish; miss the right time and perish."[74] The early awareness of the importance of timing developed into a system that relied on utilization of yinyang. Yinyang is the pattern of timing.

The *Huangdi Neijing* proclaims, "To be able to model the transformations of the yinyang of heaven and earth, is to not break from the rhythm of the four seasons. To know the reasons (*li* 理) of the twelve rhythms is a knowledge (*zhi* 知) that sages cannot miss."[75] To use yinyang to grasp rhythm is the way of the sage and the way to avoid error or fault. The *He*

---

[71] Roth, *The Huainanzi*, p. 277–279.

[72] Ziporyn (trans.), *Zhuangzi*, p. 100.

[73] Van Norden (trans.), *Mengzi*, p. 132.

[74] Graham (trans.), *The Book of Lieh-tzu*, p. 163.

[75] Zhang Yingan 張隱庵 (ed.), *Huangdi Neijing Commentaries* 黃帝內經素問集注 (Beijing: Xueyuan Press, 2002), p. 241.

Guanzi, "Tai Lu" chapter says, "Sages are those who go out with heaven and return with earth. They are with heaven and earth like yin and yang, restraining dry and moist to form models, moving according to the time (*shi* 時)."[76]

Time is the alteration of yinyang, whereas timing is how yinyang operates. To understand this connection, we must consider that, in early Chinese thought, time is not conceived of or spoken of in the abstract. The word we have been using for "timing" (*shi* 時) literally means the seasons. The word for "day" is literally the sun, *ri* 日, and the month is literally the moon, *yue* 月. An age or an era is also a generation, *shi* 世. The words for a year, *nian* (年) and *sui* (歲), both mean "harvest." Thus, to speak of next year is also to speak of the next harvest. The most central concept is *shi*, timing or seasons. Time (*shi*) in Chinese is a particular point as well as a movement.

It follows from this contextual and concrete view of time that there exists a certain configuration of forces at any given time, and these configurations are conceived of in terms of yinyang. Therefore, the *He Guanzi* answers the question, "what is yinyang?" by saying yinyang is timing.[77] The *Baihutong* uses yinyang to define a period of time: "Time/season is the period of time, the period of yinyang alterations."[78] (時者, 期也，陰陽消息之期也).We have already seen how yinyang was used to explicate changes in the natural world. Because timing dictates the pattern of these changes, it is inseparable from yinyang. The most obvious example is the steady alternation of days and the seasons. For example, the *Guanzi* says:

> Spring and autumn, winter and summer represent shifts in the Yin and Yang. The shortening and lengthening of the seasons represent the function of their beneficence. The alternations of day and night represent their transformations. Thus the Yin and Yang maintain proper order. But even if they lacked this proper order, what was excessive could not be lessened, nor what was deficient be increased. No one can add to or detract from Heaven.[79]

The chapter on distinctions among things in the *Shuoyuan* connects yinyang to time more broadly:

---

[76] X. Wang, (ed.), 王心湛, *Collected Interpretations of He Guanzi*, 鶡冠子集解 (Shanghai: Guangyi Press, 1936), p. 36.

[77] Ibid., p. 15.

[78] *Baihungtong*, p. 429.

[79] Rickett, *Guanzi*, p. 116–117.

Heaven and earth has its power (*de* 德); uniting with it generates the *qi* (氣) that has vital essence; yinyang wax and wane and then changes have timing. If the timing is attained order will follow and transformation will take place; if the timing is lost there will be disorder.[80]

(夫天地有德, 合則生氣有精矣; 陰陽消息, 則變化有時矣. 時得而治矣, 時得而化矣, 時失而亂矣).

Yinyang as a manifestation of timing reminds us that human nature has a source in heaven and earth and must operate in relation to them, forming a third. We see this in a comment from the *Liezi*: "Formerly, the sages reduced heaven and earth to a system by means of yin and yang."[81] The yinyang structure of change and temporality cannot be separated from yinyang as a strategy for acting effectively and for taking advantage of the timing of heaven. Yinyang offers a context for configuring the essential date that heaven and earth supply for human beings, who must utilize natural phenomena to guide human actions. Consider one passage from the *Guanzi*:

> Quiet your people, pay attention to the seasons, await their commands, then take action. Therefore it is said: Act in accord with whatever the Yin and the Yang send forth and follow Heaven and Earth's constant standards. Expand and contract in accordance with the Yin and the Yang, and rely on them to do what is proper.[82]

Things always exist in a moment of change (*bian* 變) with a dynamic configuration of forces, as we have seen in the *Yijing* and the idea of *xiang* (images), both of which represent this configuration through yinyang. That configuration of forces offers behavioral guidance. In fact, because yinyang refers to forces rather than static elements, all strategic uses of yinyang can be seen as appeals to proper timing.

We have seen that time and timing as they relate to acting appropriately in the face of the demands of the moment are not clearly distinguished in classical Chinese and use the same term, *shi* (時). Knowing timing means knowing how to act in accordance with the patterns of change. The world is not a set of objects with properties but a self-organizing process with a built-in engine of yinyang. Thus, in conceptualizing yinyang through timing, human beings are not simply agents manipulating a world through representational knowledge. They are participants in the

---

[80] Liu Xiang 劉向. *Shuo Yuan Yin De,* Harvard-Yenching Institute Sinological Index Series No. 1., (Beijing: Harvard-Yenching Institute, 1931), p. 178.

[81] Graham (trans.), *The Book of Lieh-tzu,* p. 18.

[82] Guanzi, p. 133.

process. The rhythms of the world provide the context for action through mutual stimulation and response.

The advantages of terrain, literally "of the earth," are the other required elements for acting effectively. Timing and terrain are in practice inseparable, as we have already seen. The sun reflects equally on all things, however, with very different effects: some places are shaded and some illuminated, some are dark and some are light. As the "Zeyang" chapter of the *Zhuangzi* says, "Yin and yang mutually illuminate, mutually cover, and mutually order; the four seasons replace each other, mutually generate and mutually destroy."[83] The earth's position as it receives sunlight makes a crucial difference. This goes back to the origin of the terms yin and yang – the sunny and shady sides of a mountain, determined by both the movement of the sun and the contours of the terrain. We have already seen the associations among yinyang, timing, and spacing. While the hexagrams represent temporal configurations, they do so through spacing, through the idea of "position" [*wei* 位].

The clearest and best-known example of the use of yinyang to align with the contours of the earth is in *fengshui* (風水), which we have already examined as an art of categorizing. One broad way to approach the benefits of terrain is through three legendary figures that became models for effective human actions. The "Zun Deyi" ("Respecting Virtue and Rightness") text recently excavated at Guodian says:

> Yu the Great's moving the waters was by following the *Dao* of water. Zao Fu's riding horses was by following the *Dao* of horses. Hou Ji's planting the earth was by following the *Dao* of the earth. There is nothing that does not have its *Dao*, but the *Dao* of human beings is nearest. Thus, gentlemen first select the *Dao* of human beings.[84]

> 禹之行水, 水之道也. 造父之禦馬, 馬也之道也. 後稷之藝地, 地之道也. 莫不7有道焉, 人道為近. 是以君子人道之取先.

These three popular heroes exemplify advantageous human action, which comes from following along with the way of things, whether of water, horses, or human beings. Water is a dominant metaphor relating to terrain. Yu the Great (大禹 Dayu) was the legendary founder of the Xia Dynasty (2070 – 1600 B.C.E.). He mastered flood control techniques to tame rivers and lakes. In *Mengzi*, chapter 3, there is an account of how bad these floods were. Originally, Yu's father Gun (鯀) was assigned

---

[83] Chen, *Commentaries on Zhuangzi*, p. 696.

[84] Liu, Zhao (ed.), *Guodian Chujian Jiaoyi* 郭店楚簡校釋, (Fuzhou: Fujian People's Press, 2003), p. 122.

by King Yao (堯) to tame the raging flood waters. Over nine years, Gun built strong dikes all over the land in the hope of containing the waters. During a period of heavy flooding, however, all of these dikes collapsed and the project failed miserably. Gun was executed by King Shun (舜). Yu learned from his father's mistakes and took a different approach to manage the water. Instead of using force to combat the floods, such as dikes to stop up the water, he used the way of *shudao* 疏導 (redirecting) and *shunni* 順逆 (following along/going against). He dredged new river channels to direct the flow of the water, going with rather than resisting the tendencies of the water. These channels served both as outlets for the torrential waters and as irrigation conduits to distant farmlands. He, thus, successfully controlled the floods. His method serves as the metaphor of flowing along in attunement with terrain to get things done with excellence, ease, and sustainability. The *Mengzi* says that Yu succeeded by using "the way of water," and "enacting what was without work."[85] The *Mengzi* uses both Yu and Houji as examples of how to arrange things by following the advantages of terrain.[86]

Through the embodiment of yinyang, one will gain a natural power from heaven and earth, be granted the ability to manage one's internal and external world, and finally, attain a kind of magical charisma. This is the ideal of the cultivated person. In the *Huainanzi*, this adaptability is described as follows: "Sages can be yin, and they can be yang; they can be weak, and they can be strong; in tempo with the times, they are active or still; in accordance with inner substance of things, they establish merit."[87]

Although this description seems to emphasize timing – suiting the demands of the particular moment – the key is in adapting to the particular contours of the situation. As Francois Jullien puts it, "As we shall see repeatedly, in China efficacy is effective through adaptation."[88]

Yinyang Strategy Factor II: Yin as Background and Non-presence

Human understanding is a matter of integrating the information that confronts us into our broader experience of life. The depth and scope of what is present is usually only a gateway into a much more vast and

---

[85] Van Norden (trans.), *Mengzi* (6B11), p. 168; (4B26), p. 111.
[86] Ibid., 3A4, p. 70.
[87] Roth, *The Huainanzi*, p. 510.
[88] Jullien, *A Treatise on Efficacy*, p. 51.

open field. All knowing is situated within unseen structures, and our orientation toward what is known always emerges from what is not fully known. Yinyang as a mode of interpretation is often vague and is always incomplete. Greater precision and completeness are added by background capacities and linkages. Yinyang strategy not only pays attention to heaven's timing and earth's advantages but also draws particular attention to background and non-present structures.

One key concept for this reliance on background factors is the term *yin* 因, which should not be confused with the yin 陰 of yinyang. In contemporary Western expression, this *yin* is similar to the idea of resourcefulness. In the *Lüshi Chunqiu*, the notion of relying on (*yin* 因) has great importance: "By employing the techniques of 'relying' [*yin*], the poor and lowly can vanquish the rich and noble and the small and weak can control the strong and big."[89] Relying is a technique or strategy for success. On what does one rely? The *Lüshi Chunqiu* says that Guanzi used the technique (*shu* 術) of relying and then explains: "The wise invariably rely on the right timing or opportunity. But there is no guarantee that the timing or opportunity will come, so one must also rely on ability, just like making use of a boat or a cart."[90] Another passage in the same section says, "The three dynasties treasured nothing as much as relying on the natural state of things. If one can treasure 'relying,' one will be undefeated."[91] What one relies on is the natural propensity of things, such as water's power or the tendencies of the human heart. We have already seen this idea in the descriptions of Yu managing the great flood. We could say that he relied on the natural tendencies of water and the contours of the terrain.

The *Lüshi Chunqiu* articulates this ability to be resourceful through examples:

> When those scrutinize the sky to recognize the four seasons by examining the zodiac constellations, this is an instance of relying on the natural state of things. When those who keep the calendars know when the first and last days of the month will occur by observing the movements of the moon, this is a case of relying on the natural state of things [*yin* 因].[92]

The uniqueness of a sage is in this ability. Another passage illuminates further:

[89] Knoblock and Riegel, *The Annals of Lü Buwei*, p. 358.
[90] Ibid., p. 360.
[91] Ibid., p. 364.
[92] Ibid., p. 367.

The true kings of antiquity acted less on their own and more by "relying on." The person of relying on has the art/technique of a sovereign; action is the way of ministers. Acting by oneself entails disturbance; reliance on others will have quiescence. Relying on winter creates cold; relying on summer creates heat – what need is there for the sovereign to act in that matter? Thus, it is said, the *Dao* of the lord is not knowing and not acting. Yet because it is worthier than knowing and acting, it attains the truth.[93]

As a strategy, relying shifts the focus away from one's own actions and powers and instead toward what is already available in a given situation. In different conditions, one needs to figure out what kinds of things can be relied on. What are the resources available? There can be different kinds of relying under different circumstances, however, everything must have something to rely on for its own existence. There is a Chinese saying, "If you live by the mountain, then you will be fed by mountains; if you live by the river, you will be fed by the river." This belief can also make clear why *guanxi* 關係 (connections) permeates all aspects of today's Chinese social life. This background is not chosen but is pre-existing. It is the unnoticed milieu that makes everything else possible. Thus, the *Lüshi Chunqiu* claims one of the five sagely things is to know the "hidden and stored."[94]

Relying, as a form of nonaction or *wuwei*, indicates the importance of trusting the rhythm, patterns, timing, and opportunities that have an inherent tendency to unfold in a given moment. This relying is different from a causal relationship that articulates a linear sequence between events. Relying is embedded in complexity; it is relying in the context of associations. What sages rely on are the yin factors: yin emphasizes background and hidden structures. The yang specifies what is dominant, open, and in front. Thus, yinyang itself presupposes the role of background knowledge. In the *Zhuangzi*, supreme brightness is the source of yang, and the gate of dark secrets is the source of yin.

An early reference to this mindfulness of the background comes from the *Daodejing*'s statement in chapter 42: "All the myriad things *fu* yin *bao* yang (負陰抱陽) [embody yin and embrace yang]."

Bao (抱), to embrace, literally refers to putting your arms around something, often in a sense of holding something valuable, as in "to *bao* your child." The myriad things all embrace or wrap their arms around the yang, which is in front. The idea of *bao* yang is derived from interface with

---

[93] Ibid., p. 416.

[94] The other things are that going first is courage, leaving last is righteousness, knowing the time is wisdom, and sharing is benevolence. Ibid., p. 251.

the sun: one faces south and embraces the direct sunlight. Another extension is confronting what is in front and seeing what is present (*you*有).

The word *fu* (負), translated here as "embodying," has more than twenty meanings in a classical dictionary. One of the main meanings of *fu* is to carry or bear something on your back, not facing you but carried in the background. Thus, this word *fu* in the *Daodejing* can be taken as *bei* 背 (on your back), a term we have already seen in *fengshui* in the phrase *beishan* (背山): relying on or backing up to a mountain. *Fuyin* (負陰) refers to things that are not confronted but still carried along. It is carrying something unseen or non-present, coordinated with *wu*, nonbeing or absence. The *fuyin* always predicates a set of situations, a unique way to get a hold of the world. By extension, it is derived from the back that is away from sun, or the absence of sunlight. Taken together, *fuyin* and *baoyang* reflect awareness of two elements: the hidden underlying order and the explicit goal in front of us.

Although *baoyang* and *fuyin* are inseparable, our natural tendency is to look toward what stands before us, what is yang. A common element of yinyang is to counteract this tendency with a focus on yin. Yin is a function that should be guarded (*shou* 守) and protected (*bao* 保) – as the *Liezi* says, "If you want to be hard (*gang* 剛), you must guard it with softness (*ruo* 柔); if you want to be strong, you must protect it with weakness (*rou* 柔). Hardness that is accumulated in softness will be necessarily hard and strength that is accumulated in weakness will be necessarily strong."[95] In action, one should "stay at the front by keeping to the rear."[96]

The necessity of considering yin factors lies on several different levels, most of which we have already addressed in more abstract terms. Emptiness (*xu* 虛) and nothingness (*wu* 無) are always intertwined with fullness (*shi* 實) and being (*you* 有). Consider, for example, a vessel or container (*qi* 器), as discussed in the *Daodejing*. A vessel only serves its purpose because of its emptiness. We have already seen the same term, *qi*, used to label concrete and functional things existing "under forms." Thus, concrete things themselves always exist through an element of emptiness. Non-presence is embedded in presence. Even though we might say that both are equally important, our tendency to see only the present and the difficulty of addressing the non-present suggests a deliberate strategy for focusing on the unseen.

This point is nicely illustrated by a special device for visualizing this natural pattern involving emptiness, known as the *qiqi* 琦器, which has

[95] Graham (trans.), *The Book of Lieh-tzu*, p. 83.
[96] Ibid., p. 158.

been restored in the Forbidden City in Beijing. This container holds a certain amount of water. If it is filled with too much water, it will tip over; if it has too little water, it will also tilt. The perfect condition will contain just the right amount of water and leave certain empty space in the container. This right amount is measured by the amount of empty space.

As these examples suggest, one must attend to yang when yin is strong and yin when yang is strong. In a sense, then, what counts as background (and, thus, as yin) in a given context alternates. We have already seen the way that something that is yin can also be considered yang (if particularly prominent) and something yang can be treated as yin (when weak and incipient). Nonetheless, because we naturally focus on what is present and available, yang, there is a priority for attention to yin as its origin. Things/events emerge from the dark or background. We pay great attention to the foreground and often ignore the background. Farmers do not simply see what will grow out of the soil, but also make an effort to cultivate the soil, that is, attending to the background. A seed has been embraced (*bao*) in the depths of the earth, however, growth and nourishment will allow it to spring up and be on display. Farming is very similar to mothering, as special attention is needed in cultivation and growth. If the world is unfolded as an explicit order, as yang, the sunlight, it is also always enfolded in an implicit order, as yin, the background. The two sides exist in a time-space continuum. It is yin that is the variable and decides the outcome of the event that actually occurs. The *Huangdi Neijing* explains how yin acts as a hidden force:

> Heaven covers while earth carries and then the myriad things are generated. If a thing has not yet come out of the soil it is called the place of yin; it is yin within yin. If it comes out of the soil it is yang within yin. Yang gives straightness while yin is the master. Thus generation relies on spring, growth relies on summer, harvesting relies on autumn, and storing relies on winter. If they lose their constancy then heaven and earth will have four blockages.[97]

This priority of the unseen yin is expressed nicely elsewhere in the same chapter of the *Huangdi Neijing*, which says, "Yin is inside but it guards yang; yang is outside but it is sent by yin"[98] (陰在內, 陽之守也; 陽在外; 陰之使也). The order of yin and yang is a natural order because everything emerges from the dark ground and hidden places. A plant comes from a seed that has been hidden in the depths of the earth. The power

---

[97] Zhang (ed.), *Huangdi Neijing*, p. 69–70.
[98] Ibid., p. 58.

of growing and nourishment below the surface allows it to spring up and be displayed.

We can also consider the relationship between *baoyang* and *fuyin* in terms of the perceiver or agent. Our knowing and understanding of what we encounter functions against a contingently existing set of background capacities and practices. In other words, our system of representation requires a nonrepresentational set of capacities to function. This yin can be seen as a horizon, in Charles Taylor's terms: "Things take on importance against a background of intelligibility. Let us call this a horizon."[99] Yinyang is a contingent framework in the sense that it always exists within a background that contains a wide range of presuppositions and abilities. Recognizing the background is a footing for the discernment of yinyang. There is a yin mode, perhaps seen as a pre-reflective mode, before awareness has occurred. There is a yang mode, a reflective mode, in which one must observe one's self and attend to the inner processes, becoming aware of what is taking place. We have a limited ability to concentrate, and we sometimes are not able to see something we are in fact looking at. Our brain is trained to see the patterns that we are used to and does not see those unexpected things and events.

However, the yinyang strategy requires one to bring the hidden yin background factors into awareness. The yinyang strategy at its core is about the background capacity and competence. The crux of yinyang is that yin symbolizes a nonrepresentational background and non-presence. Yinyang strategy moves from what is at the center of our conscious attention to the periphery. It always keeps your mind on the yin, the less obvious factor at a given moment. This orientation goes against our natural tendencies, which is to avoid the dark and unseen. It is said that one's greatest fear is the unknown. One wants to know and even clings to the illusion of knowing. This assumption creates fixed views locked in on only what immediately confronts us, and it prevents the mind from navigating outside of its own barriers.

Yinyang perception and strategy is always a process of interpretation. It presupposes knowledge of yinyang schemes or patterns. If we see a yang, we cannot be ignorant of yin-ish things, because they have always been there, in time and space. It is not so much that we build knowledge based on what we objectively perceive, but that we perceive according to what we know. All representations, whether in language, thought, or experience, only succeed in representing a set of nonrepresentational capacities. This point has been widely acknowledged in philosophy, as,

[99] C. Taylor, *The Ethics of Authenticity* (Oxford: Oxford University Press, 1991), p. 37.

for example, in John Searle's "The Hypothesis of Background." The thesis of the background is that "intentional phenomena such as meanings, understandings, interpretations, beliefs, desires, and experiences only function within a set of background capacities that are not themselves intentional."[100]

The importance of *baoyang* and *fuyin* brings out an epistemic assumption underlying yinyang thinking: any given point of knowing is only a small knot in a giant and consistent web. On the one hand, we might take this as leading to what Graham calls a "great man metaphysic": "The Great Man, by identifying himself with whole, widens his perspective to a full view of everything, with the result that he sees finite things in proportion, as only relatively great or small, good or bad."[101] On the other hand, however, this yinyang frame conceives of our surroundings as the immediately accessible portions of a to-be-known world, which extends in space and time beyond the limits of our immediate access. This directly accessible portion is like the stem of a plant: as the Chinese expression says, "following the runner is the best way to find a hidden melon" (*Shunteng mogua* 順藤摸瓜). Ordinary experience yields patterns, which lend themselves to immediate and spontaneous assimilation. The yinyang knower locates herself within this fixed and largely predictable perceptual world. This is not a mystical awareness of the whole, but rather a concrete way of interacting with particulars by tracing out their broader networks. This sense of the limits of our knowing connects closely to what we discussed earlier as *youhuan yishi* (憂患意識), the sense of care and caution toward the future.

Understanding contains an indirectness and indetermination that is not yet explicit. We might say that yinyang seeks out meaning in experience that is not immediate, but begins in the formless and meaningless, as one aspect of the intricate web of life. Practically speaking, this indicates that when one faces a task, one needs to make an intentional shift from the immediate to the wider spectrum, paying attention to the background and implicit patterns. This yinyang strategy epitomizes spontaneous cognition of environmental relations. This kind of cognitive power resides in its capacity to elucidate the relationship between a person and her surroundings. It clarifies one's existential experience and enables one to better orient oneself in one's environment. This orientation is one basis for *yinyang shu* 陰陽術 (strategy). The *Houhanshu*, thus,

---

[100] J. Searle, *The Rediscovery of the Mind* (Cambridge, MA: The MIT Press, 1992), p. 175.
[101] Graham (trans.), *The Book of Lieh-tzu*, p. 144.

refers to "the yinyang *shu* of hiding and plumbing the depths" (陰陽隱側
之術).[102] The *Huainanzi* takes the core of *shu* as "Looking at the root and
knowing the branches, observing the finger and seeing the return [path],
holding to the One and responding to the many, grasping the essentials
and ordering the details. These are called 'techniques'" [*shu*].[103]

Application of Yinyang Strategy I: Yinyang Bingfa (Military Strategy)

The *Zuozhuan* reports that the most important tasks of governing in
ancient China were ritual sacrifices (*si* 祀) and battles (*rong* 戎).[104] *Si* is
the form of worship that involves setting up correct rituals and sacrifices.
Rong are the military affairs that determine how to protect the people
and win battles. Yinyang strategy developed through this rich tradition
of military strategy, known as *Bingfa* 兵法. The meaning of the word *bing*
兵 in ancient times included a blade or weapons in general or armed
forces.[105] *Fa* 法 had a wide range of meanings, such as "model" or "law."
Here, it means a method, and *Bingfa* is usually translated as the "art of
war."

The school of military thought was one of the hundred schools in
early China, even though it was not listed among the six schools in the
Shiji. The "Yiwenzhi" chapter of the *Hanshu* summarizes the school of
military affairs: "The school of military affairs comes from the responsibilities of military officers and the position of martials. From spring
to autumn they can launch surprise attacks, hiding and transforming
their armies at the same time."[106] During the Northern Song (960–1127
C.E.), seven classical Chinese military texts were compiled for military
education, together known as the *Wujing Qishu* 武經七書 (*Seven Military
Classics*).[107] They have gained popularity in contemporary China (and

[102] Fan, *Houhanshu* (*The Book of Later Han*), p. 2735.
[103] Roth, The *Huainanzi*, p. 720.
[104] M. Li, (ed.), *Zuozhuan Yizhu* 左傳譯注, (Shanghai: Shanghai Guji Press, 1998), p. 578.
[105] L. Ling, 李零, *The Only Regulation: Sunzi's Philosophy of Conflicts* 唯一的規則:孫子的鬥
爭哲學 (Beijing: San Lian Press, 2010), p. 13.
[106] Ban Gu, *Hanshu*, p. 1762.
[107] The seven texts are *The Art of Warfare*, 孫子兵法 (Late Spring and Autumn, 770–476
B.C.E.); *Wu Zi Art of Warfare*, 吳子兵法 (Warring States Period, 475–221 B.C.E.); *Six Secret Strategic Teachings* 六韜 (Warring States Period, 475–221 B.C.E.); *Methods of Sima*,
司馬法 (Spring and Autumn, 770–476 B.C.E.); *Three Strategies of Huang Shigong*, 三略
(the Han Dynasty, 206 B.C.E.–220 C.E.); *Wei Liao-zi*, 尉繚子 (the Warring States Period,

elsewhere in the world) and are currently used in business management and administration.

The *Lüshi Chunqiu* gives an account of military matters and its fundamental principles:

> One must have moral right on one's side; one must be wise; one must have courage. ... If one is wise, seasonal changes will be understood. If seasonal changes are understood, the metamorphosis from empty to full and from ascent to descent and the techniques of first and last, far and near, releasing and keeping will be understood.[108]

Knowing the changes of the seasons and rhythms of the world is a necessary part of wisdom, and yinyang became the way to this wisdom.

The *Hanshu* analyzes military strategy into four interplaying elements: *quanmou* 權謀 (authority and schemes), *xingshi* 形勢 (circumstances and situation), yinyang 陰陽, and *jiqiao* 技巧 (skills and techniques).[109] The central point of this strategy is working with the power of the unseen to build leverage that can conquer those who might be stronger. The recipe for an effective war strategy is to find the pulse of the rhythm of change. We can briefly consider each element.

Quanmou 權謀 is the relationship between military force and state government. *Quan* 權 is power, or political position; *mou* 謀 is military strategy. Many military texts discuss employing the army in association with leading the state. The *Daodejing*, chapter 57, says "use the what is right (*zheng* 正) to govern the state, and use *qi* 奇 (surprise/strangeness) to employ the military."[110] The *Hanshu* expands this in explaining *quanmou* teaching:

> *Quanmou* is using what is right to protect the state and using surprise to employ the army. First plan and then go to battle, combining circumstances and situation, embracing *yinyang*, and using skills and techniques.[111]
> (權謀者, 以正守國, 以奇用兵, 先計而後戰, 兼形勢, 包陰陽, 用技巧者也).

One assesses the situation in terms of the strengths and weaknesses both of one's self and of one's opponent. One then finds resources and leverages them by integrating circumstances and situations (*xingshi*), yinyang, and skills and techniques (*jiqiao*).

475–221 B.C.E.); and *Duke Li of Wei Answering Emperor Taizong of Tang*, 李衛公問對 (Tang Dynasty, 618–907 C.E.).

[108] Knoblock and Riegel, *The Annals of Lü Buwei*, p. 199.

[109] Ban Gu, *Hanshu*, p. 1758.

[110] Modified translation from Hans-Georg Moeller (trans.), *Daodejing: A Complete Translation and Commentary*, (Chicago and La Salle: Open Court, 2007), p. 133.

[111] Ban Gu, *Hanshu*, p. 1758.

Xingshi 形勢, circumstances and situation, are one of the most important factors in military affairs. It discloses an underlying order that extends to the field of leadership, negotiation, and medical practice. *Hanshu* explicates *xingshi*:

> The one who has *xingshi* is just like the movement of thunder and the rising of wind, last in issuing out but first in reaching completion, separating and uniting, changing and transforming without regularity, and managing opponents through lightness and quickness.[112]

> 形勢者, 雷動風舉, 後發而先至, 離合背鄉, 變化無常, 以輕疾制敵者也.

Xing 形 is what is seen, the manifestation of fixed shape. *Shi* 勢 is hidden and in the background, something dynamic in the making. Francois Jullien states that these two notions

> lie at the heart of Chinese strategy, forming a pair: on the one hand, the notion of a situation or configuration (*xing*), as it develops and takes shape before our eyes (as a relation of forces); on the other hand, and counterbalancing this, the notion of potential (*shi*), which is implied by that situation and can be made to play in one's favor.[113]

According to Roger Ames, the term *shi* has at least four clusters of meanings: "1) aspect, situation, circumstance, conditions; 2) dispositions, configuration, outward shape; 3) force, influence, momentum, authority; and 4) strategic advantage, purchase."[114]

As in Jullien's description, *shi* is entailed in *xing*, and *xing* relies on *shi*. Their relationship is like the ocean to waves, or galloping to a horse. *Xing* is the shape of the waves or the horse itself. *Shi* is the hidden energy, the potential force in the wave or in the horse. It is powerful and is ready to mobilize a given entity. Everything should be seized both in *xing*, its manifested form, and in *shi*, its potential power to do work.

Sunzi uses an example to illustrate this *xingshi* interplay: drawing a bow, aiming it, and releasing are three steps of *xingshi*. Drawing is *xing*, aiming at the target is *shi*, and pulling the trigger is *ji* 技 (skill).[115] The *shi* is potential energy ready to be put into action. *Xing* and *shi* are interwoven into a whole: there is no *xing* without *shi*, and there is no *shi* without

---

[112] Ibid.

[113] Jullien, *A Treatise on Efficacy*, p. 17.

[114] D.C. Lau and R.T. Ames (trans.), *The Art of Warfare, A Translation of the Classic Chinese Work of Philosophy and Strategy* (New York: State University of New York Press, 2003), p. 73.

[115] R.T. Ames (trans.), *Sun-Tzu, The Art of Warfare* (New York: Ballantine Books, 1993), p. 118.

xing. *Xing* is easy to see, whereas *shi* is hard to know. Military affairs have no fixed forms, just like water has no fixed forms. This changeable form is the result of *shi*.[116] The *Daodejing* explains, "*Dao* generates them, *de* nourishes them, things shape them, and *shi* completes them."[117] Things are completed through *shi*. The importance of the terms *xing* and *shi* goes beyond just military strategy, extending to all aspects of effective governing. In the *Qian Hanji* 前漢記 (*Records of the Early Han*), the Han emperor Gaozu explains the technique, *shu*, to set policies and determine victory. The three key elements are *xing*, *shi*, and the genuine (*qing* 情).[118] In fact, the *Hanshu* defines the Daoist school by using the same three terms, explaining their relationship in terms of the *daoshu*, the Daoist strategy, which "has no fixed *shi*, no constant *xing*, and thus can seek the genuine characteristics of the myriad things."[119]

The *shu* of war relies on a general principle concerning the nature of change and how to manipulate it to one's own advantage. No situation that one confronts is independent or isolated; every event is situated and unfolds within a broad and complex configuration. Going about in the world, we need to bring the whole into focus from our own particular position. This position is like a spot in a field. This wholeness can be seized through the lens of yinyang. Thus, *xingshi* is further manifested in another indispensible tactic, the proper interplay between emptiness (*xu*) and fullness (*shi*). In the *Daodejing*, emptiness is the characteristic of *Dao* as unseen or non-present. In military affairs, emptiness and fullness (*xushi* 虛實) elucidates the relationship between oneself and others. It scrutinizes strengths and weaknesses so that a strategy for attack or avoiding schemes emerges. What is full and what is empty can only be defined relationally, through a link with otherness. Using your fullness you can attack the other's lack, or you can conceal your own emptiness. Emptiness-and-fullness is the interplay between oneself and others, and a special tactic in military affairs.

The connection between emptiness and fullness is nicely illustrated in a story from the famous *Battle of Red Cliff* (208 C.E.) in which one of the best-known strategists of all time, Zhu Geliang 諸葛亮 (181–234 C.E.), stayed up all night to devise a strategy to defeat the powerful and well-armed forces of Cao Cao 曹操 (155–220 C.E.). Zhu had a limited army and a shortage of supplies, an army of 30,000 facing an army of 100,000.

---

[116] Ibid., p. 124.
[117] Modified translation from Moeller, *Daodejing*, p. 121. (道生之, 德畜之物形之, 勢成之).
[118] Zhao Rui 赵蕤 (ed.), *Qian Hanji* (Changchun Press, 2006), p. 249.
[119] Ban Gu, *Hanshu*, p. 2713.

Zhu needed to utilize other resources, using his lack or emptiness (*xu*) to fight Cao Cao's fullness (*shi*). So he turned to the natural conditions for help, using the method of relying. He studied the weather conditions and observed the movement of a turtle, which he took as indicating a heavy fog for the next morning. He filled boats with images of soldiers made from straw and then brought them in close to Cao Cao's troops. In the fog, Cao Cao's troops took them for invading soldiers and shot 10,000 arrows into them. Zhu Geliang then had the boats return, having simultaneously gained arms for his troops and taken them from his enemy without any cost to his own side. This story became a classic model for the use of emptiness-and-fullness, making the empty appear full and using one's emptiness to attack the enemy's fullness. This interplay between emptiness and fullness is also an illustration of yinyang in operation. The story also exemplifies points of strategy discussed in earlier sections, showing how yinyang strategy skillfully uses and relies on given conditions, such as timing and the weather, all of which are in motion.

Application of Yinyang Strategy II: Charioteering

We have already seen various *shu*, methods or techniques, compared to the ability to ride a horse or steer a chariot. The horse was a very significant image in many early Chinese texts. Managing horses effectively was a necessary condition for success, and horse-driven chariots were crucial for early military battles. The horse was, thus, a symbol of military culture and could be the sign of victory as well as the image of a king. The *sima*司馬, the officers of the calvary (literally officers of the horse, *ma*), were also the officers for military affairs during the Zhou Dynasty, and the term "horse" was used to refer to military leaders in the Shang Dynasty. The horse was even a common exemplar for debates about language and logic, as Gong Sunlong's (公孫龍 320–250 B.C.E.) most famous argument was that "a white horse is not a horse." (白馬 非馬). The *Zhuangzi* goes so far as to say that the myriad thing are one horse (萬物, 一馬).[120]

The best connection between the metaphor of charioteering and the use of yinyang strategy appears in the *Huainanzi*:

> Therefore, the Great Man calmly has no worries and placidly has no anxieties. He takes Heaven as his canopy; Earth as his carriage; the four seasons

---

[120] Ziporyn (trans.), *Zhuangzi*, p. 12.

4.1. Statue of Charioteer found in the tomb of Emperor Qin
Shihuang (259 B.C.E.–210 B.C.E.) (Xi'an)

as his steeds, and yin and yang as his charioteers. He rides the clouds and
soars through the sky to become a companion of the power that fashions
and transforms us. Letting his imagination soar and relaxing his grip, he
gallops through the vast vault [of heavens]....Thus, with Heaven as your
canopy, nothing will be uncovered; With Earth as your carriage, nothing
will be unsupported; With the four seasons as your steeds, nothing will
be unemployed. With yin and yang as your charioteers, nothing will be
incomplete.[121]

The four seasons are the horses, and yinyang is the driver. In this way, the
Great Man can ride through the clouds and beyond the sky. He will go
with transformation and change, doing as he pleases and unfolding with
rhythm. He gallops over an infinitely vast land.

The *Huainanzi* here compares yinyang to *yu* 御, the skill of steering a
chariot. *Yu* is one of six ancient arts in the *Zhouli*.[122] The character for *yu*
consists of three parts: walking (*xing* 行), a rope (*sheng* 繩), and human
being (*ren* 人). Putting them together, a human being holds the reins while
riding a horse; thus, it is the art of navigating a path for a horse-drawn
chariot (Figure 4.1).[123] Of course, this can extend to navigating any path,
from one's personal life to political organizations. We can speculate: why

[121] Roth, *The Huainanzi*, p. 52.
[122] The other five arts are: rites, music, archery, calligraphy, and mathematics 禮、樂、
射、書、數.
[123] See "Briefing on Excavation of Palace No. 3 of Capital Xianyang in Qin Dynasty", 秦都
咸阳第三号宫殿建筑遗址发掘简报, Kaogu and Wenwu, 考古与文物 (*Archaeology and
Cultural Relics*), 1980, (2).

would horse riding be one of the six arts? It is about training someone to become a superb horse rider by cultivating a yinyang intelligence by which one can easily and artfully locate oneself in relation to one's *milieu*.

We see the purpose of *yu* training in the five ways the *Zhouli* gives for evaluating excellence in horse riding.[124] The first (*ming he luan* 鳴和鸞) is synchronizing the sound of two bells on the carriage. If the horse and carriage move smoothly, the bells will make rhythmic sounds that can measure the skill of the driver. The second (*zhu shui qu* 逐水曲) is passing through dangerous and complicated winding roads along a river without falling down into the water. The third (*guo jun biao* 過君表) is demonstrating good temperament by staying calm and showing sincerity and respect when passing important sites. The fourth (*wu jiao qu* 舞交衢) is crossing busy traffic intersections smoothly. The fifth (*zhu qin zuo* 逐禽左) is herding animals onto the left to put them in the best position for hunting. As we can see, the elements of horse riding go beyond winning races. In the *Hanfeizi*'s commentary on the *Daodejing*, there is a classic story about King Zhao of Jin learning the art, *shu*, of charioteering. After learning the art, King Zhao was eager to defeat his master. He requested three races with three different horses, however, he lost all three times. He was angry at the master and thought that he had not taught him a complete skill. The master told him:

> I have given you all the techniques you need to ride a horse. However, there is a deficiency in your usage of these skills. The most important thing for the art of charioteering is to have the horse peacefully reside with the chariot and to have the rider's heart/mind come together with horse. However, you only care about who is in front and who is behind. If you were behind, you worried about catching me; but if you were ahead, you worried about being caught by me. There is always a rider either ahead or behind. If all of your attention focuses on me, how can you come together with the horse? This is the reason why you lost the race.[125]

Clearly, a good horse rider must be able to peacefully work with a controlled flow that responds to unrestrained forces and variations, and not focus on one single specific external fact such as who will win the race. Skill at charioteering is not a case of courage (*yong* 勇), but rather a demonstration of a kind of intelligence (*zhi* 智), a strategy for becoming an embodied navigator.

The five preceding standards define a good charioteer. Based on the *Huainanzi*'s metaphor, we can see them as demonstrations of a kind of

---

[124] Y. Wang, 王雲五 (ed.), *Zhouli* 周禮今注今譯, *The Ritual of Zhou* (Taipei: Taiwan Commercial Press, 1972), p. 193.

[125] Chen (ed.), *Hanfeizi*, p. 93.

yinyang intelligence. This technique or *shu* can be analyzed from two distinct points of view. First, yinyang intelligence is rooted in a view of the universe as an organic self-generating system. Self-organization and self-stabilization presuppose interaction between system and environment. In the case of the *shu* of horse riding, effective interaction occurs through movement. The immediate interfaces of navigating a horse-drawn carriage include the horses and their power, the terrain, the weather, and one's purpose. The horse rider is linked to the many external factors that may disturb his or her inner state and draw out different kinds of responses. It is a kind of open system that deals with environmental disturbances and processes within it. The *Huainanzi* depicts that you feel with your hand, however, you respond through your heart/mind. This is a common saying: *dexin yingshou* 得心應手, "getting it through your heart/mind and responding with your hands." In this aspect, the world to a rider is not observed but felt. The whole nexus of senses (including vision) is a felt response. Like the sting of the sunlight or rush of the wind, the act of seeing has a similar feeling. It involves the mind and body working together. The *Liezi* presents another description of the art of charioteering: "Internally, one focuses the center of the heart/mind; externally, one unites with the will of the horse. One is able to go forward and backward but there is a center and one goes around it as if with a compass. One can take the road on a long journey yet still have strength to spare."[126]

In riding horses, one can distinguish the internal (focusing the heart) and the external (the horse itself), however, the crucial point is being able to reach the center. The *Liezi* clarifies further that one receives (*de* 得) the bit and responds with the bridle; one receives in the bridle and responds in the hand; one receives in the hand and responds with the heart/mind. This way one sees without eyes and urges without a goad; relaxed in the heart/mind and straight in posture, holding six bridles and pacing twenty-four hooves to advance, withdraw, and swing around with perfect precision. The heart/mind plays a key role in adjusting the situation. One's heart/mind is synchronized and functions with the natural flow of the horse and chariot. Here, the rider is in a condition lacking deliberateness or discursive thought but has a great awareness that allows overall optimal performance.

Zhu Xi, the influential Song Dynasty Confucian, uses the analogy of horse and rider to discuss the movement and stillness of *Taiji* (Great Ultimate) and *qi*: "The movement of *Taiji* generates yang, stillness

---

[126] Graham (trans.), *The Book of Lieh-tzu*, p. 183.

generates yin. *Taiji* is *li* (pattern); *qi* is movement and stillness. When *qi* moves, *li* moves, too. They are interdependent and cannot be separated. *Taiji* is like the horse rider and movement and stillness are like the horses. Horses hold the horse rider and the rider rides the horses."[127]

We see a conception of yinyang strategy as attunement and embodiment in the *Zhuangzi*. In chapter 24, a disciple was eager to learn and get *Dao*. He thinks that getting *Dao* will enable him to get a cauldron of water to boil in the winter and to make ice in the summer. This appears to be a good method: winter is cold, so one needs boiling water; and summer is hot, so one needs the coldness of ice. However, the master answers that this is only using yang to evoke yang and using yin to evoke yin. The getting of *Dao* is different. He begins by placing two zithers in different rooms, and when he plucks a note on one, the same note on the other resonates. He then changed the tuning of one string so that it matched no proper notes, however, as soon as he plucked it, twenty-five strings on the zither resonated with it. This one sound was like the master of all the others, simply by stimulating them to resonate along with it. [128]

The *Liezi* tells the story about making music. The spring hints at the notes of the fall; the winter hints at the notes of summer.[129] Music not only shows the root scale that is associated with the four seasons, but, more importantly, reveals a pattern of hidden forces. In this sense, yinyang is not about matching one thing to another, but rather about resonating with the hidden forces at work in any situation, using such resonances to skillfully bring about results.

The second aspect of yinyang intelligence is found in adaptivity. Horse riding works with external forces and internal constraints that lead to adaptive self-organization. In this facet, adaptation is not synonymous with stability or harmony (*he*) but is closer to functional efficiency in coping with actual environmental disturbances. It is more about efficacy than about harmony. For example, what if the horse goes slowly but the rider needs to travel faster? The rider needs to initiate a way to make the horse go as fast as it can. The rider must engage in yielding and pulling movements, a dynamic yinyang play: giving and taking, pushing and pulling with the powers of the horse. The *Liezi* explains: "equalizing the give and the pull is the ultimate principle of dealing with the world."[130] What is the "equalizing" (*jun* 均)? It is the center of the wheel that can

---

[127] Li Li (ed.), *Sayings of Zhuzi*, 朱子論類 (Beijing: Chinese Press, 1999), vol. 94, p. 2376.
[128] Ziporyn (trans.), *Zhuangzi*, p. 103.
[129] Graham (trans.), *The Book of Lieh-tzu*, p. 108.
[130] Ibid., p.104.

turn to face any direction. The rider can only reach his or her goal by working with it, negotiating all variables to attain the desired result. The rider incorporates his surroundings into his perception-response loops to maintain efficacy.

Horse riding also requires human adaptation, affecting the reorganization of inherited behavior patterns to fit the existing environmental situations. This yinyang intelligence as adaptation is an indispensable instrument for the interaction between oneself and the world. Yinyang is a configuration of forces: fundamental forces that can be exerted only by certain types of configurations and the qualities that emerge from such configurations. Only sages know how to use or obtain *Dao*. *Dao* is not just getting things but knowing how to use power, like navigating a boat in moving water, or using the wind to sail at sea.

Application of Yinyang Strategy III: Sexual Practices

We can conclude this section by commenting briefly on one other application of yinyang, in sexual practices. *Fangzhong shu* 房中術, the art or technique of the bedchamber, has a long history in China that can be traced back to the pre-Qin period. Sexual practices were considered an essential element of body cultivation, health, and overall well-being. As with other Chinese practices, such as the relationship between children and parents, what was a private affair performed in one's own personal space could also directly relate to a universal shared space linked to heaven and earth. Sexual acts are cosmically meaningful events. Therefore, sex is not just a private or personal matter but rather a contribution to or distraction from the flow of cosmic *qi*. Sexual intercourse is a specific way to promote the circulation of *qi*, both on a personal level and more broadly within the cosmos, where it helps one to attain the unification of yin and yang in heaven, earth, and the human world. Men and women play the roles of heaven and earth, and together they bring this cosmic unity and generativity into their own bedroom. Human sexuality is grounded in a cosmic structure, elevating its necessity and significance. The purpose is not simply for procreation or recreation, but for consummating and exchanging cosmic energies. Yinyang strategy is an effective way to actualize this goal and has developed in a wide variety of ways.[131] It is another tangible way to "steal" (*dao*) the yinyang *qi* of heaven and earth.

---

[131] Douglas Wile comments, "The Chinese have done for sex what they have done for the soybean. Taking the raw materials of biology beyond the realm of simple stew, they have

One of the earliest sexual texts is the *Sunü Jing* 素女經 (*Classic of the Naïve Lady*), written between the Warring States Period and the Eastern Han.[132] Sunü, traditionally seen as a goddess of sex, basically acts in this text as a sex therapist for the Yellow Emperor, offering him advice on topics from the conceptual purpose and meaning of sexual intercourse to specific sexual techniques. Yinyang provides the basic framework for her views:

> All movement in the world results from the interaction of yin and yang. When yang unites with yin, yang is transformed; when yin unites with yang, yin becomes open. Yin and yang are mutually dependent in their operations. Therefore, when man is roused, [his penis] becomes hard and strong, and when woman is moved [her vagina] becomes open and enlarged. When the two ch'i [*qi*] yin and yang mingle their ching [*jing*], then their fluids are exchanged.[133]

Sexual intercourse is a natural form of yinyang exchange and the one of the two basic natural desires of human beings, a view appearing as early as the *Mengzi* (6A4), where Gaozi says that eating and sex are human nature [食色, 性也].[134] Although sex is celebrated as something natural and valuable, it must be properly regulated and directed. In other words, there must be a *shu*, an art or technique, of sexual intercourse.

Sunü declares:

> All debility in man is due to violation of the *tao* [*Dao*] of intercourse between yin and yang. Women are superior to men in the same way that water is superior to fire. This knowledge is like the ability to blend the five flavors in a pot to make delicious soup. Those who know the *tao* [*Dao*] of yin and yang can fully realize the five pleasures; those who do not will die before their time without ever knowing this joy.[135]

According to this teaching, there is correct and incorrect sexual intercourse. If one has grasped the proper method, one will be blessed with joy in the short term and a prolonged life in a long run. If one does it

---

completely transformed it into a wide variety of nourishing new forms." D. Wile, *Art of Bedchamber: The Chinese Sexual Yoga Classics Including Women's Solo Meditation Texts* (New York: State University of New York Press, 1992), p. 5.

[132] Like many sexual texts and manuals from before the Tang Dynasty, the *Sunü Jing* only survived in the *Yixing Fang*, 醫心方, a Japanese medical text compiled by 丹波康賴 (915–995).

[133] Wile, *Art of Bedchamber*, p. 86.

[134] Van Norden (trans.), *Mengzi*, p. 145.

[135] Wile, *Art of Bedchamber*, p. 85.

incorrectly, one's body and life will be affected, possibly even leading to death. Sexual intercourse was literally a matter of life and death.

The successful yinyang strategy for sexual intercourse contains three aspects. First, the man should develop a certain psychological state before and during sexual activity. He should have strong self-control and should not be driven by rash and disorderly sexual impulses. This regulation of mental and emotional states embraces three elements: settled or stable qi (*dingqi* 定氣), serene heart/mind (*anxin* 安心), and harmonious will (*hezi* 和志). The text concludes: "If the three qi are all at their utmost, one's spirit and brightness will be united 三氣皆至, 神明統歸.[136] If one's psychological state is unperturbed, one will approach sex with restraint, which will result in greater joy in the act of intercourse. This can be seen as an application of the earlier discussion of the *xinshu*, the art or technique of the heart, in which a calm heart was a prerequisite for sensory pleasures.

The second aspect of yinyang sexual strategy involves its basic principle: the most imperative demands in sexual intercourse are for the man to refrain from ejaculation to prevent the leaking of yang body fluid, and for the woman to have multiple orgasms to release yin body fluids, for the man to gather. In this way, men could get the yin they lack while retaining as much yang as possible. Thus, protecting the leaking of yang sperm and attaining yin fluid are two vital factors in sexual practice. During sexual intercourse, the man's penis, literally called the *yangju* (yang equipment), is like fire, rising quickly to be stiff and hard, yet also easily becoming soft and dysfunctional, as a fire can be easily extinguished. Woman's vagina, *yinhu* (literally the yin house), is like water, getting wet only slowly, yet having a lasting and unlimited power to keep flowing. The *yangju* must be careful and strategic to go in and out of the *yinhu* to pick up yin energy, but not to be extinguished too early or too fast. This sexual intercourse is sometimes called *caiyinshu* 採陰術, the art of picking yin.

The act of intercourse itself is often compared to a battle. Female yin energy can be released only through orgasms. So the more orgasms a woman reaches, the more yin energy she emits. On the other hand, male ejaculation ends this process of gathering or picking yin. This is seen as failure or defeat on the battlefield. The victory for man is to let woman have multiples while guarding and prolonging his erection as long as possible. The art of picking yin requires man to carefully wrestle with his own bodily functions in contending with the body of the woman. Sunü explains:

[136] Ibid., p. 85–86.

In engaging the enemy, a man should regard her as so much tiles or stone and himself as gold or jade. When his *ching* [*jing*, sperm] is aroused, he should immediately withdraw from her territory. One should mount a woman as if riding a galloping horse with rotten reins or as if fearful of falling into a deep pit lined with knife blades. If you treasure your *ching*, your life will have no limit.[137]

It is like a "battle" between fire and water. Yang is eager to unleash sexual energy before yin discharges yin energy; but just as fire can quickly be put out by water, water can slowly boil for a while. In sexual intercourse, woman's multiple orgasms are much more important than man's ejaculation, which was considered as being defeated by the woman, or having the fire be extinguished by the water. In this sexual practice of uniting yin and yang, there are "seven ills and eight benefits" (*qishun bayi* 七損八益).[138]

The core of sexual intercourse is not about male's sexual pleasure, but rather about gaining yin energy to supplement his yang energy. In later practices of sexual alchemy, "yang is concerned only to steal a bit of like essence from the heart of yin to mend its own missing link."[139] In theory, these sexual practices were designed for the benefit of men; however, it is clear that in reality, the woman gets the most enjoyment. This was specifically recognized – for woman, sex is about pleasure, *huanxi* 歡喜, whereas for men it is about not decaying, *bushuai* 不衰. We see this in another text, the *Yufang Mijue* 玉房秘訣 (*The Secret from the Jade Room*), in which the Yellow Emperor asks: "What is the *tao* [*Dao*] of intercourse between yin and yang?" Sunü answers:

There are definite characteristics to the *tao* of intercourse by which man develops his *ch'i* [*qi*] and woman eliminates all illness. The heart is gladdened and the *ch'i* strengthened. Those who are ignorant of this *tao* will be subject to decline. If you wish to know this *tao* [*dao*], it consists in calming the mind, harmonizing the emotions, and concentrating the spirit. Neither cold nor hot, neither full nor hungry, you should settle the body and compose your thoughts. Then, with a relaxed attitude, penetrate deeply and move slowly. Thrusts and withdrawals should be sparing. If you observe these principles and are careful not to violate them, then the woman will be joyful and the man will not decline.[140]

---

[137] Ibid., p. 85.
[138] Ibid., p. 89–90. Seven ills are exhaustion of the *qi*, overflow of *jing*, weak pulse, *qi* leakage, injury to the joints, hundred blockages, and exhaustion of the blood. Eight benefits are strengthening the *jing*, claiming the *qi*, profiting the internal organs, strengthening the bones, regulating the circulation, nurturing the blood, increasing the fluids, and regulating the whole body.
[139] Ibid., p. 29.
[140] Ibid., p. 86.

Sexual potency is taken as an indication of health and youth. One excavated medical/sexual text asks simply: "Why is it that the penis, which is born together with the body, dies before it?"[141] Sexual problems are problems of yinyang. In the *Sunü Jing*, the Yellow Emperor seeks advice for sexual problems:

> Sometimes during intercourse the woman is not happy, she is not moved to passion, and her secretions do not flow. The 'jade stalk' [penis] is not strong, but small and impotent. What is the reason for this?" *Sunü* answered: "Yin and Yang respond to each other's influence. Yang without yin is unhappy; yin without yang will not rise. When the man desires intercourse but the woman is not pleased, or if the woman desires intercourse but the man is not desirous, their hearts are not in harmony and their *ching chi* [*jingqi* 精氣] is not aroused.[142]

The third aspect of the yinyang sexual strategy is specific techniques and positions. They choreograph mutual response between male and female and draw attention to integrating and intertwining movements during sexual intercourse. There are nine intercourse positions, all derived from animal movements.[143] Sexual practice, after all, is a way of assimilating yin and yang. Just as day and night come in a consistent rotation, feeding off each other's presence, yin and yang also exchange positions, movements, and flowing energy in sexual intercourse. One specific method was called "nine shallow, one deep" (*jiu qian yi shen* 九淺一深) for the movement of penis. The yang equipment moves in and out while the yin house opens and closes. When they meet each other at the proper rhythm, it necessitates the best result. When the *yangju* moves in, the *yinhu* should open to embrace it; when the *yangju* moves out, the *yinhu* needs to close to increase friction. At any given moment, yin's stillness and yang's movement also follow the proper tempo. When *yangju* moves in and out vertically, the *yinhu* should be still, and when the *yinhu* contracts back and forth horizontally, the *yangju* should be at a rest and motionless. Each rhythm involves both parts working together: yang shifts between once giving then once withdrawing, while yin swings between once locking up, then once unlocking. These movements perfectly illustrate yinyang interaction and interchange, and this opening and closing of the *yinhu* most likely provided a conceptual resource for the *Daodejing*'s image of the door or gate.

[141] Harper, p. 6.
[142] Wile, *Art of Bedchamber*, p. 86.
[143] Ibid., p. 88–89.

5   Yinyang Body: Cultivation and Transformation

Health of body and tranquility of mind are the twin goals of philosophy's quest for a blessed life.

Epicurus

The subtlety of nature is greater many times over than the subtlety of the senses and understanding.

Sir Francis Bacon

The period of the Zhou Dynasty and its decline is commonly taken as a time in which Chinese thought gradually moved toward more and more humanistic and rationalistic understandings of the world and the place of human beings in it. Around the third century B.C.E., China experienced a particular shift from a mystical–religious view of the operations of the world toward naturalistic analyses of specific causes. The rise of yinyang thinking and terminology at that time is intimately connected with this shift, as yinyang became an important conceptual tool to facilitate this transition. This shift has analogies with the step from *mythos* to *logos* in the ancient Mediterranean world, and yinyang thinking functions in ways similar to the recognition of natural laws and the reduction of phenomena to elements. It advocates a rational effort to furnish an intellectual and coherent account of the natural world and the human condition. Taking a phrase from Paul Unschuld, we can say that this period was directed toward increasing "existential autonomy," allowing human beings to take more and more control over their own lives.[1] Yinyang became the most effective and multifarious concrete conceptual tool for understanding the human body.

[1] Paul Unschuld, *Medicine in China, A History of Ideas*, 25th edition (Berkeley: University of California Press, 2010), p. xxiii.

The theorization of the human body as a yinyang construct through the systematization of Chinese medicine is the best illustration of the development of yinyang thought and practice. The *Huangdi Neijing* states simply, "A good practitioner differentiates between yin and yang when observing the complexion and feeling the pulse."[2] This view is different from earlier beliefs that illness was either a curse from the ancestors or some kind of punishment. In Shang oracle inscriptions that have been found on bone and turtle shell, it is demons and the spirits of the dead that sicken the bodies of the living. Harper clarifies this view, writing, "Demonic illness reflects the belief that something with an existence outside the body has relocated on or in the body; exorcism is a logical treatment."[3] According to Harper, the character for physician, *yi* 醫, belongs to a group of Shang terms related to weapons used in exorcisms.[4] Thus, by its etymology, *yi*, physician, refers to a "shaman who heals with exorcist techniques."[5] More broadly, one finds four causes of illness mentioned in the Shang oracles bones: (1) heaven, (2) ghost and spirits, (3) deviant behavior, and (4) changes in weather.

The trend toward naturalistic explanations for illness can be traced back to at least the late Spring and Autumn and early Warring States periods. According to the *Zuozhuan*, the six forms of *qi* provide the reasons for illness. In this sense, all kinds of diseases have a natural cause in *qi*. Paul Unschuld speculates that the first step toward such naturalistic justifications may have been through appeals to the wind as a "pathological agent" – wind was closely connected to *qi*.[6] These naturalistic explanations of illness through yinyang were part of a broader trend in explaining natural phenomena. By the third century B.C.E., anatomy, pathology, illness, diagnosis, and treatments were all given naturalistic explanations, and the demonic medicine was replaced by a single system based on yinyang.

Traditional Chinese medicine uses yinyang categories and classifications (*lei*); however, it is primarily a strategy or method (*shu*) directed toward the concrete goals of health and longevity. Both aspects are ultimately based on the relationship between yinyang in the body and

---

[2] Zhang Yingan 張隱庵 (ed.), *Huangdi Neijing Commentaries* 黃帝内經素問集注 (Beijing: Xueyuan Press, 2002), p. 65.

[3] Harper (trans.), *The Mawangdui Medical Manuscripts* (London and New York: Kegan Paul International, 1998), p. 69.

[4] Ibid., p. 163.

[5] Ibid.

[6] Unschuld, *Medicine in China*, p. 67–73.

yinyang as it operates in the natural world. The understanding of the body in Chinese medicine finds its model and resource in nature itself. Yinyang was a link for the cross-fertilization between the medical tradition of macrobiotic hygiene and the more abstract fields of philosophy and cosmology, leading to a pervasive scheme for practices of body cultivation. As Harper says, "Like the philosophers, the physician (*yi*) possessed a way (*Dao*)....The transformation of medicine from an archaic craft dominated by magic-religious belief and practice into a theoretically-grounded discipline was as much a function of the new literacy as it was of rationalizing tendencies in thought."[7]

The earliest sources we have for theories of Chinese medicine clearly point to the centrality of yinyang. One source is the various medical texts that were unearthed at Mawangdui, which are thought to have been buried in 168 B.C.E.[8] We have already seen there that Shun the emperor tells his predecessor Yao that the key to cultivating life is to investigate yinyang. The most important source for early views of Chinese medicine is the *Huangdi Neijing*. It states simply, "Human beings are born and have a bodily form, and this cannot be separated from yinyang."[9] These earliest medical texts show that yinyang was imported into pre-existing health practices and inspired a systematic theorization about human anatomy, physiological and psychological functions, pathological changes, medical diagnosis, and holistic treatment. As Harper says, the *Huangdi Neijing* is "a summation of written medical knowledge edited so as to reframe older recorded teachings in terms of theoretical innovations."[10] These texts, especially the *Huangdi Neijing*, not only lay out the conceptual foundations for Chinese medicine but also provide the most systematic early account of yinyang as both a method of understanding nature and as a strategy for living well in it.

In fact, the *Huangdi Neijing* can be taken as a treatise on yinyang theory and practice, illustrating a distinctive union between pre-qin philosophical thought and various practical techniques. Unschuld describes the basic principle of this system as one of correspondence: "The phenomena of the visible and invisible world stand in mutual dependence through their association with certain lines of correspondence. The paradigm of correspondence concludes that manipulations of one element

---

[7] Harper (trans.), *The Mawangdui Medical Manuscripts*, p. 42–43, 69.

[8] See a detailed discussion and full translation in Harper (trans.), *The Mawangdui Medical Manuscripts*.

[9] Zhang, *Huangdi Neijing*, p. 241.

[10] Harper (trans.), *The Mawangdui Medical Manuscripts*, p. 88.

in a specific line of correspondence can influence other element in the same line."[11]

This thinking paradigm assumes that all natural occurrences can be incorporated into a single system of correspondence. This system of correspondence also encodes the fact that yinyang is not a substance, thing, or fixed essence, but rather a way of unfolding and coordinating multidimensional relationships that are both complex and changing.

More specifically, the naturalistic account of the human body in the *Huangdi Neijing* rests on the following assumptions: the human body shares the same categorical structure (*xianglei* 相類) with heaven, earth, and the myriad things; the pattern of pathology is the same pattern as the changes of heaven and earth; human biological rhythm should change according to the rhythms of heaven, earth, and the four seasons. These suppositions suggest, as Unschuld says, that "the image of the body has its model outside of the body."[12] As we have seen, however, we could also say that the understanding of the natural world is modeled on the structure of the body, insofar as the cosmos itself is conceived on a biological model. These presuppositions also display a central claim in Chinese thought and culture: the unity of heaven, earth, and human being. This hypothesis relies heavily on yinyang for its rational explanation and coherence. The development of yinyang through the practices of medicine secured a permanent and powerful place for yinyang in Chinese thought and culture at the same time that it broadened and systematized the meaning of yinyang. This chapter will focus on the application of yinyang in the context of the cultivation and transformation of the body.

Yinyang Is a Spectrum Not an Entity

Like all phenomena in nature, the human body and its parts, functions, and elements can be classified according to their characteristics as either yin or yang. The *Huangdi Neijing* applies yin and yang to all aspects of the body, from the smallest things like sweat to the most vital internal organs like the heart/mind. Because the human body is a network of yinyang interactions and operations, yinyang structures all aspects of medical practice: the cause of disease is the imbalance of yinyang; the diagnostic method distinguishes yinyang; the consumption of herbs and

---

[11] Unschuld, *Medicine in China*, p. 52.
[12] Ibid., p. xii.

other types of treatments all manipulate the *qi* of yinyang. Yinyang is seen as the ultimate key to a living human organism, but not as a simple proposition or formula. Yin and yang are not fixed, and they are not simply elements within the body. Rather, yinyang can be considered as like an internal space-time structure in which yin and yang mark points in relations across a spectrum and field.[13] Thus, the same element can be yin in a certain relation but yang in another, and one can talk about yin within yang, or yang within yin. The *Huangdi Neijing* identifies at least four aspects of this yinyang spectrum. We will examine each of these in this section.

Yinyang as Relating Differences

The most important function of yinyang is as a pervasive marking of a spectrum of differences within relatedness, connection, and mutual influence. Yinyang can be applied to all things that can be differentiated as opposites, contraries, or poles. As a general scheme based on the distinction between heaven and earth, "Yinyang is the male and female, blood and *qi*. Left and right are the paths of yinyang. Water and fire are the representations of yinyang. Yinyang is the beginning and capability of the myriad things."[14]

Yinyang ties all the diversified things into a complex network that assumes difference and divergence. The unifying function of yinyang is meaningful precisely because it is built on the differences within the myriad things. One can then locate correlations between these differences: "If heaven and earth are seen as yinyang, then the sweat of yang can be named as the rain of heaven and earth; the *qi* of yang can be named as the wind of heaven and earth."[15] The human body shares the same anatomical map with the universe. We can compare them side by side through their shared conceptualizations in terms of yinyang. On a basic level, the body is perceived as having two main aspects: one is like heaven, in which there is movement such as the flow of *qi*, blood, and fluids; the other is like the earth and is what has form, such as the organs, meridians, limbs, and bones. These connections lie in the analogies and correspondences between how differences relate and interact.

---

[13] "In the yinyang doctrine, the terms yin and yang no longer retain any specific meaning themselves; they function merely as categorizing symbols used to characterize the two lines of correspondence." Unschuld, *Medicine in China*, p. 56.

[14] Zhang, *Huangdi Neijing*, p. 58.

[15] Ibid., p. 63.

The *Huangdi Neijing* gives several levels for the application of yinyang differentiation:

> If we talk about human beings as yinyang, then the exterior is yang while the interior is yin. If we talk about the human body as yinyang, then the back is yang while the front is yin. If we talk about the internal depots (*zang* 臟) and palaces (*fu* 腑) within the human body as yinyang, then the depots are yin and the palaces are yang. The five internal depots are liver, heart, spleen and kidney, and they all are yin. The five palaces are gallbladder, stomach, small and large intestines, urinary bladder and triple burner, and they are all yang.[16]

Here the human body is approached on three levels. The first level looks at the human body as a whole, with a distinction between external and internal; the second level derives from an examination of front and back; the third level pinpoints the exact body organs. Although yinyang illuminates all these levels, the division of the organs into *zang* and *fu* (depots and palaces) in terms of yinyang is the most vital hypothesis for Chinese medicine.

The five *zang* (depots) are classified as yin because they are relatively solid, resembling the solidness of the earth. These include the kidney, liver, heart, spleen, and lung. They are also taken as the interior (*nei*) parts of the body and, thus, as yin. *Fu* (palaces) are classified as yang because they resemble the movement of heaven, are hollow, and control the transport and digestion of food. These include organs such as the gallbladder, stomach, small and large intestines, urinary bladder, and the so-called triple burner.[17] They are seen as relatively exterior (*wai*) parts of the body. *Zang* and *fu* are different but intrinsically related, and they operate across a field of pairings. *Zang* organs are organs of storage; the *fu* are organs of transfer. Storage is a yin function, whereas transport and transformation is a yang function. These *zang* and *fu* organs can be further subdivided into yin and yang. The activity or function of the organ is its yang aspect, and the structure is its yin aspect. For example, the heart is defined as controlling the circulation of blood and mental activities; these activities are yang, however, the blood and the organ structure of the heart are yin. The basic functions of the body come through the excitation of yang and the restraint of yin. This system offers a way to grasp the complicated links and continual changes of the human body.

---

[16] Ibid., p. 33.

[17] The triple burner refers to three parts of the body cavity: the upper burner, which houses the heart and lung; the middle burner, which houses the spleen and stomach; and the lower burner, which houses the kidney, urinary bladder, and small and large intestines.

In any area, from the interior and the organs to the exterior and orifices, all the meridians circulate according to determinate rhythms, all in terms of yinyang.

Yinyang is the foundation for discerning diseases, for diagnosis, and for treatment. All diseases are divided into two basic kinds: yang diseases or yin diseases. The main diagnostic procedures involve distinguishing between yin and yang.[18] For example, there is the so-called *bagang bianzheng* 八綱辨証 (eight principles for differentiating symptoms) method of diagnosis, focusing on the differentiation of yinyang symptom complexes. These principles are based on a few sets of distinctions: yin and yang, which are the basic categories of diagnosis; heat and cold (*re/han* 熱寒), which determine the nature of the disease; exterior and interior (*biao/li* 表裡), which determine the location of the disease; deficiency and excess (*xu/shi* 虛實), which provide a quantitative assessment. Although the pathological conditions may differ in thousands of ways, these variations never exceed the bounds of yin and yang. That is, all can be approached through the pairing of differences.

Regarding treatment, *qi* and taste (*wei* 味) are defined as the basic ingredients of herbal medicine. *Qi* comes from heaven, so it is yang; *wei* comes from earth, so it is yin. Taking herbs in essence is to take external yin or yang to enhance or diminish the internal interplay of yinyang in the body.

Yin and yang are two dynamic states of variation, however, the elements that control these variations are countless: yinyang is affected by age, gender, the seven desires, the six excesses, diet, work, environment, and so on. These elements can be evident and clear (*ming* 明) or subtle and unseen (*shen* 神). Yinyang is an infinite classification system that extends to all aspects of human life, including human emotions and dreams. It, thus, underlies the holistic approach of Chinese medicine,

---

[18] These methods are *wang* 望, *wen* (2nd tone) 聞, *wen* (4th tone) 問, and *qie* 切. Watching is visual inspection of the body, including inspection of the physique, the facial expression, the color of the complexion, and the color, shape, and surface of the tongue. For example, in watching the skin, the practitioner should distinguish between a yang complexion, which is smooth and glistening, and a yin complexion, which is pale or ashen in color. A yellow or red complexion suggests a symptom complex of yang and heat; a blue and purple, white or dark color implies a symptom complex of yin and cold. Listening (or smelling) is gathering information about the body from the sounds of the voice, breathing and digestive system. For example, if the voice is sonorous with heavy breathing, that implies a yang condition; feeble with weak breathing suggests a yin condition. Asking is the process of determining the patient's complaint, past history and lifestyle. Feeling is taking the pulse. There are seventeen types of pulses that can occur alone or in combination.

relating both mind and body. The *Huangdi Neijing* says, "Human beings have five *zang* that transform into five *qi*. They will generate joy, anger, sadness, worry, and fear. Therefore, joy and sadness will injure the *qi*, while cold and hot will injure the forms. Extreme anger will injure the yin and extreme joy will injure the yang."[19]

Yinyang presents the common medium by which to explain the fact that physiological disruptions influence our emotions and that emotions can damage our physical health. Another passage applies yinyang analysis to dreams:

> If one has excessive yin, one will dream of fearfully crossing a flood; if one has excessive yang, one will dream of a great fire burning. If one has both an excess of yin and yang, then one will dream of killing and injuring....If the *qi* of the liver is too strong, one will be angry in a dream; if the *qi* of the lungs is too strong, one will cry in a dream.[20]

Such imbalances in yinyang can have many causes, from emotions to physiological processes to environmental influences. These causes can be expressed on many levels, including emotions and dreams.

Yinyang classification is much more complicated than a mechanistic division of elements because it necessitates a frame of reference. That is, yinyang categorization hinges on a context rather than on a fixed characterization and designation. For example, from the point of view of anatomy, liver is yin because it is one of the five depots (*zang*). From the point of view of the rhythm of the body and seasons, however, liver is yang because it represents the spring. In the frame of *zang* and *fu*, heart, lung, and liver are all yin, because they store. In the frame of inside and outside, however, they become yang:

> Thus, the back is yang and the yang within yang is the heart. The back is yang and the yin within yang are the lungs. Stomach is yin; kidney is the yin within yin; stomach is yin, liver is the yang within yin; stomach is yin, spleen is the ultimate yin of yin. Thus yin and yang, internal and external, male and female, all mutually resonate, corresponding to the yinyang of heaven.[21]

This contextualization gives flexibility to the applications of yinyang. *Zang* as yin controls the storage of *qi*, however, each organ is a system that might best be portrayed as an energy field or network. The *zang* include the pathways or system of channels that connect various parts

[19] Ibid., p. 47.
[20] Ibid., p. 151.
[21] Ibid., p. 34.

of the body. This network consists not only of its own structure but also of other elements, such as tissues, muscles, and bones. For example, to speak of an organ like the heart is to refer to a whole system and the functions it performs. The organ really refers to (1) the basic life materials like *qi*, blood, body fluids, and activity; (2) relationships, as between the exterior and interior portions of the body and the upper and lower halves of the body; and (3) multiple functions, as the heart governs blood circulation and vessels but also stores consciousness.

Yinyang Interaction and Integration

The second yinyang spectrum is situated in interactions and mutual integration. Yin cannot exist without yang; yang cannot exist without yin. Yin and yang are inherently interdependent and are seen as an interlocking ring. All patterns are based on the belief that no yin can be formed without yang and that yang fails to come into being without yin. When yin flourishes smoothly and yang generates steadily, they regulate themselves so as to maintain mutually interdependent connections. Yin and yang do not exist in isolation but in a dynamic field of interaction. The significance of this aspect of yinyang was recognized by the Nobel Prize winning physicist Niels Bohr (1885–1962), who asserted that the new development of physics forces us to "replace the ideal of causality by a more general viewpoint usually termed complimentarity."[22] The notion of "complimentarity" recognizes the fact that atoms can be separately analyzed as having contradictory properties that exist in a complimentary way. For example, physicists have concluded that light behaves either as a wave or a stream of particles depending on the experimental framework – two apparently mutually exclusive properties are interrelated at the same time. Bohr found philosophical applications for this daringly original principle, and he himself made the connection to Chinese yinyang thought. When awarded the Order of the Elephant by the Danish government, Bohr designed his own coat of arms, which featured a *Taijitu* (the yinyang symbol, which will be discussed in Chapter 6) and the Latin motto *contraria sunt complementa* (contraries are complementary) (see Figure 5.1). It would be interesting to know how much yinyang thinking actually inspired Bohr's scientific work.

In the *Huangdi Neijing*, yin and yang continuously support and consume each other, forming a changing pattern or continuum called "mutual restraint." It is not the case that yin and yang become one, but

---

[22] N. Bohr, "Causality and Complementarity," *Philosophy of Science*, 4:3 (1937): 289–298.

5.1. Coat of Arms designed by Nobel Prize winner Niels Bohr (1885–1962). Kept at Frederiksborg Castle in Hillerod, Denmark. Picture by Verner Worm, October 2011.

rather that yin multiplies yang to form a dynamic but sustainable system. In any relationship there is this mutual dependence: "Heaven covers and earth carries. Things when they have not yet come out of the ground are in the place of yin, which is called yin-within-yin. Once they have come out of the ground, they are called yin-within-yang."[23]

As Unschuld puts it: "All living beings are, therefore, brought into existence by yang influence and given a physical structure by yin influence. This process of genesis proceeds indefinitely, ensuring the continuation of existence. An imbalance of yin and yang influences leads eventually to death."[24]

This interdependence appears in another influential distinction coordinated with the yinyang relationship. Yin is the structure (*ti* 體), and

[23] Zhang, *Huangdi Neijing*, p. 69.
[24] Unschuld, *Medicine in China*, p. 199.

yang is the function (*yong* 用). *Ti* as yin refers to the tangible parts of the body, such as the organs, blood, and body fluids. *Yong* as yang refers to the abilities to act and transformational activities. Both structure and function are tied together to maximize different bodily capacities. For example, if one exercises (seen as yang) by weightlifting, then the capacity in one's bodily structure (seen as yin) will be more suitable for becoming a football player; on the other hand, if one exercises (yang) differently, for example by doing aerobic exercise, then one's capacity (yin) will be suited to running as a result of the building up of endurance and aerobic strength in the body. To strengthen yang functional performance, one must build on yin, transforming the structures. Structure and function are two complimentary forces that generate the wholeness of performance.

The interdependence and mutuality of yinyang as a complex system grounds the basic character and orientation of traditional Chinese medicine. It is well known that Western medicine builds on the model of "virus-causes-disease." Physicians seek to identify the virus that caused the disease, and then they select medicines or chemicals designed to destroy these pathogens and to cure the disease. Chinese medical practice, in contrast, employs a system of yinyang that weaves diagnosis and treatment into a continuous and integrated movement of yinyang between various environmental factors for the particular patient. Health is a way of life and not simply the absence of disease. To cure is to establish a balanced lifestyle grounded in the mutuality of yin and yang. The human body is a structured system, and therefore, it should be understood as the organic connection between different parts of the body (including thoughts and emotions), as well as the synchronization between the body and the environmental conditions within which it exists. Yinyang theory offers the fundamental principle of treatment: to attain an integrated balance both within the body and between the body and the world by adjusting the relationships of yin and yang.

This integration cannot simply be a matter of linear causality but finds its basis in the body's interconnected circuits through twelve vessels or *jingluo* 經絡, which hold a key position in Chinese medicine. The vessel theory involves two kinds of vessels (*mai* 脈) and serves as the basic anatomical and physiological model for the human body.[25] The word *mai* (vessels, channels, or veins) appears in relation to blood flow as early

---

[25] Other common translations for the word *mai* are "meridians" or "conduits." Livia Kohn (ed.), *Daoism Handbook*: Handbook of Oriental Studies, vol. 14. (Boston: Brill, 2000), p.97.

as the *Zuozhuan*. The character of *mai* itself connects with blood and the flowing of water.[26] The *Guanzi* states that *qi* flows along with blood through the *mai* (vessels) inside the body. According to Harper, early medical texts show that the "physiological theory is vessel theory, vessels are the essential structures subsuming the other constituents of the body."[27] The vessels "pervade the entire body like a network of rivers and lakes. The *qi* flows, in a cyclical rhythm, from the body's center to the extremities (hands and feet) and back, passing through the twelve major conduits associated with the yin and yang orbs."[28]

There are two systems of *mai*. One is called *jingmai*, which is like threads twisted together, and is on the left part of the body. *Jing* means a net or anything resembling a net, that is, anything with an interwoven structure. The other is called *luomai*, which is like a river flowing, and is on the right part of the body. *Luo* is flow, timing, and function. These vessels are the pathways throughout the body. All of these vessels are classed as either yin or yang, so that there are six yang *mai* and six yin *mai*. They form the interconnected circulatory system of the body. Each vessel is linked to one of the internal organs, whose physiological function influences that particular vessel. The *mai* have three functions: the communication between organs, the regulation or coordination of the activities of the *zang* and *fu* organs, and the distribution of nutrients and fluids. Threads are twisted together along the main pathways through which *qi* and blood circulate, connecting all parts of the body into an organic unit. These vessels filled with blood and *qi* inside the body dominate physiological speculation concentrated on the wholeness of the body. All acupuncture points are located on these twelve vessels. When one specific needlepoint is stimulated on that vessel, then the linked internal organ will be affected. Health is maintaining a constant supply of free-flowing blood and *qi* in these vessels, which is the foundation for both diagnosis and treatment.[29] All of these interpretations and practices take, as their focal point, the view that all components and ingredients of the human body are interrelated, interconnected, and interdependent through a flowing and changing yinyang structure. Whether or not the existence of these points or vessels can be verified by modern scientific methods, some of the acupuncture treatments have been empirically established as effective.

[26] Harper (trans.), *The Mawangdui Medical Manuscripts*, p. 83.
[27] Ibid., p. 78.
[28] F. Pregadid and L. Skar, "Inner Alchemy" in the *Daoist Handbook*, p. 97.
[29] Harper writes, "Vessel diagnosis is the only accurate way of determining the nature of a patient's illness; treatment focuses on ameliorating the morbid condition exhibited by the vessels." Harper (trans.), *The Mawangdui Medical Manuscripts*, p. 70.

The vessel theory developed from an initial awareness of physiological structures holding blood and *qi*, but it becomes the foundation for a full physiological theory, merging with cosmological views to become a new image of the body as microcosm.[30] The *Huangdi Neijing* shows these cosmological correlations:

> Huangdi asks: "Human beings have 'four vessels' and 'twelve followings.' What are they?"
>
> Qibao answers: "The four *jing* respond to the four seasons and the twelve followings respond to the twelve months. The twelve months respond to the twelve *mai*. *Mai* have yin and yang. Those who know the yang will know the yin; those who know the yin will know the yang." (知陽者知陰, 知陰者知陽)[31]

This choice of *mai* as the foundation for grasping the body reveals a fundamental orientation toward movement, patterns, and interaction, in contrast to a focus on organs or elements. It also points toward the importance of timing and rhythm, both of which were articulated through ideas of yinyang. As Harper says, the focus on *mai* as circuits "is the basis for applying a broad range of Yin and Yang and Five Agent theories to physiology."[32] The *Huangdi Neijing* says directly: "If one's vessels follow yinyang the sickness will be an easy case; if the vessels go against yinyang the sickness will be a difficult case." (脈從陰陽, 病易已; 脈逆陰陽, 病難已).[33]

The Ideal State of Yinyang Interaction "Steady Yin and Secure Yang" 陰平陽秘

The third yinyang spectrum characterizes the favorable state for yinyang relationships, consisting of dynamic equilibrium and balance. What is the ideal yinyang condition and how can one measure the loss of this state? The *Huangdi Neijing* describes it as follows:

> The essential of all yinyang is that if yang is secured then yin is affirmed. If these two are not balanced it is just like there being spring without fall or winter without summer. If they can be harmonized, this is the measure of the sage. Therefore if yang is strong but cannot be secured, the *qi* of yin will be exhausted. If yin is steady and yang is secure then the spirit will be in an order. If yinyang are separated the essence of *qi* will be exhausted.[34]

[30] Ibid., p. 82.
[31] Y. Zhang, *Huangdi Neijing*, p. 75.
[32] Harper (trans.), *The Mawangdui Medical Manuscripts*, p. 87.
[33] Zhang, *Huangdi Neijing*, p. 169.
[34] Ibid., p. 26–27.

The steady yin and secure yang (*yinping yangmi* 陰平陽秘) is regarded as the sign of health and well-being. This phrase is difficult to translate, but it is defined in modern terms as the equilibrium or balance of yinyang. The yin should be *ping*, which refers to being even, level, calm, and steady. The yang should be *mi*, which refers to being sound, dense, and secure. In the *Huangdi Neijing*, the two indicate a condition in which yin and yang work together through a process of self-adjustment. When the yang located in the body's exterior is secure or dense, it will have a protective function over the interior yin, keeping it from being harmed by external forces. On the other hand, if yin is level or steady, it will provide a foundation for the external yang. It is like the way a good personal relationship supplies a basis for someone to go out and face the challenges of the external world.

Yinping and *yangmi* is a basic need for the health and well-being of human physical and mental existence. The *Huangdi Neijing* confirms this:

> The person who has yinyang balance will have attained a harmony of *qi* of yinyang. His blood vessels are adjusted. Distinguishing his yinyang, one sees his correction of deviance, his calm appearance and actions. Examine where there is excess and deficiency: reduce what is too full and supplement what is too empty. Not too full and not too empty, attaining it through the vessels – this is called adjusting yinyang.[35]

The best way to measure or exemplify this state of yinyang interplay is through health. When this *yinping yangmi* pattern fails, proper balance will be lost, and the body diverges from its healthy state. The cause of disease is an imbalance of yinyang, either as deficiency or excess. The struggle between pathogenic and anti-pathogenic factors results in the flourishing or decline of yin and yang in the body. The *Huangdi Neijing* says:

> The deviant sickness is generated either from yin or from yang. If it is generated from yang, it is attained from wind, rain, cold, and heat. If it is generated from yin, it is attained from drink, diet, shelter, and living conditions. They can also come from yinyang joy and anger."[36]

More specifically, there are two sources for sickness or imbalances of yinyang. One is called "exogenous pathogenic factors," which come when

---

[35] Niu, Bingzhan. 牛兵占 (ed.), *Huangdi Neijing*, 黃帝内經 (Shijiazhuang: Hebei Science and Technology Press 1993), p. 168.

[36] Zhang, *Huangdi Neijing*, p. 518. The joy and anger of yinyang refer to states of emotions. Too much yang will be excessive joy; too much yin will be excessive anger.

yang is not *mi* (secure, dense, guarding). The body encounters and is harmed by external influences, such as the changing of four seasons and so on. This aspect suggests the immune system and resistance against disease. There are six influential environmental factors (also called the six deviants, *liuxie* 六邪): wind, cold, heat, dampness, dryness, and fire (風, 寒, 暑, 濕, 燥, 火). If the six deviants become abnormal or excessive, as in cases of abrupt and extreme changes in environmental conditions, or if the body's resistance is too weak to adapt to these variations, the six deviants can become pathogenic factors that destroy the physiological equilibrium of the body, thus causing disease. This is yang disease, arising because the yang of the body is not secure, or *mi*. It is significant that the fundamental cause is not the external element but rather the weakness of one's own yang *qi*, which is what renders one vulnerable to external harms.

The other sources are called endogenous factors, which come when yin is not *ping* (steady or calm). It is a case of the body's own internal weakness or disruption, which tends to produce conditions of deficiency. For example, human emotions have a bodily basis and are closely related to the functioning of the internal organs. The seven basic emotions (*qing* 情) of being pleased, angry, worried, pensive, grieving, fearful, and alarmed (喜, 怒, 憂, 思, 悲, 恐, 驚) each corresponds to yin and yang. Emotional stimuli can attack the organs, causing disease by disrupting the normal ascending and descending flow of *qi*. An extreme emotion can impair the various organs, just as a dysfunction of the organs can lead to abnormal emotions, as we have seen.

These yang forces (relating to the six deviants) and yin forces (relating to the seven emotions) have to work together to attain a balance that is healthy and sustainable. Otherwise, the body will face four basic types of imbalance or disease: yang impaired by a preponderance of yin; yin consumed by a preponderance of yang; overabundance of yang caused by a deficiency of yin; overabundance of yin resulting from a deficiency of yang. The *Huangdi Neijing* says: "If yin is excessive then it is yang disease; if yang is excessive then it is a yin disease. Yang in excess is hot while yin in excess is cold."[37] Clearly neither yin nor yang can be considered in isolation – health and illness both lie in the relationship between them.

These symptom complexes have two major variables linked to yin and yang, namely, cold and heat. A preponderance of yang leads to a heat symptom complex, and an overabundance of yin will lead to a cold symptom complex. The causes of cold and heat may be either endogenous or

[37] Ibid., p. 46.

exogenous, and they may produce symptoms on the surface (exterior) or in the depths (interior) of the body. The relationship and the balance between yin and yang are ways to delineate these conditions, as they are the manifestations of either excess or deficiency.

Since the cause of disease is the imbalance of yinyang, then the medical treatment lies in adjusting yin and yang to bring back balance: reduce the excess or superfluous and supply the insufficiency. The *Huangdi Neijing* expresses this: "Investigate their yinyang in order to distinguish hard and soft. Yang disease should be treated with yin; yin disease should be treated with yang."[38] As one would expect, a cold symptom complex should be treated with drugs that are warm or hot in nature. A heat symptom complex should be treated with drugs that are cool or cold in nature. A deficiency symptom complex should be treated with a method of increase. An excess symptom complex should be treated with a method for reducing.

Herbs function to restore the balance of yin and yang and to gain the state of *yinping yangmi*. Herbals are divided into three basic groups according to their basic nature, flavor, and effect, all of which are also classified according to yinyang. The basic nature of herbs has four types: hot, cold, warm, and cool. The yang herbs are warm or hot in nature; the yin herbs are cool or cold. There are six classes of flavors that also divide into yin and yang: herbs that are pungent, sweet, or insipid are yang; those that are sour, bitter, or salty are yin. Based on the cosmology of *qi*, these herbs have effects that can be considered as ascending or descending. Those herbs that have effects of descending and condensing are yin; herbs that have effects of ascending and dispersing are yang. All of these herbs are used to reduce what is superfluous and to replenish what is insufficient to restore the relative balance between yin and yang.

Yinyang Movement and Transformation

The relationship between yin and yang is never static, and thus, the ideal state of steady yin and secure yang is never fixed or final. The fourth spectrum for yinyang is the rhythm (*jiezou* 節奏) of change and transformation. The discussion of yinyang cosmology in Chapter 2 has shown that the world at its most macroscopic level consists of combinations of patterns of yinyang interplay that furnish an explanatory framework capable of encompassing all forces and all events. The human body seen at a microscopic level also enjoys a natural pattern of the waxing and

---

[38] Ibid., p. 67.

waning of yin and yang. In other words, the human body is a microcosm of the complex system of nature, made up of patterns of oscillation, vibration, and transformation. Living organisms contain rhythms modeled on nature.

The myriad things exist in time through yinyang. We have already examined yinyang and time/timing in the last chapter, seeing how timing is central to yinyang as a strategy. This view goes into a deeper and more specific form through the interpretation of the human body in the *Huangdi Neijing*. Like the rhythm of day and night and the changes of the four seasons, the human body functions as a natural biological clock ticking according to yinyang alternations. The alternations in the body are influenced by those of the broader natural world, with the body particularly influenced by the waxing and waning of the moon.[39] In nature, spring and summer are identified with yang, and winter and fall are identified with yin. Yin and yang exchange positions to complete a yearly cycle connected with the harvest. At every phase, there is an accomplishment at present and germination for the future. The *Huangdi Neijing* summarizes this: "Yang generates, yin grows; yang collects and yin stores. Yang transforms the yin and yin completes the form."[40] As one would expect, various illnesses thus coordinate with the seasons: "Winter sickness is because of yin; summer sickness is because of yang; spring sickness is in yin and autumn sickness is in yang."[41] Human biological changes all follow a seasonal pattern and take place in the vessels (*mai*) as pulse. There are four types of pulse, correlated with spring, summer, autumn, and winter. Spring pulses feel like the string of a musical instrument; summer pulses feel like a hook; winter pulses feel like a stone; autumn pulses feel like fur.[42] (春脈玄, 夏脈鈎, 冬脈石, 秋脈毛).

The *Huangdi Neijing* distills many specific patterns of yinyang transformation. These enrich the forms of yinyang pairing we have already seen, and it shows their application in concrete practice. We can distinguish sixteen positive and constructive yinyang transformations and eight kinds of negative and destructive changes. All of them are applied to explicate bodily change. The sixteen affirmative yinyang changes are as follows:

---

[39] Unschuld explains, "The full moon produces a repletion with the strength within body, while a new or waning moon signifies a period of weakness, of susceptibility to injury." Unschuld, *Medicine in China*, p. 70.

[40] Zhang, *Huangdi Neijing*, p. 42.

[41] Ibid., p 34.

[42] 難經 *Nan Jing*, 經脈診候

陰陽之變 alternations of yin and yang
陰陽相過 yin and yang pass by each other
陰陽相移 yin and yang move each other
陰陽相薄 yin and yang mingle with each other
陰陽相傾 yin and yang lean on each other
陰陽相持 yin and yang support each other
陰陽相得 yin and yang attain each other
陰陽相乘 yin and yang respond to each other
陰陽相貫 yin and yang thread together
陰陽和調 yin and yang harmoniously adjust
陰陽和平 yin and yang harmoniously balance
陰陽平復 yin and yang return to balance
陰陽相隨 yin and yang follow each other
陰陽往復 yin and yang cycle around
陰陽卷舒 yin and yang contract and expand
陰陽離合 yin and yang separate and join

The eight negative yinyang changes are as follows:

陰陽相離 yin and yang separate from each other
陰陽相逐 yin and yang chase each other
陰陽相失 yin and yang deplete each other
陰陽不通 yin and yang disconnect
陰陽俱盛 yin and yang simultaneously dominate
陰陽異位 yin and yang are displaced
陰陽逆順 yin and yang going against and going along
陰陽相逆 yin and yang oppose each other

The formulation of types of yinyang transformation guides the practice of acupuncture. The master of acupuncture is one who can apply the needle in a way to initiate or enhance the appropriate transformation of yinyang:

> The one who uses acupuncture masterfully induces yang from yin and induces yin from yang, using the right to manage the left and using the left to manage the right, using their own self to know others and using the manifestation to know the inside." (從陰引陽, 從陽引陰, 以右治左, 以左治右, 以我知彼, 以表知裡) [43]

The core of medical practice is in applying different methods for the transformation of yinyang. If a patient manifests symptoms of heat, the qi is too hot, which means it is too active, rising, or rapid. In that case,

[43] Zhang, *Huangdi Neijing*, p. 65.

one should be treated with cold, such as cooling herbs or foods that transform the *qi* of the patient. One needs to regulate and adjust the flow of *qi* according to the variations of the yinyang patterns. Thus, an essential phenomenon of acupuncture is *deqi* 得氣, literally "attaining *qi*." The acupuncturist administers the needle attentively to attain the arrival of *qi*.

The *Huangdi Neijing* describes the practice of acupuncture:

> Therefore if one knows yinyang, one will know where to insert the needles. One makes the diagnosis carefully and responds with timing, corresponding internally with the five depots and six palaces and externally with nerves, bones, skin and surfaces. Therefore there is internal yinyang as well as external yinyang.[44]

The quality of treatment depends on whether the patient has felt this sensation of *deqi*, attaining either *yinqi* or *yangqi* based on the diagnosis. This is the immediate effect of inserting an acupuncture needle into an acupuncture point located in the vessels in the body.

As we have seen in the previous chapter on yinyang strategy, one must act according to natural patterns and rhythms emerging from a complex and implicit background. On this model, physicians are facilitators and cultivators, rather than technicians who fix broken machines. Transforming a disrupted yinyang body into a balanced organism exemplifies yinyang strategy.

Yinyang Quantification: Three Yin and Three Yang

The *Huangdi Neijing* takes yinyang as the force of life and develops a complex and intricate yinyang theory. It introduces for the first time the notion of three yin and three yang (*sanyin sanyang* 三陰三陽), which expands the function of yinyang by adding subtle differentiations in quantity and quality. The *Huangdi Neijing* makes clear the link between quantification and the idea of "three yin and three yang":

> What does it mean that *qi* has more or less and that form has flourishing and declining?
>
> Guiyu answers: The *qi* of yin and *qi* of yang each have more or less [i.e., a quantity], and therefore we speak of the three yin and three yang.[45]

---

[44] Niu, *Huangdi Neijing*, p. 22.
[45] Zhang, *Huangdi Neijing*, p. 555.

These distinctions complicate the notion of yinyang and reveal a system that has three dimensions: quantity (*liang* 量), position or space (*wei* 位), and rhythm or timing (*shi* 時). Another important medical text written after the *Huangdi Neijing*, the *Shanghan Lun* 傷寒論 (*Treatise on Cold Damage Disorders*) written by the physician Zhang Zhongjing 張仲景 (150–219 C.E.) in the Eastern Han, used three yin and three yang to articulate a full theory for syndrome differentiation by the six vessels (*liujing bianzheng* 六經辨証). Since that time, the idea of three yin and three yang permeates all Chinese medical practice, yet it is an extremely difficult notion to grasp.

The distinction of three yin and three yang plays several roles in Chinese medicine, all of them in theorizing and specifying the connections between organs and vessels. The first point is the focus on changing of quantity (*bianliang* 變量). The three yin and three yang first demonstrate that yin and yang are not simply two qualities but that in its deeper structure, yin and yang also have variations in quantity, which involve movement through different phases. The three yin and three yang create a sixfold subcategorization of yinyang based on the rhythm of time. Thus, the yang category is further divided into great yang (*taiyang* 太陽), lesser yang (*shaoyang* 少陽), and yang brilliance (*yangming* 陽明). The yin category is similarly divided into three quantitative phases: great yin (*taiyin* 太陰), lesser yin (*shaoyin* 少陰), and a ceasing yin (*jueyin* 厥陰).

The human body can be analyzed according to its embodiment of these six structures. The sixfold categorization of yinyang corresponds to the three yang vessels and three yin vessels that run through the hands. Three yin vessels extend from the hands to the head, and the three yang vessels extend from the chest into the hands. Three yin foot vessels extend from the feet to the chest, and three yang foot vessels, from the head to the feet. These three yin and three yang physiological systems all relate to the five organ systems. The crucial aspect of these subcategories is the quantification of yinyang movement. If yinyang is a dynamic changing process, then these changes seen as *qi* movement should be measurable. Three yin and three yang serve as the measurement for these quantitative changes. In the six stages, the most important two are yang brilliance, the highest yang stage in which great yang and lesser yang are combined, and ceasing yin (*jueyin*), the lowest yang stage in which great yin and lesser yin combine. The distinction is a result of the amount of yang or yin.

The addition of quantitative change to the interaction between yin and yang allows for more specific accounts of change. Since the time of the *Zhuangzi* and the *Huainanzi*, yinyang's concentration and dispersion has been recognized as the ultimate force of growth and decay in the myriad things, however, this was only a general suggestion. The notion of three yin and three yang specifies these processes in the context of the human body. Like seasonal changes, yinyang in the body follows a cycle of generating (*sheng*), growing (*zhang*), collecting (*shou*), and storing (*cang*). With the help of great yin, lesser yin moves toward the transition to lesser yang, and this movement is called generating. With the participation of lesser yang, great yin moves toward great yang, and this process is growth. With the participation of great yang, lesser yang moves toward lesser yin, which is the process of collecting. With the participation of lesser yin, great yang moves toward great yin, which is called regenerating. These are the comprehensive three yin and three yang movements. These movements also take place in the internal organs, which align with these transformations.

The notion of three yin and three yang conceptualizes the human body through the details of seasonal change. January and February belong to lesser yang, the beginning of the yang; in the human body, this is the belly button area (*dan* 丹) and the triple burner. Its function is upward movement, and it has connections with the liver. March and April belong to great yang, the flourishing of yang, connecting with the lungs, bladder, and small intestines. May and June belong to yang brilliance, the highest state of yang, which results from the movement of lesser yang and great yang. It connects to the stomach and large intestine. July and August belong to great yin. Here, yang declines, and yin is starting. It connects with the spleen and stomach. September and October belong to lesser yin. Yang is much declined, whereas yin moves forward. This connects with the kidney and heart. November and December belong to ceasing yin. The term translated here as "ceasing" is *jue* 厥, which means short, referring to having a short time. This time connects with the liver and the area around it.

One important dimension of harmony with nature is synchronizing with nature's timing, as we have seen. One's internal biological clock should be tuned with the external rhythms of nature. The *Huangdi Neijing* maintains:

> Only sages follow nature and therefore no unusual sicknesses strike them. The myriad things will not be lost and generative *qi* will not be exhausted. If one goes against the spring *qi*, then the lesser yang will not generate liver *qi* and one will suffer internal changes. If one goes against the summer *qi*, then the greater yang will not grow, and the heart *qi* will have an internal gap. If one goes against the autumn *qi* then the greater yin will not collect and the lung *qi* will be excessive. If one goes against the winter *qi* then minor yin will not regenerate and the kidney *qi* will sink. Therefore

following the seasons of yinyang is the root of the myriad thing. Sages will nourish yang in spring and summer and nourish yin in autumn and winter. Aligning with the sinking and rising of the myriad things is the gate to generation and growth. If one goes against this root, one will injure this root and damage the core.[46]

Yinyang in Body Cultivation

We have already seen that early traditional Chinese medicine is primarily oriented toward the healthy functioning of the body as a complex system, rather than focusing on removing the elements of illness. From that orientation, it is not surprising that attempts to further cultivate the body overlap and are difficult to distinguish from the practices of medicine. That is, the early Chinese path toward health naturally suggests the attempt to perfect the body and reach a higher state of being. The significance of bodily cultivation in early Chinese thought may be difficult to appreciate from the perspective of Western philosophy. Marcus Aurelius famously advised us to consider that "the human body itself is no more than rotting meat in a bag."[47] This claim is just an extreme expression of a tendency in Western philosophy to devalue the body and to emphasize instead the soul, the mind, and reason. In contrast, the human body has always held a special place in Chinese thinking. Zhang Zailin, a contemporary scholar, has even argued that Chinese philosophy is most fundamentally a philosophy of body.[48] The central importance of the body appears most clearly in the Chinese term, *shen* 身 (body). *Shen* is the word most analogous to "self or person," which is how it is often translated, however, it refers to the body rather than the consciousness or mind. *Shen* contains a strong sense of what is close or direct. *Shen* is not simply a noun defining an object but rather a verb that indicates action and practice – the self as a living body.

The implications of the importance of the body can be seen on several levels. Most simply, many early texts emphasize the importance of the body as the locus of health and life itself. *Shen* 身 (body) is a different

---

[46] Ibid., p. 14.
[47] M. Aurelius, *Meditations: A New Translation*, G. Hays (trans.) (New York: The Modern Library, 2003), p. 108.
[48] Zhang Zailin 张再林. *Traditional Chinese Philosophy as the Philosophy of the Body* 作为身体哲学的中国古代哲学, (Beijing: China Social Science Publishing House 中国社会科学出版社, 2008), p. 5. Also, see R. Wang's book review in *Dao: A Journal of Comparative Philosophy*, 8:1 (2009), 113–6.

character from *sheng* 生 (living, life), but it has a similar sound, and *sheng*, living, is often seen in the same usage as *shen*. The body is fundamentally connected to growth and life. Although the main concern is with health and longevity, those concerns can extend toward developing what we might now deem super-normal powers, culminating in the search for immortality. We have already seen that bodily health is integrated with emotional and mental health as well. Considering this holistic approach, we can witness how all forms of self-cultivation might fall under the category of bodily cultivation, as we see in many of the key terms for cultivating the self, notions such as *anshen* 安身 (pacifying or being at peace in the body), *shoushen* 守身 (guarding the body), *guishen* 貴身 (valuing the body), *fanshen* 返身 (returning to the body), and *xiushen* 修身 (cultivating the body). All of these are prioritized in the pursuit of sagehood.[49] This focus is not so far from Jean-Paul Sartre's claim that "Body is the totality of meaningful relations to the world."[50]

On a second level, the pondering of the ultimate questions about existence in Chinese philosophy has always been intertwined with thinking through the body. As we have seen, the natural world itself is conceived primarily on a biological model, as like an organic body, and yinyang thought is based on such organic processes. The body partakes of the shape and logic of the cosmos, and the body can express the entirety of creation and cosmic change.[51] Thus, human beings should act in ways that will bring about the best alignment with the cosmos.[52] This cosmic link partly justifies the power attributed to bodily cultivation. We observe this focus on the body as far back as the *Daodejing*: "If you esteem taking care of your body more than you do taking care of the world, you can be

[49] Harold D. Roth explains that "Inner cultivation is the primary way in which human beings can realize the deepest aspects of their intrinsic nature, that part of their being is directly in touch with the way and, through it, with the inherent patterns and structures of the universe." Roth, introduction to "Originating in the Way," *The Huainanzi*, p. 43. For more of the connection between body and cultivation, see R. Wang, "The Virtuous Body at Work: The Ethical Life as Qi 氣 in Motion," *Dao: Journal of Comparative Philosophy*, 9:3 (2010), 339–351.

[50] J.-P. Sartre, *Being and Nothingness*, H. E. Barnes (trans.) (New York: Washington Square Press, 1993), pp. 430.

[51] While using quite different terms, this connection is echoed by Merleau-Ponty's claim: "If we therefore say that the body expresses existence at every movement, this is in the sense which a word express thought.... In this way the body expresses total existence, not because it is an external accompaniment to that existence, but because existence comes into its own in the body" (Merleau-Ponty, *Phenomenology of Perception*, Colin Smith (trans.) (New York: Humanities Press, 1962), p.165–166).

[52] See L. Kohn (ed.), *Daoism Handbook*.

entrusted with the world; if you love your body as if it were the world, then the world can be handed over to you."[53]

Developing a similar line of thought, the *Huainanzi* shows that the essentials of the world lie not in others but in our own bodies (*shen*) – when one can fully realize *Dao* in one's own body, then "all the myriad things will be arrayed before you."[54] Similarly, the *Lüshi Chunqiu* says, "The past sages perfected their own body (*shen*) and the world was made complete. They governed their own body and the world became well-ordered."[55]

On a third level, knowledge was thought of as closely connected to the body. We have already seen that yinyang as a strategy lies not just in conscious decisions but also in an embodied responsiveness to the world. Yinyang thought is a bodily thinking in the sense that it is not simply an activity of the mind isolated from the world and its objects. Thinking develops through bodily refinement. Early Chinese views of the body show an awareness of something like what has come to be called a "body schema," which Gallagher takes as a "system of sensory-motor processes that constantly regulate posture and movement-processes that function without reflective awareness or necessity of perceptual monitoring."[56] How does the refinement of this body schema form and change our sense of world? Body works to govern movement on the basis of integrating information received from numerous sources with the environment. It is a holistic immersion. Awareness of one's body constitutes a necessary condition for intentional action. This view echoes more recent discussions of the body in European philosophy, for example, Sartre's saying that "Body is lived and not known."[57] Merleau-Ponty writes, "There is a logic of the world to which my body in its entirety conforms, and through which things of intersensory significance become possible for us."[58] If we consider the link between body and perception, it follows that cultivating the body can modify our perception of the world.

---

[53] Hans-Georg Moeller (trans.), *Daodejing: A Complete Translation and Commentary*, (Chicago and La Salle: Open Court, 2007), p. 33.

[54] Harold Roth (trans.), *The Huainanzi: A Guide to the Theory and Practice of Government in Early China* (New York: Columbia University Press, 2010), p. 71.

[55] Knoblock and Riegel (trans.), *The Annals of Lü Buwei: A Complete Translations and Study*, (Stanford: Stanford University Press, 2000), p. 102.

[56] S. Gallagher, *How the Body Shapes the Mind* (New York: Oxford University Press, 2005), p. 37.

[57] Sartre, *Being and Nothingness*, p. 427.

[58] Merleau-Ponty, p. 174.

Self-cultivation as a holistic process based in the body has deep roots in early Chinese texts. The *Zhuangzi* celebrates a special type of human being called the *zhenren* 真人, the "true" or "genuine" person, which is the highest rank of human being. *Zhenren* are capable of lifting heaven and earth, grasping yinyang, breathing pure *qi* 氣, relying on spirit (*shen* 神), enjoying longevity, and mastering the timing of heaven (*tianshi*).[59] The *Huangdi Neijing* articulates four types of ideal human beings as "true people" 真人 (*zhenren*), "utmost people" 至人 (*zhiren*), "sagely people" 聖人 (*shengren*), and "worthy people" 賢人 (*xianren*). Three are distinguished by how they deal with yinyang: true people can master yinyang, utmost people can harmonize yinyang, and worthy people know to follow yinyang.[60] The *Huainanzi* makes it clear that "it is because sages inhale and exhale the *qi* of yinyang that none of the myriad things fail to flourish as they acknowledge potency [*de*] in harmonious compliance."[61] (是故聖人呼吸陰陽之氣, 而群生莫不顒顒然仰其德以和順).

In another story in the *Zhuangzi*, it is said that after Confucius met Laozi, he did not come out for three days. His disciples asked what he had seen. Confucius said, "I have finally seen a dragon! Coiled up, his body is complete; extended, his scaly patterns are whole. He rides on the cloudy vapors [*qi*] and is nourished by yin and yang."[62]

Laozi's strength and energy is gained through his nourishment of yinyang. In other words, yinyang inhabits one's own body. If the human body exists through movements of *qi*, then the cultivation and transformation of this *qi* will have the greatest importance.

Such classical Daoist visions of human beings were pursued and actualized in later Daoist texts, rituals, and practices. One of the most important ways bodily cultivation was analyzed was through the distinction of three elements: physical form (*xing* 形), *qi* (vital energy), and spirit (*shen* 神). *Xing* refers to shape or form – the physical, visible form of the body. It is the house or abode of life and a vessel for the Dao.[63] *Qi* is the invisible foundation and the source of life, as we have seen. Spirit (*shen*) is the psychological and divine aspects of human life and is that which regulates life.[64] If *qi* is gathered, the form will possess life; if *qi* is lost, the

---

[59] Chen Guying, 陳鼓應, 莊子今注今譯, *Commentaries on Zhuangzi*, (Beijing: Chinese Press, 1983), p. 168–169.

[60] Zhang, *Huangdi Neijing*, p. 7–8.

[61] Roth, *The Huainanzi*, p. 99.

[62] Victor H. Mair, *Wandering on the Way: Early Taoist Tales of Chuang Tzu*, (Honolulu: University of Hawai'i Press, 1994), p. 140.

[63] Kohn (ed.), *Daoism Handbook*, p. 96.

[64] Roth, *The Huainanzi*, p. 74.

form will lose life. If spirit has purified *qi*, it will be in order, however, if *qi* is turbid, spirit will be chaotic. The crucial aspect of this vision is that *qi* is the mediator between spirit and bodily form. It is through *qi* that mind and body are united and interact. The *Taiping Jing* illuminates this point: "Spirit is embodied from heaven, refined essence (*jing*) is endowed by earth; *qi* comes from balance and harmony (*zhonghe*). Spirit rides *qi* to move, and refined essence (*jing*) inhabits balance. The three of them assist one another. This will lead to longevity. This is caring for *qi*, respecting spirit and valuing refined essence."[65]

This passage emphasizes *jing* 精, translated as "refined essence," instead of bodily form (*xing*). The notion of *jing* comes from refining or selecting out the best, originally in relation to rice.[66] The rice is divided into two kinds, the best kind is *jing*, and the other is *cu* 粗, which means coarse or rough. One will pick out the best, the *jing*, and leave behind that which is rough or coarse. *Jing* refers to the best parts, what we might call the "cream of the crop," however, it also refers to what has been refined or purified. This leads to a meaning of *jing* as the pure part or essence of something. In Daoist body transformation practices, *jing* denotes blood in the female body and sperm in the male body. Both are essential parts of the human physical form. Human bodily form (*xing*) is coarse (*cu*) in comparison with the *jing*, the refined essential part.

Although *jing* is often translated as "essence," the distinction between *cu* and *jing* is fundamentally different from that between essence and existence in Western philosophy. *Jing* or essence in Chinese texts is the core of existence, however, it is a tangible entity existing in spatial and temporal configurations. That is, *jing* also is bodily functions.

We have already discussed the term *shen* in relation to the line from the *Xici* commentary of the *Yijing*, which says that what cannot be measured by yin and yang is called *shen*, numinous.[67] *Shen* can mean spirits, the divine, the obscure and immeasurable, or what happens as if by magic. *Shen* was frequently associated with *ming* 明, which encompasses meanings from brightness and illumination to insight. The character itself groups images of the sun (*ri* 日) and of the moon (*yue* 月). Both *shen* and *ming* can be either an attribute of the world or of human beings. They, thus, connect human beings with the cosmos, and together they constitute the spiritual and intellectual core of a human being. *Shenming* literally

---

[65] Yang Jilin 杨寄林 (ed.). *Taipingjing* 太平經 *Classic of Great Peace*, (Shijiazhuang: Hebei People's Press, 2002), p. 1730.

[66] Kohn (ed.), *Daoism Handbook*, p. 97.

[67] W. J. Peterson, "Making Connections," p. 104.

refers to a kind of intelligence possessed by the spirits, however, it is also attributed to sages.[68] It is a "spiritual-like intuitive clarity" attainable by human beings. Harold Roth takes the phrase *shenming* 神明 as marvelous influence, magical efficacy, or spiritual illumination. It is a way to explain the world beyond the narrow vision of human beings, pointing toward mystical experience, ineffability, noetic equality, transiency, and passivity.[69] *Shenming* is attained only through a process of cultivation and the elimination of bias. The Mawangdui medical text, "Ten Questions" (*Shiwen*), directly links this to yinyang. The Heavenly Teacher exhorts the Yellow Emperor to examine the rules of yin and yang and to "eat yin and secure yang in order to attain *shenming*."[70]

This *shenming* is also closely connected with *qi*. As a verb, *shenming* communicates two opposite qualities in the transformation *qi*, which is its condensing and extending. Condensing *qi* begins with *shen*, and extending *qi* becomes *ming*. *Ming* as extending is yang, and *shen* as condensing is yin. *Shen* frequently means the *qi* condensing or absorbing nature of the earth; *ming* denotes the *qi* extending or *qi* issuing nature of heaven. This might explain the claim in the recently discovered *Taiyi shengshui*, which says that heaven and earth assist each other and produce *shen* and *ming*, which then assist each other to produce yin and yang.[71] As we have seen, yin links to the obscure, and yang correlates to what is manifest. Thus, *shen* is the non-manifest, inscrutable aspects of *qi*, whereas *ming* involves the manifestations of *qi* as phenomena and explicit influences.

Many approaches to self/body cultivation are conceptualized through these elements. For example, the *Lushi Chunqiu* says:

> Nature [*tian*] produced the Yin and Yang principles, cold and heat, wet and dry, the transformations of four seasons, and the metamorphosis of the myriad things. Each of these can produce benefit, or it can cause harm. The sage scrutinizes what is appropriate to the Yin and Yang and discriminates what is beneficial in the myriad things in order to enhance life. Thus, the vital essence and the spirit being secure within the bodily frame, the person's life span is extended.[72]

---

[68] According to Kenneth E. Brashier, "In pre-Han and Han texts, 'spirit illumination' [shenming] could refer to either a divine being or a spirit-like intelligence ..." K. E. Brashier, "Han Thanatology and the Division of Souls," *Early China*, 21 (1996), 149.

[69] Roth, *The Huainanzi*, p. 127.

[70] Harper (trans.), "Body and Spirit" in *The Mawangdui Medical Manuscripts*, Prolegomena sect. 4.

[71] Liu (ed.), *Guodian Chujian Jiaoyi* 郭店楚簡校釋, (Fuzhou: Fujian People's Press, 2003), strip 1.

[72] Knoblock and Riegel, *The Annals of Lü Buwei*, p. 99.

There are numerous texts and complicated manuals for body cultivation in the Chinese tradition. We can consider one of the earliest classics on body cultivation, the *Zhouyi Can Tong Qi* 周易参同契 (*The Three Ways Unified and Normalized of Zhouyi*), written by Wei Boyang 魏伯陽 (151– 221 C.E.), a Daoist alchemist of the second century.[73] The *Zhouyi Can Tong Qi* grew from a combination of practical experience, magical beliefs, and naturalistic reasoning. The text integrates the thought of the *Yijing*, the vision of the Huanglao School, and the alchemical tradition into a system directed toward transforming the body so as to attain immortality. Like the classical texts the *Daodejing* and the *Zhuangzi*, the *Zhouyi Can Tong Qi* has enjoyed a significant theoretical and practical position in China, where it has been known as "the ten-thousand-year king of alchemy" (萬古丹經王). The work signifies a shift from Daoist practices of outer alchemy (*waidan* 外丹) to what is called internal alchemy (*neidan* 內丹), turning human attention to the physical body.

In ancient China, there has been a long alchemical tradition of creating elixirs (*waidan* 外丹), which synthesize herbal, animal, and mineral ingredients. These were produced according to elaborate and secret recipes to produce materials that could be eaten, drunk, or inhaled. Lacking scientific procedures for systematic testing, however, these elixirs frequently contained highly toxic substances, such as mercury. They sometimes brought death on the partakers, from emperors to practitioners, sometimes suddenly, but other times through long, painful processes. These experiences prompted practitioners to look for other paths toward immortality, leading toward the idea of internal alchemy, *neidan* 內丹. The term *neidan* can refer to a tradition or body of teachings, to specific practices and exercises, or to the inner state attained through such practices.[74] *Neidan* relies upon the body's intrinsic substances and energies, built on the belief that through continuous practice, one will be able to activate hidden internal body forces and transform the body both physically and spiritually into an everlasting existence.

This shift toward *neidan* was also linked to a philosophical change from the external to the internal, as we see in views of free wandering or play, *you* 遊, which appears as a central goal in the *Zhuangzi*. There is external wandering, which wanders outside in the world, however, there

[73] For the complete English translation, see L. Wu and T. L. Davis, "An Ancient Chinese Treatise on Alchemy Entitled Ts'an T'ung Ch'I,", *Isis* 18:2 (1932), 210–289. The biography of Wei Boyang can be found in Ge Hong's *"Biographies of Immortals"* 葛洪神仙傳 (Beijing: Xueyuan Press, 學苑出版社, 1998).

[74] Pregadid and Skar, "Inner Alchemy," in the *Daoism Handbook*, p. 481.

is also internal wandering in the body itself. The *Liezi* distinguishes external wandering, which seeks in external things, from inner wandering, which involves become sufficient in one's own body.[75] Turning to one's own body is the best way to be with *Dao*.

The *Zhouyi Can Tong Qi* is about cultivating and transforming the body, using an approach deeply rooted in yinyang thought. Pregadid and Skar explain: "The *Can tongqi* uses an obscure metaphoric structure and an extremely complex terminology to link alchemical processes with various cosmological patterns. The two main emblematic substances in its theories are mercury and lead, symbolizing Real Yin (*zhenyin*) and Real Yang (*zhenyang*), respectively."[76]

Based on a yinyang conceptual framework, the *Zhouyi Can Tong Qi* distinguishes four related elements: *qian*/heaven, *kun*/earth, *li*/fire, and *kan*/water. Heaven and earth are the structure (*ti*) of yinyang, and fire and water are the function (*yong*) of yinyang. Heaven and fire are yang, whereas earth and water are yin.

These four factors refer to trigrams from the *Yijing* (*Book of Changes*). *Qian*/heaven consists of three yang lines, whereas *kun*/earth consists of all yin lines. *Li*/fire has yang lines above and below with a yin line in the center. *Kan*/water is the inverse, with yin lines above and below and a yang line in the center. We have already discussed the *li* and *kan* trigrams as they come together to form the *jiji* hexagram (with *kan*/water above and *li*/fire below) in (Chapter 2). We have also seen them in the structure of Zhou Dunyi's *Taijitu*. The importance of these two trigrams partly originated from their role in the *Zhouyi Can Tong Qi*:

> Heaven and earth are established and the *Yi* [Changes] operates among them. Heaven and earth are the images of *qian* and *kun*. What comprises positions is the arrangement of yin and yang and their interaction. *Kan* and *li* are the function of *qian* and *kun*. These two functions have no fixed line position and flow within the six voids. They come and go without fixation, fluctuate up and down without constancy, hiding and disappearing, changing and transforming. They embrace the ten thousands things and the thread of Dao, using emptiness to form tangible things and using vessels to hold nothingness. The state of *kan* and *li* bring growing and resting.[77]

We can also consider the opening statement of the *Zhouyi Can Tong Qi*:

---

[75] B. Yang, p. 128.

[76] Pregadid and Skar, "Inner Alchemy," in the *Daoism Handbook*, p. 466.

[77] Chen Quanlin 陈全林 (ed.). *Zhouyi Can Tong Qi* 周易参同契, (Beijing: Chinese Social Science Press 中国社会科学出版社, 2004), p. 15.

Qian-heaven and Kun-earth are the gateways of change; they are the father and mother of all of the trigrams and hexagrams. *Kan*-water and *Li*-fire may be compared to the four walls of a city; their workings are like the hub of a wheel. Masculine and feminine, these four trigrams function like bellows and reeds. Controlling the way of yin and yang is like the work of a skilled driver – one holds the reins, is correct like the compass and square, and follows the tracks exactly.[78]

乾坤者, 易之門戶, 眾卦之父母. 坎離匡廓, 運轂正軸, 牝牡四卦, 以為橐籥. 覆冒陰陽之道, 猶工御者, 準繩墨, 執銜轡, 正規矩, 隨軌轍.

We see here several metaphors central to yinyang strategy as examined in the last chapter, in particular the comparison to driving a chariot.

This passage also highlights the inherent link between cosmology and *neidan* practice, linked through the four elements of nature – heaven, earth, fire, and water – which themselves are connected through yinyang. Bodily transformation is based on the belief that fire and water should interact and attain completion, as we saw in the discussion of the *jiji* hexagram. This interaction is the function and manifestation of heaven and earth. The *Zhouyi Can Tong Qi* states:

If a thing has no yin and yang it will be against the way of heaven. A hen cannot conceive by herself. There would be no healthy chickens [...]. Endowment and transformation are the nature of heaven and earth. It is just as fire moves upward and water flows downward. There is no teacher to guide them but they are self-so.[79]

Based on these cosmological links, the *Zhouyi Can Tong Qi* posits three basic constituents of *neidan*: the tripod/furnace (*dinglu* 鼎爐), the materials (*yaowu* 藥物), and the firing (*huohou* 火候). All three originally refer literally to the key elements involved in external alchemy, but they are applied to illuminate the internal process of bodily cultivation.

The first factor is the "tripod and furnace." The physical tripod used in alchemy itself was divided according to yinyang.[80] The human body is a miniature of this cauldron that has its upper head as the tripod (*ding* 鼎) and the area just below the belly button as the furnace (*lu* 爐). The 5 organs, 12 vessels, 24 vertebrae, and 360 joints are all part of this bodily *dinglu*. Nature is seen as a giant furnace that contains heaven/*qian* and

---

[78] I am grateful to Louis Komjathy for the translation of this passage.

[79] Chen (ed.), *Zhouyi Can Tong Qi*, p. 112.

[80] For more information on *Dinglu*, see I. Robinet, "Dinglu" in *The Encyclopaedia of Taoism*, edited by F. Pregadio (ed.) (New York : Routledge, 2008), p. 362.

earth/*kun*. The 4 seasons, 12 months, 24 periods, and 360 days are parts
of this natural furnace.

The second factor is the materials (*yaowu* 藥物), visualized in terms
of *kan*/fire and *li*/water. In nature, *kan* as yang is sun and fire; *li* as yin is
moon and water. It is because of the interaction between sun and moon
and fire and water, ultimately yang and yin, that the myriad things are
generated and sustained. In the human body, the heart is *kan* and the
kidney is *li*. *Kan* or heart is the home for spirit and the central controller of the human body. *Li* or kidney designates a sphere of influence
that penetrates and regulates the biological, psychological, and spiritual functions of the water phase. Kidney/water is the most potent and
foundational among the five phases, and it is the home for *jing* (refined
essence), which is sperm in the male and blood in the female. Kidney is
the source of human energy, specifically sexual energy. *Li* and *kan* (heart
and kidney) must be in a constant state of interaction.

The third factor is firing or timing (*huohou* 火候). Like external
alchemy, inner alchemy contains four stages: picking (*cai* 採), making
(*zao* 造), refining (*lian* 煉), and mixing (*hun* 混). Picking concerns the
proper measurement for the giving and taking of yinyang. The other three
stages depend on the proper firing, which requires an adjustment of yinyang. This adjustment consists of breathing exercises in which inhaling is
yang and exhaling is yin and will. All of these procedures follow yinyang
patterns to secure a successful result.

Kan-Li dynamics are at the core of another key Daoist distinction,
between the primordial state called "before heaven" (*xiantian* 先天) and
the formation of concrete things "after heaven" (*houtian* 後天). A concern
with the primordial state before the structured natural world – referred to
as what is before heaven – can be traced back to the *Daodejing* chapter 25,
which says, "There is something generated before heaven and earth [有物
混成, 先天地生]." The "Great Teacher" chapter of the *Zhuangzi* similarly
says that Dao is "generated before heaven and earth [先天地生]."[81]

We have already seen the consistent orientation toward explaining
cosmological processes through a division from oneness into multiplicity, passing through yinyang. This relationship is taken up through the
distinction between a prenatal state before heaven and a postnatal state
after heaven. As Pregadid and Skar put it:

> While yin and yang "before heaven" are in their prime state and join to
> form Oneness, in the state "after heaven," original yang is enclosed in yin

[81] Chen, *Commentaries on Zhuangzi*, p. 181.

entities (yang within yin), while original yin is found in yang entities (yin within yang). This notion underlies several modes of representation of the *neidan* process, and provides the foundations for recovering the primary constituents of the cosmos and the human person.[82]

The distinction between *xiantian* (before heaven) and *houtain* (after heaven) supports two points. First, there is something beyond this tangible world, something primordial and authentic, categorized in the *Taipingjing* as *yuan* 元 (primordial, originary, the root). The most precious elements of human life, such as *jing* 精 (refined essence), *qi* 氣, and *shen* 神 (spirit) are classified as *yuanjing, yuanqi,* and *yuanshen.* These are the manifestations of *Dao* or the intangible, unformed state of before heaven. Second, body cultivation is about returning (*fan*) to this primordial state. One must cultivate this original state (*xiantian*) by using what one has now (*houtian*).[83] Life is the interplay between *xiantian* and *houtian.* This vision is also captured in the *Fuxi xiantian* and *Wenwang houtian* cosmological emblems, which will be discussed in Chapter 6. In the framework we have seen in the *Zhouyi Can Tong Qi,* *qian* and *kun* represent the unconditioned state before heaven, whereas *kan* and *li* represent the conditioned state after heaven. Pregadid and Skar explain:

> *Kan* is the conditioned aspect of *kun,* and *li* is the conditioned aspect of *qian.* However, the yin trigram *kan* or Water enclosed a solid yang line, which is Real Fire (yang within yin) and the yang trigram *li* or Fire encloses a broken yin line, which is Real Water (yin within yang). The two inner lines symbolize the original yin and yang principles of before Heaven.[84]

These hexagrams had concrete implications for conceptions of gender and the specificity of bodily cultivation. *Kan*/water represented the female, leading to the belief that women contain a yang element inside, and therefore, it is faster for women to be transformed than for men. *Li*/fire represents the male, however, it has a yin line inside. Therefore, it takes men a longer time to attain immortality. A man's foundation is convex, and the convex organ is called the "essence chamber" (*jingshi* 精室). Woman's foundation is concave, and the concave organ is called the *zigong* 子宮, literally, the "children's palace." The vital force in men is located in the *qi* cavity; in women, the vital force is located at the point between the breasts. Through the process of body cultivation, however,

---

[82] Pregadid and Skar, "Inner Alchemy," in the *Daoism Handbook*, p. 484.

[83] See R. Wang, "Kundao: A Lived Body in the Female Daoist Text," *Journal of Chinese Philosophy*, 36:2 (2009), 277–292.

[84] Pregadid and Skar, "Inner Alchemy," in the *Daoism Handbook*, p. 486.

men and women lose their secondary sexual characteristics and reach a more androgynous ideal, with men strengthening yin and women strengthening yang. This vision supports taking sexuality as one of the most direct ways of harmonizing yin and yang. It is by the interaction between heaven and earth, male and female, that myriad things are generated and transformed. "The *Dao* of *qian* (heaven) completes the male; the *Dao* of *kun* (earth) completes the female."[85] Intercourse is necessary not only for the individual's well-being but also for the proper functioning of the universe. As the *Zhouyi Can Tong Qi* says, "*Qian* is hardness, *kun* is softness. They are mutually complementary and mutually containing. Yang endows and yin embraces; male and female are mutually necessary. This mutual need brings creation and transformation (*zaohua* 造化)."[86]

This mutuality naturally leads to what is known as the dual cultivation of male and female, in which the transformation of yang to yin and yin to yang is enabled through techniques in which a man and a woman work together, including sexual practices.[87] We read: "The male does not stay alone and the female does not live unaccompanied. Tigers, turtles and snakes are intertwined together to mutually support each other. This clarifies that male and female are jointly needed."[88]

Spirits/Souls

Understanding yinyang as a strategy and particularly as a form of bodily cultivation requires that we give up any assumed dualism, not only between body and mind but also between body and spirit. The emphasis on embodiment thought does not lead to a way of thinking that is reductionist or purely materialist in its approach to the world.[89] Yinyang body transformation brings out the linkage between our immediate presence in this earthly world and the broader indeterminate and generative foundations of nature. In the restricted sense of going beyond the normal and current limits of the body as a discrete thing, we can point to a

---

[85] Chen (ed.), *Zhouyi Can Tong Qi*, p. 9.
[86] Ibid., p. 70.
[87] Despeaux and Kohn, *Women in Daoism*, (Cambridge: Three Pines Press, 2003), p. 223.
[88] Chen (ed.), *Zhouyi Can Tong Qi*, p. 123.
[89] Harper writes, "The *Guanzi*, Neiye, provides the best testimony of the fourth century B.C. formulation of physiological theories which fused the physical and spiritual components of the human organism, and which made vapor [qi] the source of each." Harper (trans.), *The Mawangdui Medical Manuscripts*, p. 119.

transcendent dimension of body cultivation, reflected in the penetrating and pervasive power of yinyang. The physio-spiritual fusion underlying bodily cultivation in many medical and alchemical texts encompasses what we would often distinguish as spiritual practices.

There are Chinese terms that designate something like the spirit or soul, however, all are conceptualized and related to the body through yinyang. We have encountered one important term, the multilayered word *shen*, which could refer to a spirit or what goes beyond our present, cognitive ability. *Shen* can come to inhabit the human body, and this is one goal of body cultivation. Cao Wenyi 曹文逸, a female Daoist in the Song Dynasty (960-1279), takes the body as the best residence of *shen*, however, she taught that the body had to first be made clean and proper so that *shen* would come and reside.[90] We see this in the *Taipingjing*, which marks a key step in the divinification of Daoism. In this text, yinyang becomes the explicit foundation of Daoist teachings. Yinyang takes on a transcendent meaning but also becomes more specific. The *Taipingjing* states:

> For one who is being empty [*xuwu* 虚無], the inside is full and the outside is empty, their having is like empty. They return to the state of a fetus and inhabit Dao. Alone, they preserve their heart/mind and attain the "dragon's concern," and so they become the house of *shen*, gathering Dao and emptiness but wandering with *qi*. Thus they are empty. With *qi* and *shen*, their excess is always eliminated. They take the heart as center and thus attain being without deviance.[91]

There are two steps in this progression from *Dao* to *shen*. From nonaction (*wuwei*) one attains the first step, which is quietness. This state is then able to unite with *shen*, which results in leaving nothing undone (*wubuwei*). These are two interrelated fields. The first focuses on the heart/mind, is guided by emptiness, and is released from all desires, leaving only "the dragon's concern."[92] The second field is to live with *Dao*, however, this will move on with primordial *qi* (*yuanqi*) and be with *shen*. It is centered on the heart/mind, as well.

Although translated as "spirit," *shen* cannot be identified with a soul, however, yin and yang have been identified with something closer to human spirits or souls, known as *hun* 魂 and *po* 魄. In the Western

---

[90] Y. Chen, *Commentary on Lingyuan Dadaoge*, 靈源大道歌, (Beijing: Chinese Daoist Association Publishing, 1988), p. 10.

[91] *Taipingjing*, p. 1105.

[92] The "Dragon" refers to Laozi.

tradition, the soul is usually spoken of in terms of radiance and light.[93] In the early Chinese context, the soul is not a single entity but two inter-related forces, labeled as *hun* and *po*. As one would expect, indigenous Chinese views of soul were also understood through a yinyang frame-work.[94] *Hun* and *po* are manifestations of yang and yin in the realm of the human spirit. The earliest usage of the word *po* can be traced back to Zhou oracle bone inscriptions in the eleventh century B.C.E. Ying-shih Yu writes, "Etymologically, *po* means white, whiteness, or bright light and probably derives from the growing light of the new moon."[95] The chang-ing phases of the moon appeared as the periodic birth and death of its white light or *po*, so *po* became associated with yin. *Po* is responsible for growth and is patterned on the waxing and waning of moon. Therefore *po* is yin, which is how the *Shuowen jiezi* defines it: "po is the yin spirit [魄: 陰神]." Yu suggests it might have developed in the south of China and then spread to the north in sixth century B.C.E.[96] In the *Zuozhuan, po* is more fundamental and *hun* is a derivative notion:

> The first transformation in human life is called *po*, and when the *po* is pro-duced, its yang is called *hun*. By means of an abundance of material and refined essence [*jing*], the *hun* and *po* then strengthen, and so the refined essence and vigor reaches the point of spirit illumination [*shenming*]."[97]

人生始化曰魄, 既生魄, 陽曰魂, 用物精多 是以有精爽, 至於神明

Here, *hun* is the yang aspect of *po*, and *hun* as yang emerges from *po* as yin.[98] Thus, the *Shuowen Jiezi* defines *hun* by saying "*hun* is yang *qi* [魂, 陽气也]."

---

[93] Tansley says that according to the Greek tradition, "soul is a radiant body of light, which they called *augoeides*, meaning 'form of radiance.'" D. V. Tansley, *Subtle Body: Essence and Shadow* (London: Thames and Hudson, 1977), p. 6.

[94] Stevan Harrell says, "The idea of two 'souls' stems from the fundamental yin-yang dual-ism which has permeated so much of Chinese religious and philosophical thought, and which has influenced folk belief as well." S. Harrell, "The Concept of Soul in Chinese Folk Religion," *The Journal of Asian Studies*, 38:3 (1979), 521.

[95] Y. Yu, "New Evidence on the Early Chinese Conception of Afterlife – A Review Article," *The Journal of Asian Studies*, 41:1 (1981), 83.

[96] Y. Yu, "O Soul, Come Back! A Study in the Changing Conceptions of the Soul and Afterlife in Pre-Buddhist China," *Harvard Journal of Asiatic Studies*, 47:2 (1987), p. 373.

[97] Li (ed.), Zuozhuan, p. 1292.

[98] Xu Xingwu says, "According to Chinese traditional cosmology, the process of *hun* gen-erated from *po* is the process of yang generated from yin. Although *po* is yin but it is deci-sive." 徐興無 Xu Xingwu, "Concepts of 'Hun' and 'Po' as Found in the Han-Dynasty Theory of Human Nature," 漢代人性論中的"魂", "魄"觀念" *Journal of Nanjing University* 南京大學學報, 47:2 (2010), 51.

Connecting *hun* and *po* souls to yang and yin naturally sets them within a complex web of categories. *Po* is connected with the physical form (*xing*), whereas *hun* relates to *qi* (vital energy). As in the preceding passage from the *Zuozhuan*, *po* connects with *jing* (refined essence), whereas *hun* connects with *shen* (spirit). The *Huangdi Neijing* makes the same connection, although emphasizing movement more: "What follows the coming and going of *shen* is called *hun*; what enters and exists together with refined essence [*jing*] is called *po*."[99] (隨神往來者謂之魂; 並精而出入者謂之魄.)

Hun and *po* cannot be taken too strictly as discrete entities. There is significant scholarly debate about how many *hun* and *po* a person has and how they work to compose the person.[100] In most Daoist teachings, there are three *hun* and seven *po* (*sanhun qipo* 三魂七魄). These are further categorized into yin-*hun* and yang-*hun*, yin-*po* and yang-*po*. These divisions fall within the broader division between *hun* souls as yang, and *po* souls as yin. *Hun* and *po* are not independent of each other. K. E. Brashier has criticized Yu's dualistic division of *hun* and *po* based on new archeological findings and analysis of medical texts, arguing persuasively that *hun* and *po* are interconnected and are not two isolated entities.[101] In fact, *hun* and *po* are better thought of as forces rather than beings. Farzeen Baldrian-Hussein writes:

> Although the term "souls" is often used to refer to them, they are better seen as two types of vital entities, the source of life in every individual. The *hun* is Yang, luminous, and volatile, while the *po* is Yin, somber, and heavy. They are moreover to be considered the epitome of the spiritual (*shen*) and the demonic (*gui*): the *hun* represents spirit, consciousness, and intelligence, whereas the *po* represents physical nature, bodily strength and movement.[102]

This conception of *hunpo* as interrelated forces is what we would expect, given its analysis through yinyang.

Hun and *po* are active in both the human body and consciousness. In Han medical texts, *hunpo* inhabit the human body and play an essential role in the body's physiology.[103] Ying-shih Yu argues that the ancient

---

[99] Niu, (ed.), *Huangdi Neijing*, p. 29.

[100] Harrell, "The Concept of Soul," p. 521.

[101] Brashier, "Han Thanatology," p. 140.

[102] F. Baldrian-Hussein, "Hun and Po" in *The Encyclopedia of Taoism*, p. 521. Note that *gui* refers to the soul of the dead and is different than *hun* and *po*, which are the soul of living.

[103] Brashier, "Han Thanatology," p. 145.

Chinese generally believed that breathing (from heaven) and eating (from earth) were the two basic human activities governed by the souls: *po* as bodily soul (*xingpo*) and hun as breath-soul (*hunqi*).[104] *Hun* and *po* are living forces that form a union with the human body when one is alive. At death, they depart and leave the body. *The Elegies of Chu* (*Chuci* 楚辭) refers to this as "*hun* and *po* separating and leaving" (*hunpo lisan* 魂魄離散). They have their own fate. The *hun*-soul as *qi* moves quickly up to heaven, and the *po*-soul, as the heavier physical form, moves downward to earth. Therefore, one death ritual called the *fu* attempts to "summon the *hun* and return the *po*" (*zhaohun fupo* 招魂复魄).[105] There is a T-shaped painting excavated in the Mawangdui tomb in Changsha that symbolizes this kind of summoning of the soul and offers an archaeological confirmation of the *fu* ritual.

Hun and *po* are of great concern in (bodily) cultivation, because improper actions can cause the *hun* and *po* to leave the human body. One must avoid this "losing *hun* and destroying *po*" (*diuhun shipo* 丢魂失魄), a common expression even today. The *Zhouyi Can Tong Qi* makes this connection directly: "If yinyang is properly measured, then *hun* 魂 and *po* 魄 can reside. The spirit of yang (yang *shen*) is called *hun* and the spirit of yin (yin *shen*) is called *po*. The *hun* and *po* are mutually rooted."[106]

The concern for preserving the *po* goes back to the *Daodejing*, chapter 10, which asks rhetorically, "in carrying *yingpo* and embracing oneness, can you keep them from leaving?" [載營魄抱一, 能無離乎？] The *Heshang Gong Commentary* indicates that *yingpo* here refers to *hunpo*. The link to body cultivation in these passages again marks clear that even if we label *hun* and *po* as "souls," they cannot be separated from the body and bodily cultivation.

In the Daoist text *Zhonglun* 中論 (*On Balance*) by the late Han Dynasty (25–220 C.E.) scholar Xu Gan 徐幹 (170–217 C.E.), there is a dialogue explaining the *po*, giving a different approach to its role in cultivation:

> Someone asked, "Confucius said the benevolent person will have longevity but Yan Hui had an early death. It is said that 'the family which accumulates virtues must have plenty.' Yet Bi Gan 比干 and Zi Xu 子胥 suffered grand misfortune. Is it the case that sages use words to deceive later generations? The answer is this: Sages die but they are immortal. First, they have established virtue (*de*), second, they have established accomplishment, and third they have established words. Although their bodies are gone their *Dao*

---

[104] Yu, "O Soul, Come Back!" p. 374.
[105] Ibid., p. 363.
[106] Q. Chen (ed.), *Zhouyi Cantongqi*, p. 87.

still exists. This is called immortality [不朽]. The physical body form is the essence of *po*; following virtue and righteousness is the glory of the essence of *po*. Therefore, sages love their physical forms and complete them with virtue and rightness.[107]

Although the *po* is the core of the physical form, it should be formed through virtue, thus linking the body and virtue together. This passage appears to be a critique or reinterpretation of the doctrine of immortality, interpreting it in terms of lasting fame and influence rather than literally avoiding death.

---

[107] Xu Xiangling 徐湘霖 (ed.), "夭壽 chapter," *Zhonglun Xiaozhu* 中論校注 *On Balance* (Chengdu: Bashu Press, 巴蜀出版社, 2007), p. 205.

6 Yinyang Symbol: Knowing Through Visual Presentation

Now for the thinking soul images take the place of direct perceptions; and when it asserts or denies that they are good or bad, it avoids or pursues them. Hence the soul never thinks without a mental image.

Aristotle

Art is a form of magic designed as a mediator between this strange hostile world and us.

Picasso

The yinyang symbol is the most popular representation of yinyang in the West. It has been used as an icon appearing on everything from book covers, business logos, and advertisements, to earrings, candles, and tattoos. The Chinese terms yin and yang have become a part of colloquial English, partly through this image. The image can also be seen everywhere in China, from temples to the well-known yinyang soup, which swirls together green vegetables and white egg yolk. Any comprehensive investigation of yinyang must offer some account of this symbol and its significance.

Some Chinese scholars have speculated that the yinyang symbol is an image of the meeting place between the cleaner water of the Yangzi River and muddy water of the Yellow River, but it is doubtful that the Yangzi River and the Yellow River would ever have actually crossed each other. However, at Chaotianmen dock in the city of Chongqing, the Jialing River and the Yangzi River converge, and one can see the swirling point between clean water and muddy water, which does produce a spiral-like movement resembling the image of yin and yang.

The yinyang symbol is also sometimes called a fish symbol because it looks like two intertwined fish chasing each other in water. One Western scholar has even speculated that the symbol originated from the *Notitia dignitatum* of the Roman Empire.[1] One could also note that the yinyang symbol resembles what is known as the "logarithmic spiral," which has cross-cultural significance.[2] Nature exhibits logarithmic spirals from sunflowers, seashells, and whirlpools, to hurricanes and giant galaxies, so it is clear that nature itself supplies this spiral pattern. One striking feature of the logarithmic spiral is that it does not alter its shape as its size increases, a feature known as self-similarity. The yinyang symbol may be a reflection of this universal structure, just as the pairing of yin and yang in the hexagrams of the *Yijing* express common ways of binary thinking.

This chapter will look briefly at the genealogy of the yinyang symbol, showing that, although this icon was not found in early China, it stemmed from a diversified image-making tradition that developed over a long period of time. The yinyang symbol is not an aberration or something that might have been imported from elsewhere, as has been suggested, but one member of a far-flung family of symbols that evolved over time.

How can we read this circular design divided into two interlocking halves with two antithetical dots? If an image is a representation, what is this image meant to represent? Answering these questions will further our understanding of the complexity of yinyang thought and steer us toward a conclusion for this book. By placing this symbol in its historical context, we can better grasp how it gives rise to meaning and insight as a specific aspect of Chinese epistemology, which takes image making as a particular way of thinking and expressing thought.

The concern with images (*xiang* 象) and the making of diagrams (*tu* 圖) arose in part out of a concern for the limits of discursive language. If, as we have seen, yinyang reveals a self-generating and self-transforming world, then how can human linguistic tools like words capture this full living reality in its vibrant patterns or changing configurations? This concern first surfaced in the interpretation of *The Yijing* (*Book of Changes*).

---

[1] di Giovanni Monastra, "The 'Yin-Yang' among the Insignia of the Roman Empire?" *Sophia*, 6:2 (2000), [it. ed. *Futuro Presente*, a. 4:8 (inverno, 1996)]. Translated from the Italian by John Monastra.

[2] For example, the Spanish mathematician, Jacques Bernoulli (1654–1705) indicated that the logarithmic spiral "may be used as a symbol, either of fortitude and constancy in adversity, or of the human body, which after all its changes, even after death, will be restored to its exact and perfect self." Mario Livio, *The Golden Ratio: The Story of Pi, the World's Most Astonishing Number* (New York: Broadway Books, 2002), p. 116. Bernoulli asked that the following epitaph be assigned to his tombstone: "*Eadem mutato resurgo*" ("Though changing, I rise again the same").

The "Xici" commentary of *The Book of Changes,* links *xiang* explicitly
to the limits of language: "The master said, writing does not bring out
exhaustively what is said, and what is said does not bring out exhaustively what is thought. The sages set up *xiang* (images) in order to bring
out exhaustively what is thought."[3] This doubt about the human ability to express thoughts in language turns to making *xiang* (images) as a
way of deepening what can be conveyed to others, but also as a form of
thinking itself. This belief that *xiang* provide a different and sometimes
more effective form of knowledge and communication has been a common view from early in the history of Chinese thought. For example, the
Huangdi Neijing says: "For heaven, earth, and yinyang, one should not
just use numbers to reason but also use *xiang* to name them." (天地陰陽
者, 不以數推以象之謂也). [4]

We have seen that from the Han Dynasty (202 B.C.E.–220 C.E.) through
the Ming and Qing dynasties (1368–1911) there was a consistent tension
between two schools of thought in interpreting the *Yijing*: the school of
images and numbers (*xiangshu* 象數) and the school of meanings and
interpretations (*yili* 義理).[5] Both of these schools seek to codify the order
and patterns in the world through human constructs, whether to formulate this underlying pattern through numbers and visual images (*xiangshu*) or words and concepts (*yili*). Jing Fang 京房 (78–37 B.C.E.) and Meng
Xi 孟喜 (West Han Dynasty 206 B.C.E.–9 C.E.) promoted "establishing
xiang to fully get the meaning" (*lixiang jinyi,* 立象盡意), whereas Wang Bi
(王弼 226–249 C.E.), an influential commentator on the *Daodejing* and
the *Yijing*, claimed that one "gets the meaning and then forgets the *xiang*"
(*deyi wangxiang* 得意忘象).[6]

Regarding *xiang* in the *Yijing*, on the one hand, its commentaries
prognosticated on *xiang* as omens, astrological signs, and numerological devices; on the other hand, they also gave rise to what we might call
"*xiang* thinking," as embodying a particular way of reasoning. As a way
of understanding the world, this *xiang* thinking assumes that everything
carries or contains one or another form of *xiang.* Whenever we confront
a being or phenomenon, we should also seize its *xiang* representation.

[3] W. J. Peterson, "Making Connections: Commentary on the Attached Verbalizations of the
Book of Change," Harvard Journal of Asiatic Studies, 1982, 42),p. 99.

[4] Zhang Yingan 張隱庵, (ed.), *Huangdi Neijing Commentaries* 黃帝內經素問集注 (Beijing:
Xueyuan Press 學苑出版社, 2002), p. 562..

[5] For further discussion, see B. Zhu, 朱伯昆, *The Philosophical History of Yi Studies* 易學哲
學史, (Beijing: Huaxia Press 華夏出版社, 1995).

[6] Bi Wang, "Clarifying Images," in *Zhouyi Lueli* (周易略例) (Beijing: Chinese Press, 1980),
p. 607.

These *xiang* can be considered as representations based on similarity. Thus, John Henderson takes them as "the *simulacrum* or *doppelgänger* of cosmic patterns."[7] Willard Peterson states, "Being change [*yi*] is a matter of *xiang*; being *xiang* is a matter of resembling."[8]

The *xiang*, however, are not simply human creations. They exist independently of human perception as a form or shape, a pattern or configuration. The *Liji* gives a common view of *xiang* as coming from heaven/the sky (*tian*): "The earth supports the myriad things, while heaven hangs down its *xiang*. . . . Sages imitate them."[9] *Xiang*, however, are not obvious or given ready-made. From observation to taking an image is a process of articulating meanings in which one needs to figure out which *xiang* can express the best meaning, and in what way. *Xiang* can be translated as "figure" in both its nominal and verbal senses. Petersons explains: "To figure is to represent as a symbol or image, but also to give or bring into shape."[10] However, *xiang* as a figure is not to be confused with *xing* 形 (form), the term we have seen for the physical form of the body. *Xing* is more concrete and is evident in a particular structure. *Xiang*, however, is more subtle and demands a special way of knowing, if it is to be recognized. *Xiang* attempts to integrate both the particular and the whole, the general and the specific.[11]

In Chapter 3, we discussed *xiang* images, with a focus on their function as a way to classify things in their interconnectedness and relationships. In this chapter, *xiang* will be considered as visual presentations, as a medium connecting the realm of what is intelligible to the realm of what is imperfectly knowable, thus mediating between known and unknown. Rather than just discuss the yinyang symbol, we will consider the variety of attempts to diagram the structure of the universe with visual representations of yin and yang. This will both help to draw together the various

---

[7] John B. Henderson, *The Development and Decline of Chinese Cosmology* (New York: Columbia University Press, 1984), p. 12.

[8] Peterson, "'Verbalizations' of the *Book of Change*," p. 99.

[9] Wang Mengou, 王夢鷗 (ed.) *Liji*, 禮記今註今譯 (*Record of Rituals*), (Taipei: Taiwan Commercial Press, 1981), p. 421.

[10] Peterson, "'Verbalizations' of the *Book of Change*," p. 81.

[11] Zhang Zailin develops this point extensively, arguing that *xiang* thinking avoids the shortcomings of the two main schools of contemporary Western philosophy: analytical thought only sees the trees not the forest, whereas continental philosophy only sees the forest but not trees. For Zhang Zailin, *xiang* thinking can take into consideration both the specific tree as well as a giant forest. See, Zhang Zailin 张再林. *Traditional Chinese Philosophy as the Philosophy of the Body* 作为身体哲学的中国古代哲学, (Beijing: China Social Science Publishing House 中国社会科学出版社, 2008).

nuances of yinyang thought and to show the importance of diagrams (*tu*) and images as a form of thought and representation.

Genealogy of the Yinyang Symbol

There is no clear and definite way to determine the exact date of origin or the person who created the yinyang symbol as it exists today. No one has ever claimed specific ownership of this popular icon. The final form of the symbol as an independent image most likely arose in the Qing Dynasty, although something close to that image appeared as early as Zhao Huiqian's 趙撝謙 (1351–1395) *Tiandi Ziran Hetu* (天地自然河圖 *River Diagram of the Spontaneity of Heaven and Earth*), discussed later in this chapter. The image received its most common name, the *Taijitu*, from Zhang Huang 章 潢 (1527–1608), in a 7,000-page compendium that attempted to sort out Confucian materials from those of Daoist and Buddhist origin.[12] In this massive encyclopedic collection of diagrams, Zhang Huang includes a diagram he calls the "Ancient *Taiji* Diagram" (*gutaijitu* 古太極圖).

In any case, the symbol emerged from a rich textual and visual history of *xiang* making, growing out of traditions of commentary on the *Yijing*. These traditions involved intricate efforts to produce diagrams and charts linking numerical signs, circles, boxes, and lines for the sake of articulating the true patterns of the universe according to the vision of the *Yijing*. These visual presentations or *xiang* were not meant for aesthetic appreciation but rather for cosmological contemplation.

This *xiangshu* thinking became popular in the Han Dynasty and reached its peak in the Song Dynasty. In fact, making diagrams has been an integral part of intellectual work throughout Chinese history. For the school of *Xiangshu*, the way to systematize and interpret the *xiang* is to produce or draw their figurative and numerological representations. The most common effort of the *Xiangshu* school was to construct diagrams (*tu* 圖).[13] *Tu* have been seen as signifying celestial realities, deciphering terrestrial regions in a crystalline structure representing the dynamic patterns of the universe. Generations of intellectuals have labored on the formulation and creation of numerous *tu*.[14] These efforts

---

[12] Louis, Francois, "Genesis of an Icon: The Taiji Diagram's Early History," *Harvard Journal of Asiatic Studies*, **63** no. 1 (2003), p. 186.

[13] For a discussion of concept of *tu*, see Florian C. Reiter, "Some Remarks on the Chinese Word T'U 'Chart, Plan, Design,'" *Oriens*, 32 (1990), 308–322.

[14] The extent of the tradition of making *tu* is best reflected in the compilation of *tu* recently edited by Li Shen and Guo Yu, which consists of three volumes and thousands of pages.

were meant to integrate thinking and pictorial imagery, forming a genre distinct from the writing of books that attempt to explain things discursively. This genre formed early – among the manuscripts discovered at Mawangdui in 1973 in Hunan, there is one special category called *tu* (diagrams).[15] Guolong Lai explains, "Such excavated diagrams show that Warring Sates and Han authors extensively explored the advantage of a diagram as a non-linear, non-textual mode of visual communication, and used texts in conjunction with images to express complex cosmological ideas."[16] Neo-Confucians in the Song Dynasty used diagrams as a tool for the visualization of textual analysis and representations of structural aspects of a system of thought.[17] According to Francois Louis, in the tenth and eleventh centuries, *tu* were transmitted privately from master to student, playing an essential role in the pursuit of enlightenment and insight.[18]

These *tu* convey their meanings through variables of black and white, structure and lines, position and numbers, while taking yinyang as an underlying organizational code. Although *tu* are presented as pictures or charts and, thus, as descriptive, they also have a normative force, a sense of *fa* 法, serving as a model or rule. In other words, *tu* are a microcosm of the universe, and thus, they exemplify definite norms or rules for action.

This historical development in making diagrams can be traced back to the Song Dynasty Daoist monk Chen Tuan 陳摶 (906–989 C.E.).[19] It is believed that Chen Tuan lived on Hua Mountain (in what is now Shanxi Province, near the ancient capital city that is now Xi'an), and drew several *tu* in order to elucidate the *Yijing*. Though none of his *tu* have been directly passed down, he is considered the forerunner of the school of *tushu* 圖書 (diagrams and writings). It was said that he had three *tu*. The effort to rediscover these *tu* later became a popular pursuit.[20]

Zhouyi Tushuo Zonghui 周易圖說總匯, *The Complete Selection of Diagrams of the Zhouyi* (Shanghai: China Eastern Normal University Press 華東師範大學出版, 2004).

[15] Guolong Lai, "The Diagram of the Mourning System from Mawangdui," *Early China*, 28 (2003), 44.

[16] Ibid., 45.

[17] Louis, "The Taiji Diagram's Early History," 145–196.

[18] Ibid., 163.

[19] For more information on Chen Tuan, see Livia Kohn, "Chen Tuan in History and Legend," *Taoist Resources*, 2:1 (1990), 8–31.

[20] Zhu Zheng offers an account of the historical transmission of these works. According to him, Chen Tuan's *Xiantian Tu* was passed down from Zhong Fang 种放 (1014) to Mu Xiu 穆修 (979–1032) to Li Zhicai 李之才 (1045) and then came to Shao Yong. The *Hetu*

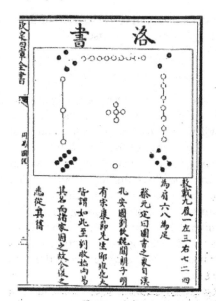
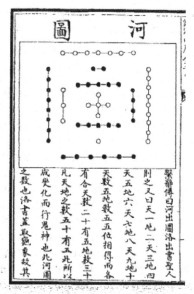

图 103 洛书 · 图 102 河图

（朱熹《原本周易本义》）

6.1. *Hetu* and *Luoshu*.

There were various approaches to the creation of diagrams, *tu*. The Qing Dynasty scholar Hu Wei 胡渭 (1633–1714), following the earlier Song Dynasty scholar Zhu Zheng 朱震 (1072–1138), distinguished three trends in making *tu* that emerged in the Song dynasty[21]: the *Hetu* 河圖 and *Luoshu* 洛書 (*The River Diagrams and Luo Writing*, Figures 6.1 and 6.2) of Liu Mu 劉牧 (1011–1064); the *Xiantian Tu* 先天圖 (*The Diagram of Before Heaven*, Figure 6.3) and *Houtian Tu* (*The Diagram After Heaven*, Figure 6.4) of Shao Yong 邵雍 (1011–1077); and the *Taijitu*, 太極圖 (*The Diagram of the Great Ultimate*, Figure 6.5) of Zhou Dunyi 周敦頤 (1017–1073). These trends eventually contributed to the formation of the first yinyang symbol, as we can see in Zhao Huiqian's *Tiandi Ziran Hetu* 天地自然河圖 (Figure 6.6) and Zhang Huang's *Gu Taiji Tu* 古太極圖 (*Ancient Diagram of Great*

and *Luoshu* tradition was handed through Li Gai to Xiu Jian to Fan Hechang, then to Liu Mu. The *Taiji tu* was carried by Mu Xiu to Zhou Dunyi. Zhu Zheng's speculations were confirmed and endorsed by Zhu Xi (1130–1200 C.E.) and have been accepted in intellectual circles since then.

[21] Wei Hu 胡渭, *Yitu Mingbian* 易圖明辨 *Clarifications of Yi Diagrams* (Taiwan: Guangwen Press, 廣文書局, 1977).

Ultimate) in the Ming Dynasty (Figure 6.7). We can consider each of these trends before turning specifically to the yinyang symbol itself.

Hetu and Luoshu (The River Diagram and Luo Writing)

Hetu and *luoshu* are believed to be the two oldest forms of numbered diagrams. Both refer to rivers: *he* 河 refers to rivers in general but also specifically the *Huang He*, the Yellow River; *Luo* 洛 is the proper name of a river in the city of Luo. The earliest occurrence of the term *hetu* is given in the "Kuming" chapter of the *Shangshu*, however, it also appears in other early classics. For example, in the *Analects*, Confucius claims, "The phoenix has not arrived; the *he* (river) has not issued its *tu* (diagram)."[22]

The "Liyun" chapter of the *Liji* mentions that the *hetu* appeared on the back of a dragon-like horse.[23] The *Xici* commentary on the *Yijing* also mentions both forms of diagrams as coming from rivers: "The *tu* was produced from the Yellow River and *shu* was produced from the Luo River. Sages model them."[24]

The *Hanshu* makes the strong claim that "when the world has the way, then the river brings forth a diagram [*tu*] and the Luo brings forth a document [*shu*]."[25] These images took on a variety of different functions. According to Michael Saso, *hetu* appears with two different roles in early texts, sometimes as a kind of precious object that gives legitimacy to a rule, usually associated with heaven's approval, and other times as a chart of the eight trigrams from the *Yijing*.[26] The *hetu* is usually presented with its companion chart, the *luoshu*. The two are complementary, with the *hetu* emphasizing permanence and the *luoshu* depicting change.[27] The *luoshu* was supposedly first seen on the back of a tortoise. Although *luoshu* are mentioned very early in Chinese history and were supposed to have been transmitted secretly for thousands of years, they first started to appear publically in the tenth century.[28]

[22] B. Liu 劉寶楠 (Qing Dynasty), *Analects* 論語正義 (Beijing: Chinese Press, 1990), p. 333.

[23] Wang, *Liji*, p. 386.

[24] Gao Heng 高亨, *Commentary on Zhouyi* 周易大傳今注 (Jinan: Qilu Press, 1998), p. 405.

[25] Ban Gu 班固, *Hanshu* 漢書 (*The Book of Han*), commentary by Yan Shigu 颜师古, (Beijing: Chinese Press, 1962), chapter 75, p. 3189.

[26] Michael Saso, "What Is the Ho-t'u?" *History of Religions*, 17 (February–May 1978), 406–407.

[27] Ibid., 402.

[28] Schuyler Cammann, "The Magic Square of Three in Old Chinese Philosophy and Religion," *History of Religions*, 1 (Summer 1961), 45.

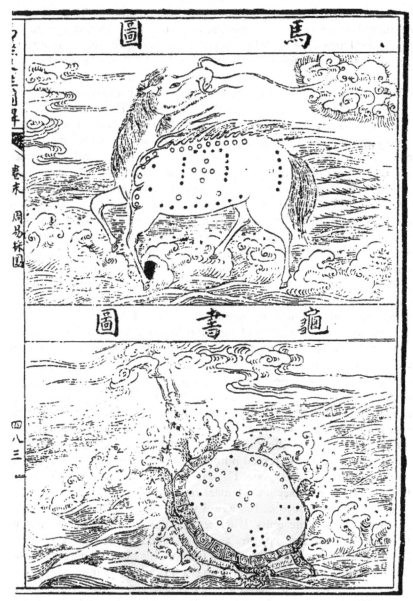

6.2. *Horse Diagram* and *Tortoise Diagram*. Zhouyi Tushu Zonghui, 周易圖書總匯, p. 181.

The ancient forms of the *hetu* and *luoshu* are unknown, but in the tenth century, such *tu* were used for meditative purposes in Daoist and Buddhist practice.[29] During the Song Dynasty, the *hetu* took on a new meaning and became a particular form of diagram. Liu Mu 劉牧, (1011–1064) composed a *hetu* that was said to present the image of heaven through a series of fifty-five spots that had been seen by Fuyi on the back of a dragon horse (*long ma* 龍馬) that emerged from the Yellow River (Figure 6.2).

Yin and yang form the core framework for this *tu*. The dark dots and even numbers represent yin, and the bright dots and odd numbers symbolize yang. The numbers are defined according to yin and yang functions. The yang odd numbers 1, 3, 5, 7, and 9 are associated more with initiation, birth, and generation and are called the numbers of generation (*shengshu* 生數). The yin even numbers 2, 4, 6, 8, and 10 are associated more with completion and results and, thus, are called the numbers of completion (*chengshu* 成數). The dots are joined together in pairs to form a mathematical pattern but also to represent the generative forces of the universe that come through the interaction of yin and yang.

In the *hetu*, all the yang numbers together add up to twenty-five, and all yin numbers add up to thirty. Together, they add up to a total of fifty-five, which is considered heaven's number (*tianshu* 天數). The *hetu* of heaven is organized in a pattern, and the fifty-five spots are grouped into ten subsets. There are several mathematical patterns in the *hetu*. For example, the sum total of even numbers on the top and the bottom equals the sum total of odd numbers on the top and the bottom. Yin and yang are thus balanced. Furthermore, the order of the numbers does not progress in a linear fashion, from small to large, but rather in different phases. The number is divided into either yang-odd number or yin-even number to form a movement of different configurations.

The *luoshu* also represented numbers with dots, having forty-five dots that are organized in a square. The earthly number (*dishu* 地數) is forty-five, and as we have seen, the square represents the earth. The diagram consists of nine groups of black and white circles or dots. Each group has from one to nine units. If we replace the dots with the equivalent numbers, the diagram appears as the so-called magic square of three: the sum of every row and column is fifteen. This magic square expresses the Chinese tendency to divide things into groups of nine equal units with a center. We see this emphasis on nine in spatial categorizations in particular: the nine continents, the nine territories, the nine provinces of the Middle Kingdom, and the nine divisions of heaven. In fact, this

[29] Louis, "The Taiji Diagram's Early History," p. 162.

luoshu design was also termed the "The Celestial Numbers of the Nine Halls" because it shows how an ideal house should be organized. It, thus, depicts yin and yang not only in mathematical terms but also in spatial terms, once again being both descriptive but also prescriptive in setting a model for the construction of human spaces.

The *hetu* and *luoshu* share many features.[30] Both are representations of the relationship of yin and yang in pairs of odd and even numbers centering around a middle number. As Schuyler Cammann puts it, they both "symbolize the world in balanced harmony around a powerful central axis."[31] The two diagrams are also complementary. The *hetu* was associated with circularity, the stars, the rules of mathematical astronomy, the eight trigrams, and the legendary sage king Fu Xi. The *luoshu* was associated with squareness, the earth, the rules of geographical measurement, the grid form of nine squares (*jiuzhou* 九洲), and the sage king Yu.

If we consider image making as a way of representing the complexity of yinyang, the *hetu* and *luoshu* illustrate the use of images to integrate intersections of accounts based on yinyang, numbering systems, and spatial locations. Kidder Smith describes the results: "Thus the diagram functions as a matrix wherein disparate numerological phenomena, representing a multitude of processes, relationships, and points of view, can be successfully integrated, and myriads of disparate things successfully contemplated."[32]

The idea of arrangements of numbers in symmetrical figures to produce a balanced harmony may be common across cultures, as we see it also among the Pythagoreans in ancient Greece. There are crucial differences, however, in how these numbers were seen in relation to the phenomenal world. Mou Zongsan (1909–1995), a leading twentieth-century Chinese philosopher, brings out this contrast well, while also emphasizing the importance of numbers (*shu*) in Chinese thought. According to Mou Zongsan, the ancient Chinese view that everything consists of numbers means that numbers communicate the order of generation and completion. In his words:

> The natural generations and completions (*shengcheng*) have mathematical orders, and numbers were used to express these orders. Numbers, though,

---

[30] It should be noted that the names of the two diagrams were sometimes switched. In the beginning, it was said that *hetu* is the number forty-five and *luoshu* is the number fifty-five. However, Liu Mu reversed the order, and Zhuxi confirmed this change. Since then, the *hetu* is the number fifty-five.

[31] Cammann, "The Magic Square of Three," p. 48.

[32] Kidder Smith, *Sung Dynasty Use of the I Ching* (Princeton NJ: Princeton University Press, 1990), p. 122.

cannot generate the myriad things; rather, number is the result of the natural order of generation and completion. This view is more insightful than the Greek philosopher Pythagoras's view that number is the model for everything. Chinese treat generation and completion as the fundamental basis, that is, they focus on concrete facts, whereas Pythagoras treats abstract numbers as the fundamental basis, that is, he focuses on the abstract form. This is obviously the fallacy of misplaced concreteness.[33]

Although both Chinese thinkers and Pythagoras see the significance of numbers, Pythagoras identified numbers as things in themselves and emphasized their eternality as fixed relations, whereas Chinese took them as constructs emerging from patterns of change. They valued numbers as a way of understanding the function, order, and movement of yinyang to relate different phenomena as a coherent whole.

Shao Yong's Xiantian Xue 先天學 (The Learning of Before Heaven)

Shao Yong 邵雍 (1011–1077) is known as "one of the six masters of the Northern Song" and as a founding figure of Neo-Confucian thought.[34] He was also a numerologist and his book, *Huangji Jingshi* 皇極經世 (*The Sublime Principle Which Governs All Things Within the World*), develops a complex cosmology based on numerological charts.[35] His system organizes historical and natural phenomena into a coherent whole that is based on numbers and expressed by the hexagrams of the *Yijing*. Shao Yong's important contribution to the *xiangshu* tradition is his new theory of *xiantian xue* 先天學 (*The Learning of Before Heaven*) and his elaboration of several influential diagrams, *tu*. Shao Yong draws the eight trigrams into two *tu* named as *xiantian* 先天 (before heaven) and *houtain* 后天 (after heaven), the first attributed to Fu Xi and the second to King Wen. We have already discussed the terms *xiantian* and *houtian* in the previous chapter. The distinction between the two originated from Daoism, but Shao Yong visualized this distinction as a way of interpreting the *Yijing*.[36] For Shao Yong, these two diagrams transform the conceptual system of

---

[33] Zongsan Mou, *The Natural Philosophy and Ethical Meanings of the Book of Changes* (Taibei: Wenjing Press, 1988), p. 48.

[34] The other five are Zhou Dunyi, Zhang Zai, the two Cheng brothers, and Sima Guang.

[35] Michael D. Freeman says that it "contains a rigid, mechanistic and esoteric cosmology based upon numerological charts." "From Adept to Worthy: The Philosophical Career of Shao Yung," *Journal of the American Oriental Society*, 102 (1982), 484.

[36] For a discussion of Shao Yong's sources, see Smith, *Sung Dynasty Uses of the I Ching*, p. 112, and Freeman, *The Philosophical Career of Shao Yung*, p. 482.

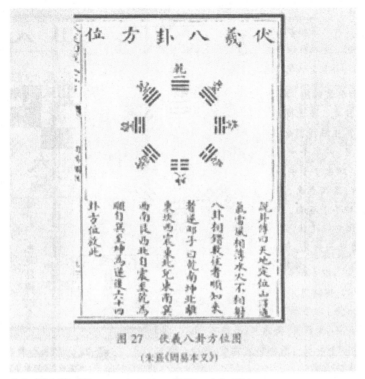

6.3. The Fu Xi arrangement of The eight Trigrams.

Zhu Xi, 朱熹 *Zhouyi Benyi* 周易本義, *Sikuquanshu* 四庫全書, 經部, p. 3.

the *Yijing* into visual presentations, revealing the basic forces of the universe. We can begin by considering the two diagrams.

The *xiantian tu* was also called the "Fu Xi Arrangement of The Eight Trigrams" (Figure 6.3). It reflects the points of Fu Xi's compass that guides the directions of changes. South (*qian/tian*) is up and north (*kun/di*) is below, forming a north-south axis; fire (*li*) is on the east and water (*kan*) is on the west, forming the east-west axis. These four cardinal trigrams set up the basic matrix of directions. The mountain-lake pair of trigrams and thunder-wind pair are placed in between. The *xiantian* diagram circles around the center. It goes from the top, *qian*, through the decline of yang, to the bottom of fullest yin, *kun*, then back up as the decline of yin leads back to the fullest yang, *qian*. This is how time flows and revolves, modeling the slow revolution of the heavens toward the left

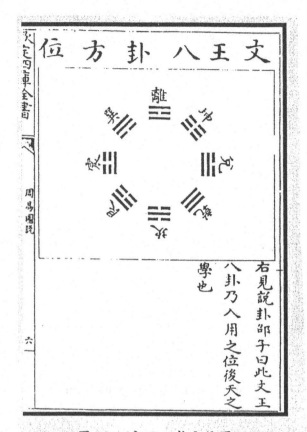

图 30   文王八卦方位图

(朱熹《周易本义》)

6.4. The King Wen arrangement of the eight Trigrams.
Zhu Xi, 朱熹 *Zhouyi Benyi* 周易本義, *Sikuquanshu* 四庫全書, 經部, p. 6.

when one looks at the pole star.[37] Going from the bottom up is called rising. Going from the top down is called descending. Rising is called giving birth (to yang). Descending is called declining (from yang). Therefore, yang is born below and yin is born above. *Yin* gives birth to yang, yang gives birth to yin. Yin again gives birth to yang, yang again gives birth to yin. Through this movement, the myriad things are generated. This cyclical progression and alternation is inexhaustible.

[37] Smith, *Sung Dynasty Uses of the I Ching*, p. 119.

The image can be read in several ways. As Francois Louis describes, this arrangement shows a cycle of the waxing and waning of yin and yang as one goes around the circle, whereas, at the same time each trigram is set across from its opposite on the other side of the circle.[38] Richard Wilhelm points out that the circle can be read as unfolding in either direction, so that "a double movement is observable: first, the usual clockwise movement, cumulative and expanding as time goes on, and determining the events that are passing; second, an opposite, backward movement, folding up and contracting as time goes on, through which the seed of the future take form."[39] In addition to showing the cyclical rising and falling of yin and yang, this arrangement is also meant to illustrate the interaction between yin and yang forces underlying natural cycles, such as the phases of day, month, and year. South and east are mainly yang, however, hiding in them is the birth of yin; north and west are mainly yin, however, hiding in them is the power of yang.

The *houtian* diagram is also named the "King Wen Arrangement of The Eight Trigrams" (Figure 6.4).

It follows a different arrangement, based on a statement in the "Shuogua" of the *Yijing*: "*Zhen* (thunder) is at the east. *Xun* (wind) is at the southeast. *Li* (fire) is the trigram of south. *Qian* (heaven) is the trigram of northwest. *Kan* (water) is the trigram of north. *Gen* (mountain) is the trigram of northeast."[40] The King Wen arrangement has fire (*li*) at the top and water (*kan*) at the bottom. It depicts the temporal progression between the cardinal trigrams and the seasons, thus explaining the basic patterns of the natural world. As Louis explains, the trigram *zhen* (thunder) represents spring, and thus, it is the beginning and is placed in the east. The circle is then read clockwise from that position. The only complementary pair hexagrams that are placed opposite each other in the diagram are *li* (fire), placed in the south, and *kan* (water), placed in the north. Thus, these represent yin and yang most directly in the diagram.[41] The arrangement of the eight trigrams is still extremely significant for the performance of ritual in temples today.[42]

In terms of the expression of yinyang thought, Shao Yong's most important contribution is in presenting the trigrams in a circular arrangement. This illuminates the way that different configurations of yinyang lead

---

[38] Louis, "The Taiji Diagram's Early History," p. 149.

[39] R. Wilhelm and C. F. Baynes (trans.), *The I Ching or Book of Changes* (New Jersey: Princeton University Press, 1950), p. 267.

[40] Gao, *Commentary on Zhouyi*, pp. 456–457.

[41] Louis, "The Taiji Diagram's Early History," p. 156.

[42] Saso, "What Is the Ho-t'u?" p. 404.

into each other, following a cyclical pattern or rise and decline. This shift toward circular depictions of yin and yang is continued in the well-known yinyang symbol. Before Shao Yong, there were presentations of binary permutations from *Taiji* to the eight trigrams, based on the statement in the "Xi Ci" that "*Taiji* generates the two modes [yinyang]. The two modes generate the four images [*xiang*]. The four images then generate the eight trigrams."[43] Shao Yong repositioned from this linear sequence to two circular arrangements of trigrams coded according to yinyang. This integration of the eight trigrams into a circle makes an important step in the visualization of yinyang movement. In fact, the *Zhouyi Can Tong Qi*, which we discussed in the last chapter, made some steps in this direction by arranging two trigrams (*kan* and *li*) in a circle as the way of expressing the cyclical alternation of yin and yang. In Zhu Xi's edition of the *Zhouyi Can Tong Qi*, he explains that "Heaven and earth establish the positions, and the changes take place between them. Heaven and earth means *qian* and *kun*. Establishing the position means arranging the position of a yin and yang pair."[44]

For Shao Yong, the circular arrangement of the *xiantian* and *houtian* diagrams reveals that cosmological patterns are cyclical.[45] The heavens continually circle in their course and carry within them regulated movements. The sun and moon make their rounds in circular motions as well as in the cycles of hours, days, months, and years. This means that yin and yang are never entirely separated: even when the yang is almost fully eclipsed at the height of yin, a fragment of it lingers and gradually becomes bigger to eventually take the central place.

Shao Yong not only uses the circle to describe the movement temporally, he also discloses a numerical sequence in the spatial positions. He

[43] Gao, *Commentary on Zhouyi*, p. 354.

[44] Ibid., p. 165.

[45] The priority of cyclical motion in understanding the cosmos also appears in ancient Western cosmology; for example, Plato's *Timaeus* describes the universe as "a circle moving in a circle." Plato, *Timaeus*, Benjamin Jowett (trans.) (Indianapolis: Bobbs-Merrill, 1949), p. 16. Aristotle states that "circular motion is necessarily primary. For the perfect is naturally prior to the imperfect, and the circle is a perfect thing." Aristotle, *De Caelo*, "Aristotle Selection," in W. D. Ross (ed.) (New York: Scribner's, 1927), p. 126. Time itself is a circle measured by heaven. The word for the yearly unit of time, *annus*, was taken from the word *annulus*, "ring." John Swan, an early seventeenth-century Cambridge philosopher, interprets the term: "In Latin the year is called *annus*, because we may say of it, *revolvitur ut annulus*. For, as in a ring, the parts touch one another, circularly joining each to the other; so also the year rolls it self back again by the same steps that it ever went." S. K. Heninger, Jr., *The Cosmological Glass* (San Marino, CA: Huntington Library Press: 2005) p. 4.

produced the diagram that arranges all sixty-four hexagrams into a circle and then arranges them again in a square in the center of the circle. When the Jesuit missionary Joachim Bouvet (1656–1730) sent this diagram to the German philosopher and mathematician Leibniz (1646–1716), Leibniz saw the diagram as representing a version of his newly discovered binary arithmetic, a system for representing all numbers through combinations of two symbols. If one replaces the broken-line yin symbol with 0 and the straight-line yang symbol with 1, one ends up with the numbers 0 to 64 in order.[46]

Zhou Dunyi's Taijitu

The third important development in image making comes from Zhou Dunyi, another forerunner of Neo-Confucianism in the Song Dynasty. We have already encountered his *Taijitu* (Taiji Diagram) in Chapter 2.

The origin of the *Taijitu* is generally taken to be another image, the *Wujitu*, which was attributed to Chen Tuan. We can briefly consider the relationship between the two images as a way of seeing how even similar images of yinyang could take on quite different meanings. The *Wujitu* was meant to describe the progression of the Daoist practice of *neidan* 內丹 (inner alchemy).[47] The *Wujitu* consists of the exact same five images as the *Taijitu*, however, the diagrams differ in two crucial ways (Figure 6.5b). First, all of the inscriptions in the *Wujitu* are different. Second, the *Wujitu* should be read from bottom to top, the opposite direction from Zhou Dunyi's *Taijitu*. The first image at the bottom of *Wujitu* is the gate of the mysterious female, the starting point of alchemical cultivation and refinement. The second image describes a cyclic progression with two continuous movements. Beginning on the right side, one cultivates *jing* 精 (refined essence) into *qi* 氣 (energy or vital force) and then refines this *qi* into *shen* 神 (spirit). The third image illustrates the connection between *qi* and the five elements and how they all return to the origin. The fourth image is fashioned from the two trigrams, *Kan* and *Li*, of the

---

[46] For a discussion and image of the document received by Leibniz, see F. Perkins, *Leibniz and China: A Commerce of Light*, (New York: Cambridge University Press, 2004), p.116-18. See also Zhonglian Shi, "Leibniz's Binary System and Shao Yong's Xiantian Tu," in Li and Poser (eds.), *Nueste uber China*.

[47] The origin of this diagram has been debated for centuries. The dominant view is that this is the Daoist diagram and Zhou Dunyi took it and gave a Confucian span. However, Li Shen recently presented strong evidence that Zhou Dunyi, in fact, discovered this diagram and Daoists then borrowing it from him. See Shen Li 李申, *The Examination of Yi Diagrams* 易圖考 (Beijing: Peking University Press, 1993).

6.5a. Zhou Dunyi's *Taijitu*.

Yijing. This image is also called *shui huo kuang kuo tu* 水火匡廓圖, the *Diagram of the Framework of Water and Fire*, which plays an important role in body cultivation in the *Zhouyi Can Tong Qi*, as we have seen.

The inscription states, "take *kan* (water) to fill in *li* (fire)." The fifth image is the culmination of this journey, when one has reached the highest stage of inner alchemy. Chen Tuan's *Wujitu* reflects the Daoist practice of self-cultivation or "inner alchemy," consisting of three stages: cultivating refined essence to transform it into *qi* (煉精化氣), cultivating *qi* to transform it into spirit (煉氣化神), and cultivating spirit to return to emptiness (煉神還虛). The *Wujitu* equips disciples with a map outlining the crucial points in the progression by which the body and self is cultivated and transformed. This journey leads practitioners to return back to the "Infinite" or the "Void."[48]

[48] See Robin Wang, "Kundao: A Lived Body in the Female Daoist Text," *Journal of Chinese Philosophy*, 36:2 (June 2009), 277–292.

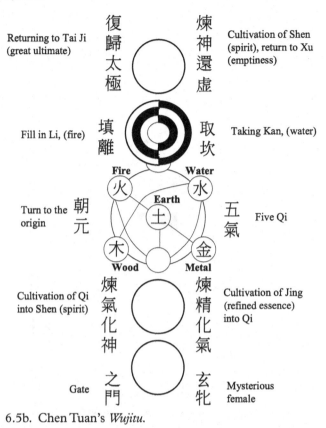

Returning to Tai Ji (great ultimate) 復歸太極

煉神還虛 Cultivation of Shen (spirit), return to Xu (emptiness)

Fill in Li, (fire) 填離

取坎 Taking Kan, (water)

Fire 火 **Earth** 土 **Water** 水

Turn to the origin 朝元

五氣 Five Qi

Wood 木 **Metal** 金

Cultivation of Qi into Shen (spirit) 煉氣化神

煉精化氣 Cultivation of Jing (refined essence) into Qi

Gate 之門

玄牝 Mysterious female

6.5b. Chen Tuan's *Wujitu.*

Although Zhou Dunyi's *Taijitu* seems to contain essentially the same images as Chen Tuan's *Wujitu*, reading from top to bottom rather than bottom to top yields a dramatic change in perspective. The *Wujitu* emphasizes return to the unifying origin, whereas Zhou Dunyi's *Taijitu* emphasizes instead the movement from the unitary source into a diversified world. However, both make use of images to convey their point of views.

The Emergence of the Yinyang Symbol

Taken together, the three sets of diagrams explored here render how Song Dynasty thinkers employed nondiscursive ways of thinking to search for the ultimate meanings of the universe and the place of human beings within it, developing images with representations of yinyang

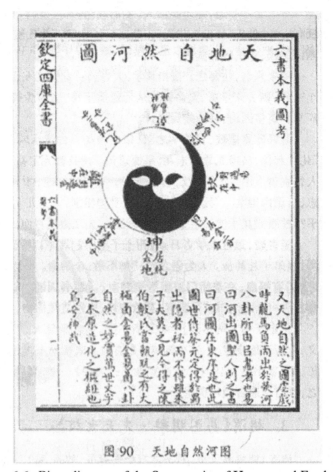

图90　天地自然河图

6.6. River diagram of the Spontaneity of Heaven and Earth.

Zhao Weiqian 趙撝謙, *The Essence of the Six Books* 六書本義, *Siku Quanshu*, 四庫全書, p. 1.

relations as their basic elements. These thinkers ultimately believed that the essential aspects of various orders of reality could be incorporated into a system so comprehensive as to transcend the limits of discursive argument and so complete as to be practically a *simulacrum* of the cosmos as a whole. Beyond discursive descriptions and arguments, the patterns of the universe could also be articulated in figurative and numerological terms.

Out of this conceptual tradition, the prototype for the yinyang symbol was formed in Zhao Huiqian's work from the Ming Dynasty, the *Liushu Benyi* 六書本義 (*The Essence of the Six Books*) (Figure 6.6).

The image itself appears in a diagram called the *Tiandi Ziran Hetu*, which we might translate as "The River Diagram of the Spontaneity of Heaven and Earth."[49] Zhao described the image in terms of the sun and the moon and the alternation of brightness and darkness: "The sun has no waxing or waning and the moon adheres to the way of a vassal in that its light brightens and dims according to its distance from the sun."[50] Calling the first yinyang symbol a *hetu*, a "river diagram," of heaven and earth, shows that Zhao placed it in the lineage of *hetu*, however, he gives it in the shape of a circle. He thus integrates elements of Liu Mu's *hetu*, Shao Yong's circular form, and Zhou Dunyi's sequence of the *Taijitu* to produce this new image with interlocking spiral halves. This circle is dynamically divided into two swirling halves surrounded by the eight trigrams outside the circle. Zhao followed the Chinese etymological tradition and believed that in their earliest forms, the trigrams and the characters for the various elements of nature were written in the same way and came from the same origin. Louis clarifies this and its connection to the *hetu* tradition:

> Linking his paleographic observations to the *xiantian* trigram charts of Song, Zhao correlated the origin of the Chinese script with the origin of cosmological symbols and diagrams, and fittingly began his section of tables and charts with our *taiji* diagram. To Zhao Huiqian, this was a primal image of natural creation comparable to one of the divinely revealed charts of mythical times, the famed *hetu*.[51]

Like other image makers, he treated it not as an illustrative diagram in a book but as a rare physical object with mystical value. This original yinyang symbol is more complicated and integrated with the words surrounding it, in contrast with the current free-standing yinyang icon.

Reading the Yinyang Symbol

The efforts of making different *tu* disclose a tacit insight that thinking is not simply a mental process above or beyond perception, but rather it

---

[49] Although most scholars consider this to be the first yinyang symbol, there is still debate about this among Chinese scholars. See Li, *The Examination of Yi Diagrams*.

[50] Weiqian Zhao 趙撝謙, *The Essence of the Six Books*, *Siku Quanshu*, 四庫全書本 (1781), p. 1.

[51] Louis, "The Taiji Diagram's Early History," p. 172.

is an essential ingredient of perception itself. Visual perception is visual thinking. This view underlies the whole *xiangshu* tradition. For these early Chinese texts, the world is not structured according to a Pythagorean dichotomy between a heavenly order of rationality and a terrestrial disorder of irrationality. There are not two qualitatively different realms – one the calculable order of the heaven that appeals to our thought and the other a variety of earthly shapes and events impinging upon our observation and sensual experience. The world of the senses is pervasive throughout the interplay of cosmic forces, which rule the stars in the heaven, the seasons on the earth, and the smallest elements in human beings. Of course, the epistemic value of images and diagrams has been recognized in various ways in the tradition of Western philosophy, going back to Plato's discussion of the Divided Line and "The Allegory of the Cave" in the *Republic*. Contemporary virtue epistemology has particularly questioned the narrowness of defining knowledge only as a justified true belief.[52] The virtues of the mind presuppose a broader conception of knowledge that draws in both perception and understanding, which is explained in terms of making a connection between the parts and the whole.

The development of various diagrams in Song Dynasty can, thus, be seen as expressing a particular conception of knowledge and knowing, a thinking model presupposed in the symbol itself. As our analysis of the *tu* should suggest, visual thinking clearly has been an important tradition in the study of the *Yijing*. The yinyang symbol must be "read" in that context.

Paul Ricoeur (1913–2005) once claimed, "The symbol gives rise to the thought."[53] How does the yinyang symbol communicate the originality of yinyang thought? We can begin with the obvious. The yinyang symbol portrays the world as fundamentally constituted by and ordered according to two forces, yin and yang, symbolized by the dark and light swirls. These forces are not dualistic, however, as the image shows them as interdependent, reciprocal, and intertwined. Within the strongest moment of yang, one finds a small circle of yin, and within the strongest moment of yin, one finds a small circle of yang. Moreover, yin is shown as gradually transforming into yang, while yang is transforming

---

[52] Robert C. Robert, "The Concept of Knowledge: Plato and Aristotle as Resources for Contemporary Virtue Epistemology" (lecture, Loyola Marymount University, Los Angeles, CA, April 13, 2005).

[53] P. Ricoeur, *The Symbolism of Evil*, Emerson Buchanan (trans.) (Boston: Beacon Press, 1967), p. 347.

into yin. If we imagine that a line drawn from the center of the circle to its periphery represents the configuration of a particular thing, event, or moment in time, then each thing is shown to be constituted by both yin and yang, dark and light, at any given moment and position.

Second, the yinyang symbol is meant to illustrate change. Everything participates in a universal ebb and flow, returning to their opposites, and back again. As Louis describes it, "Its two curved, interlocking geometric shapes depict a rotating, self-creating cycle of complementary opposites, of mutually dependant entities whose beginning are the other's ending."[54] The yinyang symbol represents the waxing and waning of yin and yang, which implies an understanding of gradual and cyclical quantitative change. Yin and yang are eternally oscillating between each other, explaining the enormous diversity of circumstances in life. At any given point, yin-dark or yang-bright is in the process of change. This difference is implicit in any state of being – there are no fixed points or frozen moments. Once again, if we imagine that a line from the center to the periphery represents a moment in time, that moment leads immediately into the next configuration. This depiction of a continuum of change is one of the main advantages of the yinyang symbol over early arrangements of the trigrams or hexagrams of the *Yijing*. Although meant to show continual change, the representation of that change as the trigrams necessarily implies discrete conditions – one jumps from one hexagram to another. The sixty-four hexagrams allow more stages of change in between, however, they still signify a continuum in terms of discrete moments or symbols. The yinyang symbol permits a presentation of the full continuum of yinyang relations, representing all gradations of change. Things exist in phases. Space is conceived as a field, defined by positions and goals. Time is conceived as a string, moved in a circle. Although it is impossible to fully represent change in a symbol that is itself static, we can also consider the "performance" of this diagram – the sage's brush produces the symbol in one continuous motion.

Third, even though we can think about the yinyang symbol as two teardrop-shaped parts, namely yin-dark and yang-bright, when they are brought together, they form a circle. Now the emergent properties of a circle are different from either of these two constituents. If the circle were a hoop, it could rotate or roll and neither of the two parts could do these things. The whole emergent regularity is more than the sum of its parts. The symbol not only emphasizes the wholeness of the universe, but also shows the element of "thirdness" involved in yinyang thought.

[54] Louis, "The Taiji Diagram's Early History," p. 175.

The yinyang interaction itself goes beyond being merely complementary and mutually supporting. Yin and yang together fashion a new existence, which is not simply half bright circle and half dark circle. Yinyang ultimately generates 生 (*sheng*) things to emerge, exist, and endure.

The fourth point is the emergence of consistent patterns. One aspect of the thirdness of this symbol is the constant configuration of the two forces. It is like the standing wave that emerges in a moving stream, where the water particles are constantly changing while the pattern persists.

At its core, yinyang thought takes the world as a net shaped by thousands of diverse things and events but linked through consistent patterns, movements, and forces. Yinyang provided the most efficient way to get hold of this web. Yinyang thought not only presents a coherent worldview, however. It also embraces skills that measure one's aptitude for being and doing. Yinyang thought constructs knowledge into simple, integrated, and flexible patterns that are broadly applicable to wide ranges of phenomena. This expansive application is reflected in the multiple and diverse contexts in which the symbol itself has appeared. In fact, yinyang is a kind of art (*shu*) of living, something difficult to describe because it can only be fully known through practice. Yinyang thought does not claim that the world is "over there" for us to grab or take as an object; rather we are already within the world, participating in it. In terms of the diagram, we ourselves are already inside the circle, which means we both play a role in generation and change and are shaped by these forces. At a fundamental level, yinyang thought focuses on the ways that human life is infused with connections to our surroundings on many levels, and each of these relationships is shaped by our own participations.

We can conclude that reading the yinyang image also illustrates the way in which yinyang is interpreted and applied. The image conveys meaning primarily in an analogical mode of presentation. We have seen that yinyang thought relies on our accumulated common sense data and takes observable patterns in nature as its starting point and, from there, builds a system of classification by which to make sense of the myriad things. The symbol helps bring to our attention the way that words and concepts limit our knowledge to a finite set of distinctions and fixed categories, while images grant an infinite scope for comprehending the texture of reality. This allows one to perceive and think about the world in a three-dimensional space, something seen in what is called "spatial intelligence."

The yinyang symbol illuminates different events from all possible directions. This comprehensive whole undergoes constant phases of changes that need to be recognized. Yinyang represents these stages or phases

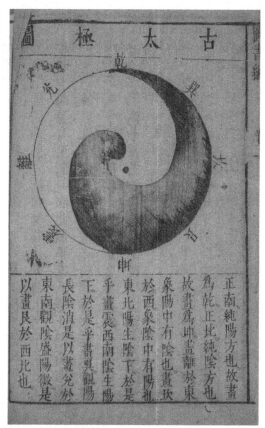

6.7. Ancient Taijitu, Zhang Huang 章潢 (1527–1608),
Ming Dynasty.

and relates them to others. We, thus, should not comprehend the *tu* as
figures illustrating doctrines already formulated in discourse, but rather
recognize them as symbols that direct our thought to be guided by living
reality, working from the symbols themselves and the visual thinking to
which they give rise. The yinyang symbol, like other *tu*, is only an invita-
tion for perceivers to think and meditate, to contemplate human beings
and the world. It cannot be simply defined through the question "what
does it mean?" because the yinyang symbol denotes nothing in terms of
fixed human abstraction. How one interprets it at any moment depends
on where one draws the boundaries among things and events.

Similarly yinyang thought is applied from a certain point of view and with specified purposes in mind. This is best illustrated by the way the same phenomenon can be described as yin in one way and yang in another. This complex flexibility explains why yinyang thought was able to permeate so many aspects of Chinese culture and civilization, and it is what this book has attempted to articulate and present.

Bibliography

Allan, Sarah. "Sons of Suns: Myth and Totemism in Early China," *Bulletin of the School of Oriental and African Studies*, **44** (1981), 290–326.

The Way of Water and the Sprouts of Virtue, (Albany: SUNY Press, 1997).

Ames, Roger T. (trans.), *Yuan Dao, Original Dao: Trace to Its Root*, (New York: Ballantine Books, 1998).

Aristotle. *The Complete Works of Aristotle*, Jonathan Barnes (ed.), (Princeton, NJ: Princeton University, 1984).

Aurelius, Marcus. *Meditations: A New Translation*, Gregory Hays (int.), (New York: The Modern Library, 2003).

Baldrian-Hussein, Farzeen. "*Hun* and *Po* 魂•魄 Yang Soul(s) and Yin Soul(s); Celestial Soul(s) and Earthly Soul(s)" in Fabrizio Pregadio (ed.), *The Encyclopedia of Taoism*, (New York: Routledge, 2008), pp. 406–09.

Ban, Gu. 班固.(Han Dynasty) *Hanshu* 漢書 *(The Book of Han)*, Commentary by Yan Shigu 颜师古 (Tang Dynasty), (Beijing: Chinese Press, 1962).

Bennett, Steven J. "Patterns of the Sky and the Earth: A Chinese Science of Applied Cosmology," *Chinese Science*, **3** (March 1978), 1–26.

Berling, Judith A. "Paths of Convergence: Interactions of Inner Alchemy Taoism and Neo-Confucianism," *Journal of Chinese Philosophy*, **6** (1979), 123–48.

Black, Alison Harley. "Gender and Cosmology in Chinese Correlative Thinking" in Caroline Walker Bynum et al. (eds.), *Gender and Religion: On the Complexity of Symbols*, (Boston: Beacon Press, 1989), pp. 166–95.

Bodde, Derk, "Types of Chinese Categorical Thinking" in Charles Le Blanc and Dorothy Borei (eds.), *Essays on Chinese Civilization*, (Princeton, NJ: Princeton University Press, 1981), pp. 351–72.

Bokenkamp, Stephen. *Early Daoist Scriptures*, Peter Nickerson (contributor), (Berkeley: University of California Press, 1997).

Brashier, Kenneth E. "Han Thanatology and the Division of 'Souls'," *Early China*, **21** (1996), 125–58.

Brindley, Erica. "'The Perspicuity of Ghosts and Spirits' and the Problem of Intellectual Affiliations in Early China," *Journal of the American Oriental Society*, **129** no. 2 (2009), 215–36.

Broman, Sven. "Studies on the Chou Li," *Bulletin of the Museum of Far Eastern Antiquities*, **33** (1961), 1–89.

Cammann, Schulyer. "The Magic Square of Three in Old Chinese Philosophy and Religion," *History of Religions*, **1** (1961), 37–80.

Cassier, Ernst. *The Philosophy of Symbolic Forms*, Ralph Manheim (trans.), 3 vols., (New Haven: Yale University Press, 1955), vol. II: *Mythical Thought*.

Chan, Alan K. L. "Harmony as a Contested Metaphor and Conceptions of Rightness (yi) in Early Confucian Ethics," in R. A. H. King and Dennis Schilling (eds.), *How Should One Live? Comparing Ethics in Ancient China and Greco-Roman Antiquity*, (Berlin: De Gruyter, 2011), pp. 37–62.

Chen, Daqi 陳大齊. *Mengzi Dai Jie Lu* 孟子待解錄, (Taibei: Taiwan Shangwu Yinshuguan, 1980).

Xunzi Xueshuo 荀子學說, (Taibei: Zhonghua Wenhua Chuban Shiye Weiyuanhui Chubanshe, 1954).

Chen, Guying 陳鼓應. *Commentaries on Zhuangzi*, 莊子今注今譯, (Beijing: Chinese Press, 中華書局, 1983).

Chen, Lai 陳來. *The World of Ancient Thought and Culture: Religions, Ethics and Social Thought in the Spring and Autumn Period*, 古代思想文化的世界：春秋時代的宗教倫理與社會思想, (Beijing: SDX Joint Publishing Company, 2009).

Chen Li, (ed.), *Baihutong*, 白虎通, *Comprehensive Discussions in the White Tiger Hall*, (Beijing: Chinese Press, 中華書局, 1997).

Chen, Qiyou 陳奇猷. (ed.) *New Annotation of Hanfeizi* 韓非子新校注, (Shanghai: Shanghai Guji Press, 2000).

Chen, Quanlin 陈全林 (ed.). *Zhouyi Can Tong Qi* 周易參同契, (Beijing: Chinese Social Science Press 中国社会科学出版社, 2004).

Cheng, Chungying. "Paradigm of Change (Yi) in Classical Chinese Philosophy," *Journal of Chinese Philosophy*, **36** no. 4 (December 2009), 516–30.

Ching, Julia. *Mysticism and Kingship in China*, (Cambridge, MA: Cambridge University Press, 1997).

Czikszentmihalyi, Mark. *Material Virtue: Ethics and the Body in Early China* (Leiden: Brill, 2004).

Dai, Zhen 戴震. *Meng Zi Zi Yi Shu Zhen* 孟子字義疏證, Wenguang He 何文光 (ed.), (Beijing: Chinese Press 中華書局, 2008).

De Bary, William Theodore and Irene Bloom. *Source Book of Chinese Tradition* (New York: Columbia University Press, 2000).

Despeaux, Catherine and Livia Kohn. *Women in Daoism* (Cambridge: Three Pines Press, 2003).

Dong, Zhongshu. *Chunqiu Fanlu* 春秋繁露義證 *Luxuriant Dew of the Spring and Autumn Annals*, Si Yu (ed.) (Qing Dynasty), (Beijing: Chinese Press 中華書局, 1996.)

Fan, Hua 范曄. *Houhanshu* 後漢書 *The Book of Later Han*, (Beijing: Chinese Press 中華書局, 1965).

Forke, Alfred. *The World-Conception of The Chinese: Their Astronomical, Cosmological and Physico-Philosophical Speculations* (London: Late Probsthain & Co., 1925).

Freeman, Michael D. "From Adept to Worthy: The Philosophical Career of Shao Yung," *Journal of the American Oriental Society*, **102** (1982), 477–91.

Fung, Yu-lan. *A Short History of Chinese Philosophy*, (New York: The Free Press, 1997).

Gallagher, Shaun. *How the Body Shapes the Mind*, (New York: Oxford University Press, 2005).

Gao, Xing. "The Conceptual Source of Sanyin and Sanyang," *Chinese Archives Traditional Chinese Medicine*, **24** no. 8 (August 2006).

Gao, Heng 高亨, *Commentary on Zhouyi* 周易大傳今注 (Jinan: Qilu Press, 1998).

Girardot, Norman. *Myth and Meaning in Early Taoism: The Theme of Chaos (hundun)*, revised edition, (Magdelena, NM: Three Pines Press, 2008).

Graham, Angus C. (trans.). *Chuang-Tzu: The Inner Chapters*, (Indianapolis: Hackett Publishing, 2001).

The Book of Lieh-tzu: A Classic of The Tao, (New York: Columbia University Press, 1990).

Disputers of the Tao: Philosophical Argument in Ancient China (Chicago and La Salle: Open Court, 1989).

Yin-Yang and the Nature of Correlative Thinking, series 6 (Singapore: Institute of East Asian Philosophies Occasional Paper and Monograph, 1986).

Granet, Marcel. *La pensée Chinoise (Chinese Thought)* (Paris: Albin Michel, 1999).

Grimshaw, Jean. *Feminist Philosophers: Women's Perspectives on Philosophical Traditions* (Brighton: Wheatsheaf Books, 1986).

Guisso, Richard W. "Thunder Over the Lake: The Five Classics and the Perception of Woman in Early China" in Richard Guisso and Stanley Johannesen (eds.), *Women in China: Current Directions in Historical Scholarships* (Youngstown, NY: Philo Press, 1981), pp. 47–61.

Guo, Zhicheng 郭志成 and Tao Guo 郭韜. *Zoujin Fuxi: Pojie Yixue Qiangu Zhimi* 走進伏羲 - 破解易學千古之謎 (Wuchang: Guangming Daily Press, 2003).

Hall, David L. and Ames, Roger T. *Thinking Through Confucius* (Albany: SUNY Press, 1987).

Hansen, Chad. *A Daoist Theory of Chinese Thought: A Philosophical Interpretation* (New York: Oxford University Press, 1992).

Harper, Donald. (trans.), *The Mawangdui Medical Manuscripts* (London and New York: Kegan Paul International, 1998).

"The Sexual Arts of Ancient China As Described in a Manuscript of the Second Century B.C.," *Harvard Journal of Asiatic Studies*, **47** (1987), 459–98.

Harrell, Stevan. "The Concept of Soul in Chinese Folk Religion," *The Journal of Asian Studies*, **38** no. 3 (1979), 519–28.

He, Xiaoxi and Jie Luo. 中國風水史, *History of Chinese Fengshui* (Beijing: Jiuzhou Press, 2007).

Henderson, John B. *The Development and Decline of Chinese Cosmology* (New York: Columbia University Press, 1984).

Heng, Kuan 桓寬 (Han Dynasty). *On Salt and Iron* 鹽鐵論 Zhenghan Li 林振翰 校釋 (Qing dynasty) (commentary), (Taipei: Commercial Press, 1934).

Heninger, S. K., Jr. *The Cosmographical Glass: Renaissance Diagrams of the Universe* (San Marino: Huntington Library, 1977).

Henricks, Robert. "The Dao and the Field: Exploring an Analogy" in Gary D. Deangelis and Warren G. Frisina (eds.), *Teaching the Daodejing* (New York: Oxford University Press, 2008), pp. 31–47.

Hsu, Dau-lin. "Crime and Cosmic Order," *Harvard Journal of Asiatic Studies*, **30** (1970), 111–25.

Hu, Shi 胡适 *Zhongguo Zhexueshi Dagang* 中國哲學史大綱 (Beijing: Dongfang Chubanshe, 2003).

Hu, Wei 胡渭. *Yitu Mingbian* 易圖明辨 *Clarifications of Yi Diagrams* (Taiwan: Guangwen Press 廣文書局, 1977).

Huang, Hui 黃暉. *Corrections and Explanations of the Lun Heng (Vol.1)*, 論衡校釋 (Beijing: Chinese Press, 中華書局, 1996).

Inoue, Satoshi 井上聰 - 日. *Xianqin Yinyang Wuxing* 先秦陰陽五行 (Wuhan: Hubei Education Press, 1997).

Jiao, Xun 焦循. *Mengzi Zheng Yi* 孟子正義, 2 vols. (Beijing: Chinese Press, 1987).

Johnston, Ian. *The Mozi: A Complete Translation* (New York: Columbia University Press, 2010).

Jullien, Francois. *A Treatise on Efficacy: Between Western and Chinese Thinking*, Janet Lloyd (trans.), (Honolulu: University of Hawai'i Press, 2004).

Kauffman, Stuart A. *The Origins of Order: Self-Organization and Selection in Evolution*, (New York: Oxford University Press, 1993).

Knoblock, John (trans.). *Xunzi: A Translation and Study of the Complete Works*, 3 vols. (Stanford: Stanford University Press, 1988–1994).

Knoblock, John and Jeffrey Reigel (trans.). *The Annals of Lü Buwei: A Complete Translations and Study* (Stanford: Stanford University Press, 2000).

Kohn, Livia. "Chen Tuan in History and Legend," *Taoist Resources*, **2** no. 1 (1990), 8–31.

(ed.). *Daoism Handbook*, Handbook of Oriental Studies, Section 4 China, 27 vols. (Leidan: Brill, 2000), vol. XIV.

"Yin and Yang: The Natural Dimension of Evil" in Robert S. Cohen and Alfred I. Tauber (eds.), *Philosophies of Nature: The Human Dimension* (New York: Kluwer Academic Publishers, Boston Studies in the Philosophy of Science, 1997), pp. 91–105.

Kuhn, Thomas. *Structure of Scientific Revolution*, 2nd edition (Chicago: University of Chicago Press, 1970).

Lai, Guolong. "The Diagram of the Mourning System from Mawangdui," *Early China*, **28** (2003), 43–99.

Lederman, Leon M. and Christopher T. Hill. *Symmetry and the Beautiful Universe*, 2nd edition (New York: Prometheus Books, 2004).

Lewis, Mark Edward. *The Construction of Space in Early China*, Series in Chinese Philosophy and Culture (Albany: SUNY, 2005).

Li, Deshan 李德山 (ed.), *Wenzi* 文子: *Twenty-two Classics* 二十二子详注全译 (Harbin: Heilongjiang People Press, 黑龍江人民出版社, 2002).

Li, Disheng 李滌生. *Xunzi Jishi* 荀子集釋 (Collected Explanations of Xunzi) (Taibei: Xuesheng Shuju, 1979).

Li Li (ed.), *Sayings of Zhuzi*, 朱子語類 (Beijing: Chinese Press, 中華書局1999).

Li, Mengsheng. 李夢生 (ed.), *Zuozhuan Yizhu* 左傳譯注 (Shanghai: Shanghai Guji Press 上海古籍出版社, 1998).

Li, Shen 李申. *Examination of Yitu* 易圖考, (Beijing: Peking University Press 北京大學出版社), 2001.

Li, Shen 李申 and Guo Yu 郭彧 (ed.), *The Complete Collections of Images of Zhouyi* 周易圖說總匯, (Shanghai: China Eastern Normal University Press, 華東師範大學出版社), 1998.

Li, Quan 李筌. (ed.) *Huangdi Yinfujing Jizhu* 黃帝陰符經集注 (*Collected Commentaries on the Yellow Emperor's Book of Secret Correspondence*) (Shanghai: Shanghai Guji Press, 上海古籍出版社, 1990).

Li, Shen and Yu, Guo. (ed.), *Zhouyi Tushu Zonghui* 周易圖書總匯 (*The Complete Selection of Diagrams of Zhouyi*, (Shanghai: China Eastern Normal University Press 華東師範大學出版, 2004).

Liang, Qichao. 梁啟超. 陰陽五行說之來歷 "The Origin of Yinyang and Wuxing" in Gu Jiegang 顧頡剛(ed.), in *The Debate on Ancient History* 古史辨, (Shanghai: Shanghai Guji Press, 上海古籍出版社,1982), vol. V.

Ling, Li 李零. *The Only Regulation: Sunzi's Philosophy of Conflicts* 唯一的規則:孫子的鬥爭哲學 (Beijing: San Lian Press, 2010).

Liu, Daling and Hu Hongxia, *The Selection of Sex Antiques Collected by China Sex Museum* (Hong Kong: Wenhui Press, 2000).

Liu, Gang 刘刚. *The Concept of Dao's Coming into Being: From The Religious and Scientific Perspective* 道观念的发生:基于宗教知识的视角 (Beijing: Guangming Daily Press 光明日报出版社, 2009).

Liu, Guozhong 刘国忠. *Research on The Great Meaning of Wuxing* 五行大义研究 (Shenyang: Liaoning Education Press,辽宁教育出版社, 1999).

Liu, Shu-hsien. "The Use of Analogy and Symbolism in Traditional Chinese Philosophy," *Journal of Chinese Philosophy*, 1 (June–September 1974), 313–38.

Liu, Xiang 劉向 (Han dynasty). *Shuo Yuan Yin De* 說苑引得, Harvard-Yenching Institute Sinological Index Series No. 1. (Beijing: Harvard-Yenching Institute, 1931).

Liu, Xiaogan 刘笑敢. *Laozi Gujin* 老子古今 (*Laozi, Past and Present*) (Beijing: Chinese Academy of Social Sciences Press, 2006).

Liu, Xuyi 刘绪义. *The World of Heaven and Human Being: A Study of The Origin of Pre-Qin Schools*, (Beijing: Beijing People's Press, 2009).

Liu, Yang. *On the Cultural Connotation of Yin and Yang and Their English Translation* (Changsha: Hunan University Press, 2010).

Liu, Zhao (ed.). *Guodian Chujian Jiaoyi* 郭店楚簡校釋 (Fuzhou: Fujian People's Press, 2003).

Livio, Mario. *The Golden Ratio: The Story of Phi, the World's Most Astonishing Number* (New York: Broadway Books, 2002).

Lloyd, G. E. R. *Adversaries and Authorities: Investigations into Greek and Chinese Science* (New York: Cambridge University Press, 1996).

Loewe, Michael. *Early Chinese Texts: A Bibliographical Guide* (Berkeley: Institute of East Asian Studies, 1993).

Loewenstein, P. J. "Swastika and Yin-Yang," *China Society Occasional Papers* (n.s.), no. 1 (London: China Society, 1942).

Lou Yulie 樓宇烈 (ed.). *Wáng Bì Collected Explanations* 王弼集校 (Beijing: Chinese Press, 1999).

Louis, Francois. "Genesis of an Icon: The Taiji Diagram's Early History," *Harvard Journal of Asiatic Studies*, **63** no. 1 (2003), 145–96.

Lu, Yulin 陆玉林 and Youbo Tang 唐有伯. *School of Yin Yang in China* 中国阴阳家. (Beijing: Religious Culture Press 宗教文化出版社, 1996).

Luoshu 洛書 and Han Pengjie 韓鵬杰 (eds.). *The Complete Works of Zhouyi*, 周易全書 (Beijing: Tuanjie Press 團結出版社, 1990).

Machle, Edward J. *Nature and Heaven in the Xunzi: A Study of the Tian Lun* (Albany: SUNY Press, 1993).

Major, John S. "Astrology in the Huai-nan-tzu and Some Related Texts," *Society for the Study of Chinese Religions Bulletin*, **8** (Fall 1980), 20–31.

Heaven and Earth in Early Han Thought (Albany: SUNY Press, 1993).

Makeham, John. "Transmitters and Creators: Chinese Commentators and Commentaries on the Analects," *Vol. 228 of Harvard East Asian Monographs* (Cambridge: Harvard University Press, 2003).

Mitchell, W. J. T. *Iconology: Images, Text, Ideology* (Chicago: The University of Chicago Press, 1987).

Moeller, Hans-Georg (trans.). *Daodejing: A Complete Translation and Commentary* (Chicago and La Salle: Open Court, 2007).

Mou, Zhonshan. *The Natural Philosophy and Ethical Meanings of the Book of Changes* (Taibei: Wenjing Press, 1988).

Nakayama, Shigeru, "Characteristics of Chinese Astrology," *Isis* **57** (Winter 1966), 442–54.

Needham, Joseph. *Science and Civilization in China*, 7 vols. (New York: Cambridge University Press, 1956).

Niu, Bingzhan 牛兵占. (ed.), *Huangdi Neijing*, 黃帝內經 (Shijiazhuang: Hebei Science and Technology Press, 1993).

Pang Pu 庞朴. *On Oneness Divided into Threeness* 浅说一分为三 (Beijing: Xinhua Press, 新华出版社, 2004).

Pankenier, David W. "The Cosmo-Political Background of Heaven's Mandate," *Early China*, **20** (1995), 121–76.

Parrish, David M. D. *Nothing I See Means Anything, Quantum Questions, Quantum Answers* (Boulder: Sentient Publications, 2006).

Peng, Lin 彭林. *A Study of the Main Thought and the Date of the Zhouli*, 周礼, 主体思想与成书年代研究, (Beijing: China Renmin University Press 中国人民大学出版社, 2009).

Perkins, Franklin. *Leibniz and China: A Commerce of Light* (New York: Cambridge University Press, 2004).

Peterson, Willard J. "Making Connections: 'Commentary on the Attached Verbalizations' of the *Book of Change*," *Harvard Journal of Asiatic Studies*, **42** no. 1 (June 1982), 67–116.

Pfister, Lauren. "Philosophical Explorations of the Transformative Dimension in Chinese Culture," *Journal of Chinese Philosophy*, **35** no. 4 (December 2008), 663–82.

Pines, Yuri. *Foundations of Confucian Thought: Intellectual Life in the Chunqiu Period, 72-453 B.C.E.* (Honolulu: University of Hawai'i Press, 2002).

Plato. *The Symposium*, R. E. Allen (trans.), (New Haven: Yale University Press, 1993).

Porkert, Manfred. *The Theoretical Foundations of Chinese Medicine: Systems of Correspondence*, East Asian Science Series (Cambridge, MA: The MIT Press, 1974).

Pregadio, Fabrizio (ed.). *The Encyclopedia of Taoism* (New York: Routledge, 2008).

Pu Ang. Wenhua Yiyu 文化一隅 *Culture One Corner* (Zhengzhou: Zhongzhou Guji Chubanshe, 2005).

Puett, Michael J. *To Become a God: Cosmology, Sacrifice and Self-Divination in Early China* (Cambridge: Harvard Asia Center Publication, 2002).

Pulleyblank, E. G. "The Chinese Cyclical Signs as Phonographs," *Journal of the American Oriental Society*, **99** (1979), 24–38.

Queen, Sarah A. *From Chronicle to Canon: The Hermeneutics of the Spring and Autumn Annals According to Tung Chung-shu* (New York: Cambridge University Press, 1996).

Reiter, Florian. "Some Remarks on the Chinese Word T'u, 'Chart, Plan, Design," *Oriens*, **32** (1990), 308–27.

Rickett, Allyn. (trans.). *Guanzi, Political, Economic, and Philosophical Essays from Early China* (New Jersey: Princeton University Press, 1998).

Ricoeur, Paul. *The Symbolism of Evil*, Emerson Buchanan (trans.), (Boston: Beacon Press, 1967).

Robinet, Isabelle. "The Place and the Meaning of the Notion of Taiji in Taoist Sources prior to the Ming Dynasty," *History of Religions*, **29** (1990), 373–411.

Rong, Gen 容 庚, *Bronze Code* 金文编 (Beijing: Chinese Press, 1985).

Roth, Harold D. (trans.). *The Huainanzi, A Guide to The Theory and Practice of Government in Early China* (New York: Columbia University Press, 2010).

Original Tao: Inward Training (nei-yeh) and the Foundations of Taoist Mysticism (New York: Columbia University Press, 1999).

Rubin, Vitaly A. "The Concepts of Wu-Hsing and Yin-Yang," *Journal of Chinese Philosophy*, **9** (1982), 131–57.

Ryden, Edmund (trans.). *The Yellow Emperor's Four Canons: A Literary Study and Edition of the Text from Mawangdui* (Taipei: Guangqi Press, 1997).

Sartre, Jean-Paul. *Being and Nothingness*, Hazel E. Barnes (trans.), (New York: Washington Square Press, 1993).

Saso, Michael. "What is the Ho-t'u?" *History of Religions*, **17** (February–May 1978), 399–416.

Schinz, Alfred. *The Magic Square: Cities in Ancient China* (Stuttgart: Edition Axel Menges, 1990).

Schipper, Kristofer. *The Taoist Body* (Berkeley: University of California Press, 1993).

Schwartz, Benjamin I. "On the Absence of Reductionism in Chinese Thought," *Journal of Chinese Philosophy*, 1 (December 1973), 27–44.

The World of Thought in Ancient China (Cambridge: Harvard University Press, 1985).

Shi, Zhonglian. "Leibniz's Binary System and Shao Yong's Xiantian Tu," in Wenchao Li and Hans Poser (eds.), *Das Nueste über China* (Stuttgart: Franz Steiner Verlag, 2000).

Shih, Joseph. "The Notion of God in Ancient Chinese Religion," *Numen*, 16–17 (1969–1970), 99–138.

Shu, Jingnan 束景南. *Zhonghua Taijitu yu Taiji Wenhua* 中華太極圖与太極文化 (Suzhou: Suzhou University Press 蘇州大學出版社, 1994).

Sima, Guang 司馬光, *Collected Commentaries of Tai Xuan* 太玄集注, Shaojun Liu 劉韶軍 (ed.), (Beijing: Chinese Press 中華書局, 2003).

Sima, Qian, 司馬遷. *Shiji* 史記 (*Records of the Historians*) (Beijing: Chinese Press, 中華書局, 2003).

Sivin, Nathan. "Chinese Alchemy and the Manipulation of Time," in Nathan Sivin (ed.), *Science and Technology in East Asia* (New York: Science and History Publications, 1977), pp. 108–22.

Smith, Kidder. *Sung Dynasty Uses of the I Ching* (Princeton, NJ: Princeton University Press, 1990).

Sun, Bin. *The Art of Warfare, A Translation of the Classic Chinese Work of Philosophy and Strategy*, D. C. Lau and Roger T. Ames (eds.), (New York: SUNY Press, 2003).

Sun-Tzu. *The Art of Warfare: The First English Translation Incorporating the Recently Discovered Yin-chueh-shan Texts*, Roger Ames (ed.), (New York: Ballantine Books, 1993).

Sun, Yirang 孫詒讓. *Mozi Xiangu* 墨子閒詁 (*Leisurely Notes on the Mozi*), (Shanghai: Shanghai Books 上海書店, 1935).

Szabo, Sandor P. "The Term Shenming – Its Meaning in The Ancient Chinese Thought in a Recently Discovered Manuscript," *Acta Orientalia Academiae Scientiarum Hungaricae*, 56 no. 2–4 (2003), 251–74.

Tan, Rongfu 譚戒甫. *Mo Bian Fa We* 墨辯發微, (Beijing: Chinese Press 中華書局, 2004).

Tang, Chun-I. "Chang Tsai's Theory of Mind and Its Metaphysical Basis," *Philosophy East and West*, 6 no. 2 (July 1956), 113–36.

Tansley, David V. *Subtle Body: Essence and Shadow* (London: Thames and Hudson, 1977).

Taylor, Charles. *The Ethics of Authenticity* (Oxford: Oxford University Press, 1991).

Todes, Samuel. *Body and World* (Cambridge, MA: The MIT Press, 2001).

Tsuchiya, Masaaki. "Confessions of Sins and Awareness of Self in the *Taipingjing*" in Livia Kohn and Harold D. Roth (eds.), *Daoist Identity:*

Cosmology, Lineage, and Ritual, (Honolulu: University of Hawai'i Press, 2002).

Unschuld, Paul U. *Medicine in China, A History of Ideas,* 25th edition (Berkeley: University of California Press, 2010).

Nature, Knowledge, Imagery in an Ancient Chinese Medical Text (Berkeley: University of California Press, 2003).

Van Norden, Bryan (trans.). *Mengzi, with Selections from Traditional Commentaries,* (Indianapolis: Hackett Publishing, 2008).

Vaught, Carl G. *Metaphor, Analogy, and the Place of Places: Where Religion and Philosophy Meet* (Waco: Baylor University Press, 2004).

Von Senger, Harro. *The Book of Strategems: Tactics for Triumph and Survival,* Myron B. Gubitz (trans.), (New York: Penguin Books, 1993).

Wang, Bi (commentary). *Zhouyi Lueli* 周易略例, Youlie Lou (ed.), (Beijing: Chinese Press, 中華書局, 1980).

Wang, Chong 王充. *Lun Heng* 論衡, (Beijing: Chinese Press 中華書局, 1990).

Wang, Mengou, 王夢鷗 (ed.) *Liji,* 禮記今註今譯 (*Record of Rituals*), (Taipei: Taiwan Commercial Press, 台灣商務印書館, 1981).

Wang, Qiaohui 王巧慧. *The Naturalistic Philosophy of Huainanzi* 淮南子的自然哲学思想, (Beijing: Science Press 科学出版社, 2009).

Wang, Robin. "Dong Zhongshu's Transformation of Yin/Yang Theory and Contesting of Gender Identity," *Philosophy East and West,* 55 no. 2 (April 2005), 209–31.

"Zhou Dunyi's Diagram of the Supreme Ultimate Explained (Taijitu shuo): A Construction of the Confucian Metaphysics," *Journal of History of Ideas,* 66, No. 3 (July 2005), 307–23.

Wang, Shishun 王世舜 (ed.), *Shangshu Yizhu* 尚書譯注, (Sichuan: Sichuan People Press, 1986).

Wang, Xinzhan 王心湛 (ed.). *Collected Interpretations of He Guanzi* 鶡冠子集解, (Shanghai: Guangyi Press 广益书局, 1936).

Wang, Yanxiang 王延相. *The Collection of Wang Yanxiang,* Vol. 1, 王延相集(一), Xiaoyu Wang 王孝魚 (ed.), (Beijing: Chinese Press 中華書局, 2009).

Wang, Yiwen 王宜文 and Chunyan Lu 路春艳. *The Collection of Chinese Classic Aesthetic Concepts* 中国古典美学范畴集粹, (Beijing: Normal University Press北京师范大学出版社, 2000).

Wang, Yunwu 王雲五 (ed.). *Liu Xiang: Shuoyuan* 說苑, (Beijing: Commercial Press 商務印書館, 1937).

Zhouli Jinzhujinyi 周禮今注今譯, (*The Commentaries on Ritual of Zhou,*), (Taibei: Taiwan Commercial Press, 1972).

Ware, James R. *Alchemy, Medicine and Religion in the China of A.D. 320: The Nei Pien of Ko Hung (Pao-p'u tzu),* (Cambridge, MA: The MIT Press, 1966).

Weber, Max. *The Religion of China: Confucianism and Taoism,* Hans Gerth (trans.), (New York: Macmillan, 1964).

Werner, E. T. C. *Myths & Legends of China* (New York: George G. Harrap & Co. Ltd., 1922).

Wile, Douglas. *Art of the Bedchamber: The Chinese Sexual Yoga Classics Including Women's Solo Meditation Texts,* (Albany: SUNY Press, 1992).

Wilhelm, Richard (German trans.). *Book of Changes*, Cary F. Barnes (English trans.), (New York: Pantheon Books, 1950).

Wu, Guoyi 鄔國義,*Guoyu* 國語譯注 (Shanghai: Shanghai Guji Press 上海古籍出版社, 1994).

Wu, Lu-Chiang, Tenney L. Davis and Wei Po-Yang. "An Ancient Chinese Treatise on Alchemy Entitled Ts'an T'ung Ch'I," *Isis*, **18** no. 2 (October 1932), 210–89.

Xiao, Hanming 蕭汉明. *Yinyang: Great Transformation and Human Life* 阴阳大化与人生, (Guangzhou: Guangdong People's Press 广东人民出版社, 1998).

Xu, Fuguan 徐復觀. *History of Chinese Discussions on Human Nature*, 中國人性論史, (Shanghai: Huadon Normal University Press, 1982).

Xu, Fuhong 許富宏. (ed.), *Gui Guzijishi*, 鬼谷子集釋 (*Master of Spirit Valley)*, (Beijing: Chinese Press 中華書局, 2008).

Xu, Shen 許慎. *Shouwen Jiezi* 說文解字, Duan Yucai 段玉裁 (ed.), (Shanghai: Shanghai Guji Press, 上海古籍出版社, 1981).

Xu, Xiangling 徐湘霖. (ed.), *Zhonglun Xiaozhu* 中論校注 *On Balance* (Chengdu: Bashu Press, 巴蜀出版社, 2007).

Xu, Xing-wu 徐兴无. "Concepts of 'Hun' and 'Po' as Found in the Han-Dynasty Theory of Human Nature," 汉代人性论中的"魂"、"魄"观念, *Journal of Nanjing University (Philosophy, Humanities and Social Sciences)*, **47** no. 2 (2010).

Yabuuti, Kiyosi. "Chinese Astronomy: Development and Limiting Factors," in Shigeru Nakayama and Nathan Sivin (eds.), *Chinese Science: Explorations of an Ancient Tradition*, MIT East Asian Science Services, vol. 2. (Cambridge, MA: The MIT Press, 1973), pp. 91–103.

Yang, Bojun, 杨伯峻 (ed.) *Liezi Jishi*, 列子集釋, *Commentaries on Master Lie*, (Beijing: Chinese Press 中華書局, 1979).

Yang, Jilin 杨寄林 (ed.). *Taipingjing* 太平經 *Classic of Great Peace*, (Shijiazhuan: Hebei People's Press 河北人民出版社, 2002).

Yang, Kuan. *History of the Warring States* 战国史, (Shanghai: Shanghai People's Press 上海人民出版社, 1955).

Yang, Xuepeng 楊學鵬. *Yinyang Qi yu Bianliang* 陰陽氣與變量, (Beijing: Chinese Science Press 中國科學院印刷廠, 1993).

Yates, Robin D. S. *Five Lost Classics: Tao, Huang-Lao, and Yin-yang in Han China*, (New York: Ballantine Books, 1997).

Yuan, Jinmei. "'Kinds, *Lei* 类' in Chinese Logic: A Comparison to 'Categories' in Aristotelian Logic," *History of Philosophy Quarterly*, **22** no. 3 (July 2005), 181–99.

Yu, Ying-Shih. "New Evidence on the Early Chinese Conception of Afterlife – A Review Article," *The Journal of Asian Studies*, **41** no. 1 (1981), 81–85.

"O Soul, Come Back! A Study in the Changing Conceptions of the Soul and Afterlife in Pre-Buddhist China," *Harvard Journal of Asiatic Studies*, **47** no. 2 (1987), 363–95.

Zhang, Qianyuan. *The Meaning beyond Images: Zhouyi's Meanings and Images and Chinese Aesthetics of Calligraphy and Paintings*, (Beijing: Chinese Bookstore, 2006).

Zhang, Qicheng 張其成. Yifi yu Yitu 易符与易圖, (Beijing: China Bookstore 中國書店, 1999).

Zhang, Xianglong 張祥龍, "The Status and Consequences of 'Gender Difference' in Chinese and Western Philosophy" '性別'在中西哲學裡的地位及其思想後果, *Jiangsu Social Sciences*, **6** (2002), 1–9.

Zhang, Yingan 張隱庵, (ed.), *Huangdi Neijing Commentaries* 黃帝內經素問集注 (Beijing: Xueyuan Press 學苑出版社, 2002).

Zhang, Zai 張載 (Song Dynasty). *The Complete Collections of Zhang Zai's Work* 張載集, (Beijing: Chinese Press 中華書局, 1976).

Zhang, Zailin 张再林. *Traditional Chinese Philosophy as the Philosophy of the Body* 作为身体哲学的中国古代哲学, (Beijing: China Social Science Publishing House 中国社会科学出版社, 2008).

Zhao, Rui 赵蕤 (ed.). *Qian Hanji*, 前漢記 (Jilin: Changchun Press, 2006).

Zhou Zhenfu 周振甫. Zhouyi Yizhu 周易譯注 (*Explanations of Zhouyi*) (Beijing: Chinese Press, 2001).

Book of Songs Annotation 詩經譯注 (Beijing: Chinese Press, 2002).

Zhu, Bokun 朱伯崑. *The Philosophical History of Yi Studies* 易学哲学史 (Beijing: Huaxia Press 华夏出版社, 1995).

Zhu, Xi 朱熹. *The Essential Meanings of the Zhouyi* 周易本义 (Beijing: Chinese Press, 中華書局 2009).

Ziporyn, Brook. *Ironies of Oneness and Difference: Coherence in Early Chinese Thought – Prolegomena to the Study of Li* (Albany: SUNY Press, Forthcoming).

(trans.). *Zhuangzi: The Essential Writings with Selections from Traditional Commentaries*, (Indianapolis/Cambridge: Hackett Publishing Company, Inc. 2009).

Index

acupuncture, 190–1
alchemy, 190, 192, 193, 217.
  See also neidan
Ames, Roger, 151
an 暗 (dark, hidden), 121
Analects, 32, 45, 106, 208
analogy and analogical reasoning, 22, 89,
  156–7, 224. *See also* reasoning
ancestor worship, 110
Ancient Taiji Diagram 古太極圖, 207–208
animals, classification of, 88–9.
  See also horses
archaeology. *See* bronze inscriptions;
  Guodian; Mawangdui
Aristotle, 44, 66, 201, 216n45
art, 60, 117–19. *See also* music
astrology, 26–7, 30, 34, 35, 45–6, 111

Bacon, Sir Francis, 163
Baihutong 白虎通 (*Comprehensive
  Discussions in the White Tiger Hall*), 27,
  105–106, 135, 139
Baldrian-Hussein, Farzeen, 198
bao 抱 (embrace), 144–5
baohan 包含 (mutual containment), 9
baoyang 抱陽 (embrace yang), 145, 147,
  148
Beijing (city), 113–14, 146
ben 本 (roots), 6, 50
benevolence. *See ren*
benxing 本性 (innate nature), 101
Bernoulli, Jacques, 202n2
bian 變 (change), 66, 72, 140, 182.
  See also change; *hua*
bianyao 變爻 (changing lines), 72
bilei 比類 (comparing categories), 86, 91,
  92, 93

Bingfa 兵法 (*The Art of War*), 149–53
Bloom, Irene, 76
Bodde, Derk, 39, 86, 96
body: and concepts of female and
  femininity, 55–9; and cosmology, 5, 44;
  fundamental importance of in Chinese
  thought, 21; and image of Nüwa and
  Fuxi, 103; interaction and integration
  in concept of, 171–8; movement
  and transformation of, 178–81; and
  musical instruments, 117; relation of
  spirits and souls to, 195–200; schema
  of, 186; and spectrum of differences,
  166–81; three yin and three yang,
  181–4. *See also* medicine; self and
  self-cultivation; *shen*
Bohr, Niels, 171, 172
Bouvet, Joachim, 217
Brashier, Kenneth E., 189n68, 198
bronze inscriptions, 22
buce 不測 (incommensurate), 72
Buddhism and Buddhist philosophy, 41,
  74–5, 79–80, 210
burial practices, 109–12
Bu Zixing, 113n111

Cai Yong 蔡邕, 117–18
calendars and calendrics, 26, 27,
  35. *See also* seasons; time and
  timing
Cammann, Schuyler, 211
cang 藏 (storing), 93, 183
Cantongqi. *See Zhouyi Can Tong Qi*
Cao Cao 曹操, 152–3
Cao Wenyi 曹文逸, 196
categorization. *See lei*
causality, and concept of *lei*, 92–3